Jaina
Logic and Epistemology

Sri Garib Das Oriental Series No. 209

Jaina Logic and Epistemology

EDITED BY

V.N. Jha

Sri Satguru Publications

A Division of

Indian Books Centre

Delhi - India

Published by :
Sri Satguru Publications
A Division of :
Indian Books Centre
Indological and Oriental Publishers
40/5, Shakti Nagar,
Delhi-110007
(INDIA)

ISBN 81-7030-518-7

First Edition : Delhi, 1997

Published by Sunil Gupta for Sri Satguru Publications a division of Indian Books Centre, 40/5, Shakti Nagar, Delhi-110 007, India and printed at D.K.Fine Art Press, Delhi-110 0052

CONTENTS

Preface

This volume contains papers presented at the National Seminar on Jaina Logic and Epistemology held at our Centre from 27th to 29th March 1995.

The growth of Indian philosophical Systems has been due to meaningful interaction among systems thoughts. Unfortunately, that tradition of interaction has been discontinued due to various political, social, economic and religious reasons. It is necessary to revive that golden tradition of interaction amongst various orthodox and heterodox systems of Indian philosophy. No growth is possible without this. Keeping this in mind the National Seminar was organized and the present volume is the outcome of that exercise. One will find that in this volume various aspects of logic and epistemology in Jaina tradition have been touched upon.

This Seminar was organized with the financial support of the Indian Council of Philosophical Research, New Delhi. I sincerely thank the authorities of the ICPR, particularly Prof. Mrinal Miri, President of the ICPR for extending their support. I also thank the Indian Books Centre for coming forward to bring out the proceedings of the Seminar in the form of the present volume. My sincere thanks are also due to the contributors to this volume.

I hope the volume will inspire the scholars in the field to take up further research in the area of Jaina Logic and Epistemology.

V.N.JHA

Director, Centre of Advanced Study in Sanskrit

University of Poona,

Pune

The Concept of Pratyakṣa In Jaina Epistemology-

L.V. Joshi

In order to attain eternal bliss, a man must possess three things, according to Jaina epistemology, viz. right faith, right knowledge and right conduct.[1] Here one of the factors that lead to emancipation is right knowledge. Now in order to understand the nature of right knowledge, we should go to the epistemology as adopted in the Jaina philosophy.

The Tattvārthasūtra enumerates five types of knowledge : (1) Sense-experience, (2) Verbal Knowledge, (3) Extra-sensory perception, (4) मनःपर्यय penetration in other's mind and (5) Omniscience, i.e. केवलज्ञान.[2]

In Jaina epistemology, these five types of knowledge, constitute the two *pramāṇas*.[3] The first two out of these five types of knowledge, i.e. मतिज्ञान and श्रुतज्ञान form the indirect or परोक्ष प्रमाण; while the remaining three, viz. अवधिज्ञान, मनःपर्यय and केवलज्ञान give rise to the direct or प्रत्यक्ष प्रमाण.

It may be noted here that in Jain epistemology, *pramāṇa* is of the nature of knowledge alone. Hence all the Jaina thinkers have emplyoed the word '*jñāna*' in the definition of pramāṇa.[4] As in the Śāṅkara Vedānta, *Jñāna* in the Jain epistemology is identified with Ātman.[5] This signifies that to understand the nature of knowledge in Jaina epistemology is to comprehend the nature of Ātman.

In order to enable a man to attain the true knowledge; and through it, to obtain emancipation, सिद्धसेन दिवाकर like the Buddhist logician दिङ्नाग, differentiated for the first time, the principles of logic from the sphere of religion and metaphysics.

It may be noted here that, during the Jaina Āgama period, the independent thinking in regard to epistemology, does not seem to have begun. Moreover, it is interesting to note here that there is a unique way to regard some knowledge as *pramāṇa* and the other as not-*pramāṇa*. If a person has wrong faith, then the knowledge whatever he possesses is taken as ignorance. For example, the *pramāṇas* like inference etc. are considered invalid, since they are adopted by the man who has wrong faith.[6]

It may be remarked here that in accordance with this Jaina view, जिन himself is regarded as स्वतः प्रमाण; i.e. intrinsically valid knowledge.[7]

In the Nyāyāvatāra of सिद्धसेन दिवाकर the *pramāṇa* has been defined as this— *Pramāṇa* is the knowledge which illumines itself and other objects without any obstruction. It is divided into two types - (1) प्रत्यक्ष (i.e. direct knowledge) and (2) परोक्ष (indirect knowledge). This division of *pramāṇa* is based on the two types of object, प्रत्यक्ष and परोक्ष as they are ascertained.[8]

Here the न्यायावतारविवृति explains the word अक्ष in प्रत्यक्ष as synonym of जीव. And this प्रत्यक्ष is regarded as transcendental in the Jaina epistemology. But if we takethe word प्रत्यक्ष in the sense of sensuous perception, then the word अक्ष in प्रत्यक्ष signifies the sense-organ.[9]

This means that the प्रत्यक्ष in Jaina epistemology is divided into two types: (1) transcendetal perception, i.e. पारमार्थिक प्रत्यक्ष and (2) an ordinary perception, i.e. सांव्यवहारिक प्रत्यक्ष. That knowledge which is acquired through Ātman alone, without the help of any sense-organ is the transcendal perception or पारमार्थिक प्रत्यक्ष; where as the knowledge generated by sense-organs is known as practical perception or सांव्यवहारिक प्रत्यक्ष.

Here in the definition of *pramāṇa* the term स्वपराभासि i.e. the knowledge which illumines itself as well as the object to the known, is employed with the intention to refute the Buddhist as well as the Naiyāyika view. The Buddhist believes that the knowledge is only self illuminous, while the Naiyāyika holds that the knowledge illumines the objects only; and not itself.[10] The Jaina view says that if the knowledge is not self luminous, it cannot illumine the objects. Hence in Jaina epistemology, the knowledge is compared with a lamp which illumines itself as well as the object around it.[11]

सिद्धसेन दिवाकर while defining the प्रत्यक्ष, takes प्रत्यक्ष in its ordinary sense. He defines the प्रत्यक्ष– Such a knowledge which cognises object, not beyond the range of the senses, is प्रत्यक्ष; the other is known as परोक्ष in reference to the manner of taking the cognizance.[12]

Here it may be noted that उमास्वाति takes the प्रत्यक्ष in the sense of Jaina tradition, as we have already marked (p. 2). But सिद्धसेन दिवाकर (5th or 6th century A.D.) introduces the प्रत्यक्ष, perhaps for the first time in the sense of ordinary perception.

In the Jaina epistemology, the ordinary perception ascertains an object along with its colour, form, genus etc. Here सिद्धसेन attempts to repuditate the Buddhis view which holds that the प्रत्यक्ष is devoid of any conceptual construction and non-illusive. This view cannot be maintained since it is not based on sound logic.[13]

Again, it is interesting to note here that the knowledge which is designated as परोक्ष also could be said as प्रत्यक्ष, because that परोक्ष knowledge also is self-cognised. In fact, a certain knowledge is designated as परोक्ष, only because it apprehends that the knowledge in Jaina epistemology is always प्रत्यक्ष. However on account of the object to be known being two fold, direct and indirect, the knowledge also is called प्रत्यक्ष and परोक्ष.

It is also remarkable that in the Jaina epistemology, the प्रत्यक्ष also can be परार्थ i.e. for the sake of others, just as the परार्थानुमान.[15] For instance, the deposition of a witness is taken by a judge as equivalent to perception.

According to अनुयोगद्वार, the प्रत्यक्ष has two varieties: (1) इन्द्रियप्रत्यक्ष and (2) नोइन्द्रियप्रत्यक्ष. The first includes all the five types of sensuous perceptions, whereas the second i.e. नोइन्द्रियप्रत्यक्ष incorporates in it the अवधिज्ञान, मनःपर्यय and केवलज्ञान.[16]

Again, it may be noted here that the knowledge that arises from Ātman alone, is the प्रत्यक्ष in the true sense, since it makes an object directly apprehended. And the knowledge which is generated through the mediation of the senses, is also called प्रत्यक्ष; known as सांव्यवहारिक. But this does not mean that the sensuous cognition is illusory.

The Jaina epistemology does not recognise प्रत्यक्ष as निर्विकल्प and सविकल्प. But it admits the four stages in the process of perceptual cognition- viz. (1) अवग्रह ("There is something" mere sensation) (2) ईहा -integrative action of the mind, (3) अवाय, ascertainment, and (4) धारणा, retention of what is experienced.

Now let us have a glance on the definitions[17] of the प्रत्यक्ष given by श्रीमाणिक्यनन्दिन् in his परीक्षामुखसूत्र. As he says, the प्रत्यक्ष is a knowledge with clarity. This clarity means a shining without mediation of any other knowledge i.e. directly or a shining endowed with particularity of the thing.

हेमचन्द्राचार्य defines the प्रत्यक्ष -when the right determination of an object becomes clear, it is called प्रत्यक्ष.[18] Then he elucidates the word 'विशदः' in the definition. He says that when there is no requirement of any other प्रमाण, and the knowledge arises independently, it is called clear, or we can say that when an object appears in the knowledge "this is", it is called clarity.[19]

Then हेमचन्द्राचार्य gives the definition of the principal perception.[20] When the veil which shrouds the knowledge is totally removed, the manifestation of the nature of the consciousness or Ātman, is called the principal perception. It is also called केवलम् because, there is not any help of the sense-organs etc., and also because, it has all as its object, and it is extraordinary.[21]

By obtaining such a perception, a man can be omniscient. In this context हेमचन्द्राचार्य quotes the view held by कुमारिलभट्ट. According to it, ब्रह्मा, विष्णु and महेश्वर can be omniscient, since their bodies consist of Vedas. But how can a man be omniscient?

Against this, हेमचन्द्राचार्य becomes enraged saying that, oh sinner of cencuring omniscient, are you blaming gods?[23]

Now let us consider about the result of knowledge or so to say, of प्रमाण. The immediate result of प्रमाण is the removal of ignorance. And the effect of केवल प्रत्यक्ष is the bliss and equanimity, whereas the result of ordinary perception is the knowledge or awareness to accept or to reject something.[24]

Now, we may note here certain features that are peculiar to Jaina epistemology. The Jaina epistemology has divided the प्रमाण into two divisions. Hence it is convenient to include any number of प्रमाण; in either of these two.

Moreover, the Jaina epistemology has regarded the transcendental perception or पारमार्थिक प्रत्यक्ष as the highest; and consequently it has relegated the ordinary प्रत्यक्ष to the position of परोक्ष.

Thus we conclude here that the Jaina Āgama has admitted five types of knowledge मतिज्ञान etc. and the first two are regarded as परोक्ष, and the rest i.e. अवधि, मनःपर्यय and केवल as प्रत्यक्ष.

Later on the Jaina scholars have attempted to incorporate these five types of knowledge in the four *pramāṇas* as they were prevalent in other branches.

Umāsvāti has followed the आगम tradition, and सिद्धसेन दिवाकर, the founder of the Jaina epistemology has deviated from the आगम tradition.

It is a unique characteristic that in the Jaina epistemology चरित्र or character has been given more importance than knowledge.

Thus we see that the concept of प्रत्यक्ष has a unique position. On the one hand, the आगम tradition has to be preserved, and on the other hand, ordinary प्रत्यक्ष has to be admitted in order to protect the Jaina principles.

Footnotes

1. सम्यग्दर्शनज्ञानचारित्राणि मोक्षमार्गः।।1।। - *Tattvārtha-sūtra*, Umāsvāti, विवेचक पं. सुखलालजी, अहमदाबाद गुजराती आवृत्तिः तृतीया, 1954 p. 4.

2. मतिश्रुतावधिमानःपर्यायकेवलानि ज्ञानम्।।1-9।। तत्त्वार्थ Ibid.

3. आद्ये परोक्षम्।।1-11।।, प्रत्यक्षम् अन्यत्।।1-92।।, *Tattvārthasūtra*, Ibid.

4. Introduction p. 68, by Pt. Dalasukh Malavania *Nyāyāvatāra vārtikavṛtti* of Śrī Śāntisūri, Singhi Jaina Śāstra Śikṣāpīṭha, Bharatiya Vidya Bhavan Bombay, 1949.

5. See Intro. by Dalasukh Malavania, p. 134, Ibid.

6. अप्रमाणानि कुतः? मिथ्यादर्शनपरिग्रहात्, विपरीतोपदेशाच्च। मिथ्यादृष्टेः हि मतिश्रुतावधयः नियतमज्ञानमेव। - तत्त्वार्थभाष्य, 1-92, टिप्पण 4, प्रस्तावना, तदेव, तत्त्वार्थवार्तिकवृत्ति, पृ. 111.

7. नमः स्वतःप्रमाणाय वचःप्रामाण्यहेतवे।
   जिनाय पञ्चरूपेण प्रत्यक्षात् पक्षदेशिने।। - मंगलपद्य, शान्तिसूरि's न्यायावतारवार्त्तिकवृत्ति, तदेव पृ. 11.

8. प्रमाणं स्वपरामासि ज्ञानं बाधविवर्जितम्।
   प्रत्यक्षं च परोक्षं च द्विधा मेयविनिश्चयात्।।1।।, *Nyāyāvatāra*, Siddhasena Divākara, edited by Satya Ranjan Banerjee, Calcutta, Revised Edn. 1981, p. 7.

9. तत्र सिद्धान्तप्रसिद्धपारमार्थिकप्रत्यक्षापेक्षया अक्षशब्दो जीवपर्यायितया प्रसिद्धः। इह तु व्यवाहारिकप्रत्यक्षप्रस्तावात् अक्षध्वनिः इन्द्रियवचनो गृहयते। ततश्च अक्षं प्रति गतम् प्रत्यक्षम्। - न्यायावतारविवृत्ति (सिद्धर्षि या चन्द्रप्रेमसूरि 905 A.D.), p. 1, Ibid, Intro. p. xxix, and Footnote 3.

10. स्वपराभासि इत्यनेन ये स्वाभासि एव ज्ञानं मन्यन्ते, ते ज्ञानवादिनो बौद्धाविशेषाः, ये च पराभासि एव मीमांसकनैयायिकादयः ते निरस्ताः। - न्यायावतारविवृत्ति, तदेव पृ. 1.

11. स्वप्रकाशाभावे परप्रकाशायोगात्, न हि प्रदीपः स्वरूपम् अनुद्द्योतयन् घटादि-उद्द्योतने व्याप्रियते। - न्यायावतारविवृत्ति, तदेव पृ. 1.

12. अपरोक्षतयाऽर्थस्य ग्राहकं ज्ञानमीदृशम्।
    प्रत्यक्षम् इतरत्ज्ञेयम्, परोक्षं ग्रहणेक्षया।। - न्यायाव. 4।।

13. ग्राहकमिति (-अपरोक्षतयार्थस्य ग्राहकं ज्ञानम् ईदृशम्-) निर्णायकं द्रष्टव्यम्,

निर्णयाभावेऽर्थग्रहणायोगात्। तेन यत् तथागतैः प्रत्यपादि, प्रत्यक्षं कल्पनापोढम् अभ्रान्तमिति तदपास्तं भवति। तस्य युक्तिरिक्तत्वात्। न्याया. विवृति तदेव पृ. 3।

14. (प्रत्यक्षात्) इतरत् असाक्षादर्थग्राहकं ज्ञानं परोक्षमिति ज्ञेयम्। अवगन्तव्यम्, एतदपि स्वसंवेदनापेक्षया प्रत्यक्षमेव। - न्याया. विवृति, पृ. 3 तदेव।

15. परस्य तदुपायत्वात् परार्थत्वं द्वयोरपि।।11।। - न्याया. प्रत्यक्षप्रतीतं पुनर्दर्शयन् एतावद् वक्ति, पश्य, राजा गच्छति। - न्याया. विवृति पृ. 7 तदेव।

16. प्रस्ता. पृ. 80, श्री दलसुख मालवणिया, न्यायावतारवार्त्तिकवृत्ति, भारतीयविद्याभवन, बम्बई, 1949 A.D. Edn. I

17. विशदं प्रत्यक्षम् 1.1.2-3; प्रतीत्यन्तर-अप्यवधानेन विशेषवत्तया वा प्रतिभासनं वैशघम्।।2-4; इन्द्रियअनिन्द्रियनिमित्तं देशतः सांव्यवहारिकम्।।2-5।। - श्रीमाणिक्यनन्दि's परीक्षामुखसूत्र, (with प्रमेयकमलमार्तण्ड) ed. महेन्द्रकुमार शास्त्री by प्रभाचन्द्र

18. विशदः प्रत्यक्षम् ।।1-1-13।। - 'सम्यगर्थनिर्णयः' इति प्रमाणसामान्यलक्षणमनूद्य 'विशदः' इति विशेषलक्षणं प्रसिद्धस्य प्रत्यक्षस्य क्रियते।। - स्वोपज्ञवृत्ति, प्रमाणमीमांसा, हेमचन्द्राचार्य, सं. पं. सुखलाल जी, संचालक सिंघी जैन ग्रन्थमाला, अहमदाबाद - कलकत्ता 1939 स्रिष्टाष्द प्रथमावृत्ति, पृ. 9।

19. प्रमाणान्तरानपेक्षा इदन्तया प्रतिभासो वा वैशद्यम् - ।।1-1-14।। - न हि शाब्दानुमानादिवत् प्रत्यक्षं स्वोत्पत्तौ शब्दलिङ्गादिज्ञानं प्रमाणांन्तरमपेक्षते। प्र. मी. स्वोपज्ञवृत्ति, पृ. 10।

20. तत् सर्वथावरणविलये चेतनस्य स्वरूपाविर्भावो मुख्यम् केवलम्।।15।। - तत् इति प्रत्यक्षपरामर्शार्थम् ...... दीर्घकालनिरन्तरसत्कारासेवितरत्नत्रयप्रकर्षपर्यन्ते .... ध्यानबलेन निःशेषतया (बहुमाम) ज्ञानावरणादीनां प्रक्षये सति चेतनास्वभावस्य आत्मनः प्रकाशस्वभावस्य ... सतः एव आवरणापगमनेन .. आविर्भूतं स्वरूपं, मुखमिव शरीरस्य, सर्वज्ञानानां प्रधानं मुख्यं प्रत्यक्षम्। - स्वोपज्ञवृत्ति। तदेव पृ.10

21. तच्च इन्द्रियादिसाहायकविरहात् सकलविषयत्वात् असाधारणत्वात् च केवलम् इत्यागमे प्रसिद्धम्। - प्र. मी. स्वोपज्ञवृत्ति, तदेव पृ. 10

22. अथापि वेददेहत्वात् ब्रह्मविष्णुमहेश्वराः।
कामं भवन्तु सर्वज्ञाः सार्वज्ञ्यं मानुषस्य किम्।। - स्वोपज्ञ. पृ. 12

23. आः सर्वज्ञापलापपातकिन् दुर्वदवादिन् मानुषत्वनिन्दार्थवादापदेशेन देवान् अधिक्षिपसि।- स्वोपज्ञवृत्ति, प्र. मी. पृ. 13 तदेव।

24. प्रमाणस्य फलं साक्षाद् अज्ञाननिवर्तनम्।
केवलस्य सुखापेक्षे शेषस्यादानहानधीः।।रतान्यायावतार।(उपेक्षा मध्यस्थवृत्तिता-विवृत्ति) पृ. 22 तदेव।

अनुमान में हेतु विचार : जैन न्याय के संदर्भ में

- प्रद्युम्न शाह सिंह

अनुमान प्रमाण के तीन मूल आधार हैं : हेतु पक्ष साध्य। उसका प्रधान आधार-स्तम्भ हेतु है। हेतु को न्यायशास्त्र में लिङ्ग एवं साधन भी कहा जाता है। उसके बिना अनुमान की कल्पना ही नहीं की जा सकती। हेतु के बिना केवल विज्ञप्ति व उदाहरण आदि से साध्य की सिद्धि नहीं हो सकती। अन्य दर्शनकारों ने हेतु के त्रिलक्षणपंचलक्षण किए हैं, पर स्याद्वादमतावलम्बियों को 'अन्ययानुपपत्ति' रूप हेतु का एक ही लक्षण इष्ट व पर्याप्त है। इस लक्षण के विपरित आदि वृत्ति होने पर हेतु स्वयं हेत्वाभास बन जाते हैं।

हेतु के स्वरूप की त्रिलक्षण (पक्षधर्मत्व, सपक्षसत्व और विपक्षासत्व) और पंचलक्षण (पक्षधर्मत्व, सपक्षसत्व, विपक्षासत्व, अबाधिविषयत्व और असत्प्रतिपक्षत्व) की मान्यता अधिक प्रचलित है। किन्तु इसके अतिरिक्त दार्शनिकों ने हेतु का एकलक्षण, द्विलक्षण, त्रिलक्षण, पंचलक्षण, षड्लक्षण और सप्तलक्षण भी स्वीकार किया है। विभिन्न दर्शनों में हेतु लक्षण निम्न प्रकार हैं :

एकलक्षण	–	अन्यथानुपपत्ति - जैन
द्विलक्षण	–	साधर्म्य, वैधर्म्य - नैयायिक
त्रिलक्षण	–	प्रसिद्ध, सत्, असन्दिग्ध, पक्षधर्मत्व, सपक्षसत्व, विपक्षासत्व नैयायिक उद्योतकर बौद्ध
पंचलक्षण[1]	–	पक्षधर्मत्व, सपक्षधर्मत्व, विपक्षाद्व्यावृत्ति, अबाधित-विषयत्व, असत्प्रतिक्षत्व) नैयायिक जयन्तभट्ट

षड़लक्षण[2] – पक्षधर्मत्व, सपक्षसत्व, विपक्षासत्व अबाधितविषयत्व, विवक्षित्रैकसंख्यत्व और ज्ञातत्व) बौद्ध धर्मकीर्ति

सप्तलक्षण[3] – पक्षधर्मत्व आदि... 3, अन्यथानुपपन्नत्व, ज्ञातत्व, अबाधितविषयत्व असत्प्रतिपक्षत्व, पक्षधर्मत्वादि)

सप्तलक्षण को वादिराज ने उद्धृत करके उसका खण्डन कर अन्याथानुपपति को ही सिद्ध किया है।

न्यायदर्शनोक्त पंचावयव (प्रतिज्ञा, हेतु, उदाहरण, उपनय, निगमन) में हेतु दूसरा अवयव है। गौतम ने उदाहरणसाधर्म्य (सादृश्य) एवं उदाहरणवैधर्म्य (वैसादृश्य) से साध्य को सिद्ध करने वाले साधन को हेतु कहा है।[4] वात्स्यायनभाष्य में हेतु के दोनो लक्षणों को व्याख्यायित किया गया है। उसके अनुसार-उदाहरण सामान्य (साधर्म्य) से साध्यधर्म का ज्ञान कराने वाला साधन हेतु है।[5] अर्थात् साधन करने योग्य पक्ष में साध्य धर्म को जानकर तथा उदाहरण में भी उसी धर्म को जानकर उसकी सिद्धि करने वाले वचन का नाम हेतु है। जैसे शब्द अनित्य है, उत्पत्ति धर्मवाला होने से, यह प्रतिज्ञा का साध वचन है, क्यों कि जहाँ उत्पत्तिधर्मत्व (घटत्व) है वहाँ अनित्यत्व (घटविनाशत्व) होता है। और उदाहरण वैधर्म्य से भी प्रस्तुत साध्य का ज्ञान कराने वाले साधन को हेतु कहते हैं।[6] कैसे? शब्द अनित्य है, उत्पत्ति धर्मवाला होने के कारण क्योंकि अनुत्पत्ति धर्मवाले द्रव्य नित्य होते हैं जैसे आत्मा आकाश आदि। इस प्रकार, साध्य की सिद्धि करने वाला अवयव हेतु होता है, यह दोनों विशेष लक्षणों में रहने वाला हेतु का सामान्य लक्षण है। उदाहरण के समान धर्म होने से साध्य का साधक एवं उदाहरण के विरुद्ध धर्म होने से साध्य का साधक क्रमशः साधर्म्य हेतु एवं वैधर्म्य हेतु होता है। देखें : उदाहरण के सदृश धर्मवाला होने से साध्य का साधक हेतु साधर्म्य हेतु कहलाता है, जैसेः साध्य है- शब्द अनित्य है, हेतु है- उत्पत्ति धर्मवाला होने के कारण। उदाहरण के विरुद्ध धर्म वाला होने से साध्य का साधक हेतु वैधर्म्य हेतु कहलाता है, जैसेः साध्य है- शब्द अनित्य है, हेतु है उत्पत्ति धर्म से रहित होने के कारण।

यहाँ यह उल्लेखनीय है कि गौतम के न्यायसूत्र पर बौद्धदार्शनिक नागार्जुन (ल. 300 ई.) ने जो आक्षेप किये उनका उत्तर वात्स्यायन (400 ई.) ने दिया।[7] बौद्ध न्याय के पिता कहे जाने वाले तार्किक दिङ्नाग (500 ई.) ने एवं उनके शिष्य शंकरस्वामी (ल. 5वीं शती उत्तरार्द्ध) ने 'न्यायप्रवेशसूत्र' में त्रिरूप हेतु बतलाये हैं।[8]

तीन रूप कौन हैं? वे हैं : पक्षधर्मत्व, सपक्षसत्व और विपक्षासत्व। वात्स्यायन व दिङ्नाग लगभग एक ही शताब्दी के हैं। शंकरस्वामी ने वात्स्यायन के मत का निरास किया है अतः वे उत्तरवर्ती ही हैं। उन का पक्षधर्मत्व एवं विपक्षासत्व हेतु वात्स्यायनोक्त हेतुओं (साधर्म्य, वैधर्म्य) का समर्थन है किन्तु उन्होंने अनुमान ज्ञान के लिए सपक्षसत्व को प्रस्तुत किया। उनके अनुसार पक्ष धर्मी के रूप में प्रसिद्ध है।[9] प्रसिद्ध का प्रयोग इसलिए है कि स्वयं पक्ष में साध्य का होना इष्ट होता है। सपक्ष सामान्य साध्यधर्म का समानार्थी होता है। जैसे- शब्द अनित्य है इस साध्य का समानार्थी घट आदि अनित्य है।[10] विपक्ष वह है जहाँ साध्य नहीं रहता। जैसे जो नित्य है वह अकृतक देखा जाता है आकाश की तरह।[11] यहाँ कृतकत्व अथवा प्रयत्नानन्तरीयकत्व सपक्ष ही है विपक्ष में वह नहीं है।[12]

आचार्य समन्तभद्र ने आप्तमीमांसा में कहा है कि एक ही वस्तु में विशेषण होने से नास्तित्व अपने प्रतिषेध्य अस्तित्व का अविनाभावी है। जैसे हेतु में वैधर्म्य साधर्म्य का अविनाभावी होता है।[13] जैन न्याय का विकास सिद्धसेन दिवाकर (वि. 5वीं शती) के 'न्यायावतार' से हुआ। सिद्धसेन ने हेतु के दो प्रकार के प्रयोग का निरूपण करते हुए कहा हैः तथोपपत्ति-साध्य के सद्भाव में ही होना, तथा अन्यथानुपपत्ति-साध्य के अभाव में नहीं होना, इन दो रूप से हेतु का दो प्रकार का प्रयोग (वचन-रचना) होता है। इन दोनों प्रकार के प्रयोगों में से किसी एक के द्वारा भी साध्य की सिद्धि हो सकती है।[14] सिद्धसेन के मत को पुष्ट करने वाले तथा 'न्यायावतार' की कारिकाओं के स्पष्ट टीकाकार सिद्धर्षिगणी (ई. 8-10) ने अपनी टीका में कहा हैः वचन रचना भी दो तरह की हो सकती है, एक तो जिसमें हेतु का साध्य के सद्भाव में ही होना बताया गया है, जैसे- अग्निरत्र, धूमस्यतथैवोपपत्तेः- यहाँ अग्नि है धूम की अग्नि के द्वारा ही उत्पत्ति होने से। यहाँ हेतु जो धूम है, उसका साध्य जो अग्नि उसके सद्भाव में ही रहना बताया गया है, इसी का नाम है तथोपपत्ति रूप प्रयोग या अन्वय प्रयोग। दूसरे जिसमें हेतु का साध्य के अभाव में न होना ही या न रहना ही बताया गया हो, जैसे- 'अग्निरत्र धूमस्यन्यथानुपपत्तेः'- यहाँ अग्नि है, क्योंकि बिना अग्नि के धूम की उत्पत्ति नहीं हो सकती। यहाँ हेतु- धूम का साध्य (अग्नि) के अभाव में उत्पन्न न होना या न रहना ही बताया गया है। इसी को कहते हैं अन्यथानुपपत्तिरूप प्रयोग या व्यतिरेक। साध्य की सिद्धि तथोपपत्तिरूप प्रयोग और अन्यथानुपपत्तिरूप प्रयोग इन दोनो से ही होती है, इसलिए दोनो में से किसी एक का ही प्रयोग करना चाहिए, दोनो का एक साथ नहीं।

प्रयोग का फल है साध्य का सिद्ध करना। यदि वह एक से ही हो जाता है, तो दूसरे का प्रयोग निरर्थक हो जाता है।[15] तथोपपत्ति एवं अन्यथानुपपत्ति रूप हेतु के दोनों भेद गौतम एवं वात्स्यायन द्वारा कहे गये हेतु के दो भेदों, साधर्म्य व वैधर्म्य के सदृश ही हैं। केवल शब्द भेद है। सिद्धर्षिगणी की टीका के अनुसार : हेतु का साधारण लक्षण 'असाधारण धर्म' बतलाया गया है। स्वार्थनुमान के सम्बन्ध में वही अन्यथानुपपन्नत्व-साध्य के बिना उत्पन्न नहीं होना-रूप से कहा गया है। उसकी प्रतीति नहीं होना, उसमें संदेह होना, या उसकी विपरीत समझ बैठना, ये तीन हेत्वाभास हैं, क्योंकि ये तीनो सम्यग् हेतु नहीं होते हुए भी हेतु के समान मालूम पड़ते हैं।[16]

स्वामी पात्र केसरी (वि. 6-7 वीं शती) का 'त्रिलक्षण कदर्थन' नामक ग्रंथ विख्यात है किन्तु सम्प्रति वह उपलब्ध नहीं है। बौद्धदर्शनाचार्य शान्तरक्षित (8 वीं शती) में अपने प्रसिद्ध ग्रंथ 'तत्त्वसंग्रह' में अनुमान परीक्षा के अन्तर्गत पात्र स्वामी के मत को अभिव्यक्त करने वाली (1363 से लेकर 1378 तक) 16 कारिकाओं को उद्धृत किया है। आचार्य कमलशील (750 ई. लगभग) ने 'तत्त्वसंग्रह' पर 'पत्रिजका' टीका लिखी है। जिसमें उन्होंने शान्तरक्षित रचित कारिकाओं का ग्रंथिभंग किया है। पात्रस्वामी ने हेतु के त्रिलक्षण का खण्डन किया है। 'तत्त्वसंग्रह' के अनुसार निम्न श्लोक में पात्रस्वामी त्रिरूप लिङ्ग का खण्डन करते हैं :

अन्यथानुपपन्नत्वं यत्र तत्र त्रयेण किम्?
नान्यथानुपपन्नत्वं यत्र तत्र त्रयेण किम्?[17]

अर्थात् जहाँ अन्यथानुपपत्ति है वहाँ त्रैरूप्य हेतु मानने से कोई लाभ नहीं, और जहाँ अन्यथानुपपत्ति नहीं है वहाँ त्रैरूप्य मानना व्यर्थ है। पात्रस्वामी के अनुसार अन्यथानुपपत्ति ही एक मात्र हेतु का स्वरूप हो सकता है, त्रैरूप्य आदि नही। अन्यथानुपपत्ति रूप हेतु के एक लक्षण को परवर्ती जैनाचार्यों अकलंक,[18] कुमारिनन्दि, वीरसेन, विद्यानन्द ने भी माना एवं पुष्ट किया है। सिद्धसेन पात्रस्वामी के पूर्ववर्ती आचार्य माने जा सकते हैं।

पक्षधर्मता के अभाव में भी संस्थान क्रम ज्ञान होता है जैसे- एक मुहूर्त के बाद रोहिणी नक्षत्र का उदय होगा, क्योंकि कृत्तिका का उदय हो चुका है'[19] इस अनुमान में पक्षधर्मता नहीं है, क्योंकि यहाँ रोहिणी नक्षत्र पक्ष है और उसका भविष्य में उदय होना साध्य है तथा 'कृत्तिका का उदय' हेतु है। 'कृत्तिका का उदय' हेतु

रोहिणी पक्ष में नहीं रहता, क्योंकि कृत्तिका का उदय कृत्तिका का धर्म है न कि रोहिणी का। अतः यहाँ पक्षधर्मता सम्भव नहीं है फिर भी वह हेतु साध्य की सिद्धि करता है। रोहिणी उदय (साध्य) का कृत्तिकोदय (हेतु) के साथ अन्यथानुपपन्नत्व होने के कारण वह सद्हेतु गमक है। दूसरा उदाहरण, गर्भस्थ मैत्रीपुत्र श्याम होगा क्योंकि वह मैत्री का पुत्र है, अन्य पुत्रों की तरह। इस असद् अनुमान में पक्षधर्मत्व, सपक्षसत्व और विपक्षासत्व तीनों हैं। परन्तु तत्पुत्रत्व का श्यामत्व के साथ अविनाभाव नहीं है और इसलिए तत्पुत्रत्व हेतु श्यामत्व का गमक नहीं है।[20] उस गर्भस्थ बालक में 'मैत्र का पुत्रत्व' रूप हेतु रहता ही है, क्योंकि वह मैत्र का पुत्र है। सपक्ष हैं उसके अन्य भाई, चूँकि वे भी मैत्र के पुत्र हैं, अतः उनमें भी मैत्रतनयत्व हेतु रहता ही है। विपक्ष है मैत्र के सिवा किसी का गौराङ्ग बालक। चूँकि वह मैत्र का पुत्र नहीं है इसलिए उसमें 'मैत्रपुत्रत्व' रूप हेतु नहीं रहता। इस तरह त्रैरूप्य के होते हुए भी यह हेतु सम्यक् हेतु नहीं है।; क्योंकि जो-जो मैत्र का लड़का हो वह काला ही हो ऐसी कोई व्याप्ति नहीं है, फलतः सर्वत्र हेतुओं में अन्यथाऽनुपपन्नत्व के सद्भाव से गमकता एवं सद्भाव से अगमकता होती है। पात्रस्वामी ने त्रिलक्षण का खण्डन करते हुए तीखे शब्दों का प्रयोग भी किया है। धर्मकीर्ति ने 'प्रमाणवार्तिक' में जैनमत का निराकरण 'एतेनैव यद्हीकाः किलप्यश्लीममाकुलम्' उक्त शब्दों से प्रारम्भ किया। फलतः पात्रस्वामी और अकलंकभट्ट आदि जैन तार्किकों ने भी तीक्ष्णायुक्त शब्द प्रयोग किये। तात्पर्य यह कि पात्रस्वामी कमलशील से पूर्व और धर्मकीर्ति के उत्तरवर्ती आचार्य हैं। त्रिलक्षण के निरास में उनकी निम्न कारिकाएँ भी दृष्टव्य हैं:

अन्यथानुपपन्नत्वे ननु दृष्टा सुहेतुता,

नासति त्र्यंशकस्यापि तस्मात्क्लीबास्त्रिलक्षणाः। 20

अन्यथानुपपन्नत्वं यस्यासौ हेतुरिष्यते,

एकलक्षणकः सोऽर्थश्चतुर्लक्षणको न वा। 21

तेनैकलक्षणो हेतुः प्राधान्याद् गमकोऽस्तु नः

पक्षधर्मादिभिस्त्वन्यैः किं व्यर्थैः परिकल्पितैः। 22

अन्यथानुपपन्नत्व ही सद्हेतु है फिर त्रिलक्षण हेतु की क्या आवश्यकता। अन्यथानुपपन्नत्व के न होने पर मैत्रीतनयत्व में त्रिरूप लिङ्ग के होने पर भी साध्य का सद्अनुमापक हेतु नहीं हो पाता।[21] जो अन्यथानुपपत्ति अन्वय

(सपक्षेसत्त्वम्) व्यतिरेक (विपक्षासत्त्वम्) के योग से होती है वह एकलक्षण से समर्थित है वहाँ द्विलक्षण, त्रिलक्षण, चर्तुलक्षण की कोई आवश्यकता नहीं।[22] वही एकलक्षण (अन्यथानुपपन्नत्व) हेतु साध्य का गमक है तो पक्षधर्मता आदि की परिकल्पना अन्यों ने क्यों की।

आचार्य विद्यानन्द ने पात्रस्वामी का अनुसरण करते हुए न्यायोक्त हेतु के पंचलक्षण का खण्डन करते हुए प्रमाणपरीक्षा में लिखा है :

अन्यथानुपपन्नत्वं यत्र किं तत्र पञ्चभिः,
नान्यथानुपपन्नत्वं यत्र किं तत्र पञ्चभिः।

जहाँ अन्यथानुपपत्ति है वहाँ हेतु के पञ्चलक्षण मानने से क्या लाभ? जहाँ अन्यथानुपपत्ति नही है वहाँ हेतु के पञ्चलक्षण मानने से क्या लाभ। इन्होंने अन्यथानुपपन्नत्व को हेतुलक्षण मानने के अतिरिक्त धर्मकीर्ति के उस त्रैरूप्यसमर्थन की भी समीक्षा की है जिसमें उन्होंने असिद्ध, विरुद्ध, अनैकान्तिक हेत्वाभास का निराकरण एवं शेषवदनुमान का निरास किया है।[25] धर्मकीर्ति ने असिद्ध के निरास के लिए पक्षधर्मत्व, विरुद्ध के व्यवच्छेद के लिए सपक्षसत्व और अनैकान्तिक हेत्वाभास के लिए विपक्षासत्व की सार्थकता बताई है। विद्यानन्द का कहना है कि अकेले अन्यथानुपपत्ति के सद्भाव से ही तीनो दोषों का परिहार हो जाता है। जो हेतु असिद्ध, विरुद्ध या अनैकान्तिक होगा उसमें अन्यथानुपपत्ति रहती ही नहीं। अन्यथानुपपन्नत्व से जब तीनो आभास दूर किए जा सकते हैं तब उनके आभास के लिए हेतु के अनेक लक्षण निकालना संभव नहीं।

माणिक्यनन्दी की हेतु की परिभाषा हैः जो साध्य के साथ अविनाभावी होना निश्चित हो अर्थात् साध्य के बिना न रहे उसको हेतु कहते है।[26] इनके अनुसार हेतु ही साध्य का गमक होता है। साध्य और साधन का अविनाभावी होना अत्यावश्यक है अविनाभाव को वादी प्रतिवादी दोनो पक्षों के तार्किक मानते हैं।

धर्मकीर्ति के अनुसार अविनाभाव दो सम्बन्धों पर आधारित हैः तदुत्पत्ति और तादात्म्य।[27] जिन दो वस्तुओं में कार्यकारणभाव होता है उनमें तदुत्पत्ति सम्बन्ध माना गया है जैसे धूम और वह्नि। यथा सत्त्व और क्षणिकत्व अथवा शिंशपात्व और वृक्षत्व। इन दो सम्बन्धों को छोड़कर अन्य कोई सम्बन्ध या प्रमाण अविनाभाव का नियामक (स्थापक) नहीं है। न ही दर्शन (अन्वय या प्रत्यक्ष) से उसकी स्थापना सम्भव है न अदर्शन (व्यतिरेक या अप्रत्यक्ष-अनुपलम्भ) से।

न्यायबिन्दु में धर्मकीर्ति कहते हैं : जो जहाँ पर स्वभाव से प्रतिबद्ध नहीं होता उसका अप्रतिबद्ध विषय में अव्यभिचार के नियम का अभाव होता है।[28] स्वभाव प्रतिबन्ध साध्य अर्थ में लिङ्ग का होता है। क्योंकि वास्तव में साध्य और लिङ्ग का तादात्म्य है और साध्य अर्थ से लिङ्ग की उत्पत्ति होती है।[29]

माणिक्यनंदि ने सहक्रमभाव नियम को अविनाभाव का आधार माना है। जिसमें तदुत्पत्ति या तादात्म्य नहीं है उनमें भी क्रमभाव नियम या सहभावनियम रहने से अविनाभाव प्रतिष्ठित होता है और उसके आधार पर हेतु साध्य का अनुमापक होता है। त्रिरूपता हेतु का असाधारण धर्म नहीं क्योंकि वह हेतु और हेत्वाभास दोनों में रहता हैः जैसे- 'बुद्धि असर्वज्ञ है क्योंकि वक्ता है' इस अनुमान में पक्षधर्मत्व, सपक्षसत्त्वादि तीनों रूप होने पर भी अन्यथानुपपन्नता के अभाव में गमक नहीं माना जा सकता। दूसरी ओर पक्षधर्मता आदि तीन पर भी संस्थानक्रम ज्ञान रूप अनुमान होता है जैसे- शकट का उदय होगा क्योंकि कृत्तिका का उदय हो चुका है। सपक्षवृत्तित्व के न रहने पर भी हेतु सद्हेतु माना जाता है।

साध्य के रहने पर ही हेतु के धर्मी में रहने का नाम त्रैरूप्य है। साध्य के न रहने पर हेतु का रहना ही बाधा है। ऐसी स्थिति में त्रैरूप्य और बाधित्व एक साथ रह ही नहीं सकते।

आचार्य प्रभाचन्द्र[31], अनन्तवीर्य[32], अभयदेव[33], देवसूरि[34] ने अन्यथानुपपत्ति को हेतु का लक्षण माना है। हेगचन्द्राचार्य[35] ने बताया साधनत्व को प्रकट करने वाली विभक्ति जिसके अन्त में हो ऐसा साधन का कथन 'हेतु' कहलाता है। उन्होंने स्वोपज्ञ वृत्ति में कहा- साधनत्व को प्रकट करने वाली विभक्ति पंचमी अथवा तृतीया मानी गई है। इन दोनो में से किसी विभक्ति वाले तथा पूर्वोक्त लक्षण से युक्त साधन का कथन करना हेतु है। धूम, शब्द के हेतुत्वनिराकरण के लिए 'साधनत्वाभिव्यंजक विभक्त्यन्तम्' इस पद का प्रयोग किया है और साध्य के साथ जिसकी व्याप्ति न हो वह हेतु नहीं हो सकता, यह बतलाने के लिए 'साधन वचन' इस पद का प्रयोग किया है। ऐसा हेतु तथोपपत्ति और अन्यथानुपपत्ति के भेद से दो प्रकार का कहा गया है; जैसे 'धूम अग्नि के होने पर ही हो सकता है (तथोपपत्ति) और धूम अग्नि के अभाव में नही हो सकता (अन्यथानुपपत्ति) है। धर्मभूषण[36] यशोविजय चारुकीर्ति आदि जैन तार्किकों ने अन्यथानुपपत्ति रूप एक ही हेतु का लक्षण स्वीकार किया है।

उपरोक्त अध्ययन-विवेचन से स्पष्ट होता है कि जैन्र चिन्तकों ने द्विलक्षण, त्रिलक्षण, चर्तुलक्षण, पंचलक्षण, षड़-सप्त लक्षणों को अव्याप्त तथा अतिव्याप्त शान्तरक्षित (बौद्धतार्किक) अन्यथानुपपन्नत्व रूप हेतु के एक लक्षण का खण्डन करने के लिए तीन विकल्प प्रस्तुत करते है : यथा आप अन्यथानुपन्नत्व सामान्य या विशेष के साथ ग्रहण करते हैं या साध्यधर्मी में अथवा दृष्टान्तधर्मी में।

(1) सामान्य या विशेष के साथ अन्यथानुपपन्नत्व ग्रहण करने पर–

1. सामान्य के साथ अन्यथानुपपन्नत्व लिया जाय तो यह साध्यधर्मी (पर्वतादि) में हेतु की सत्ता के प्रकाशित न होने से भी वह विवक्षित अर्थ की सिद्धि नहीं करा सकता है,[37] जैसे- चाक्षुषत्व हेतु अनित्यत्व के साथ अन्यथानुपपन्न है किन्तु इतने मात्र से वह शब्द की अनित्यता का ज्ञापक नहीं हो सकता है। इससे स्पष्ट होता है कि चाक्षुषत्व हेतु शब्द रूपी पक्ष में न रहने के कारण उसकी अनित्यता का ज्ञापक नहीं हो सकता।[38]
2. ऐसा कहने पर कि हेतु का धर्मी में रहना आवश्यक है इसीलिए चाक्षुषत्व, शब्द का अनित्यत्व ज्ञापित नहीं करता है क्योंकि शब्द रूपी पक्ष में उसका रहना नहीं होता तो उस स्थिति में प्रकारान्तर से हेतु के त्रैरूप्य को स्वीकृति मिल जाती है।[39]
3. अन्यथानुपपत्ति से अन्वय (पक्ष में रहना) तथा व्यतिरेक (विपक्ष में असत्व) का ग्रहण होता है, अतः हेतु का पक्ष में रहना आवश्यक है। जिससे उसका पक्ष- धर्मत्व स्वयं सिद्ध है।[40]
4. आचार्यो की मान्यतानुसार : ग्राह्यधर्म (पक्षधर्मता) से जो व्याप्त होगा वह हेतु होगा।[41]

(2) साध्यधर्मो (पर्वतादि) में अन्यथानुपपन्नत्व ग्रहण करने पर–

1. जिस प्रमाण से धर्मी (पक्ष में) हेतु का साध्य के प्रति नान्तरीयकत्व (अन्यथानुपपन्नत्व) का ज्ञान होता है उसी प्रमाण से पक्ष में साध्य का ज्ञान हो जाना चाहिए ऐसी स्थिति में हेतु अनावश्यक है।
2. अविनाभावी होने के लिए हेतु और साध्य को पहले से सिद्ध होना चाहिए। क्योंकि साध्यधर्मी में साध्य का अविनाभावी होना ही हेतु का लक्षण है। यदि साध्य (अग्नि) सिद्ध नहीं तब हेतु भी सिद्ध नहीं है। अतः हेतु असिद्ध है।[42]

3. ऐसा कहने पर कि अन्य प्रमाण से साध्य की सिद्धि है इसलिए हेतु भी सिद्ध हो गया तब हेतु अनावश्यक हो जाता है। यह कहने पर कि हेतु के द्वारा साध्य की सिद्धि की जायेगी तब अन्योन्याश्रय दोष का निवारण कठिन हो जायेगा।[43] हेतुसिद्धिपूर्विका साध्य की सिद्धि और साध्यसिद्धिपूर्विका हेतु की सिद्धि, इस प्रकार एक की सिद्धि दूसरे के अधीन होने के कारण अन्योन्याश्रय दोष हो जाता है।[44]

(3) दृष्टान्तधर्मी (महानसादि) में अन्यथानुपपन्नत्व ग्रहण करने पर–

1. यदि दृष्टान्तधर्मी में हेतु का अन्यथानुपपन्नत्व मानें, साध्यधर्मी के साथ न मानें, तो साध्यधर्मी में हेतु के द्वारा साध्य की प्रतिपत्ति नहीं हो सकती।[45]

जैनाचार्यों ने न हेतु के पाँच रूपों को स्वीकार किया न तीन। उनके अनुसार अन्यथानुपपत्ति के रहने पर त्रैरूप्य के अभाव में भी अनुमति होती है। जैसे चाक्षुषत्वात् इस असिद्ध अनुमान में साधन (चाक्षुषत्व) का साध्य (अनित्यत्व) के साथ अविनाभाव सम्बन्ध नहीं है। शब्द अनित्य है क्योंकि चाक्षुष है (यहाँ चाक्षुषत्व हेतु शब्द में अविद्यमान है)। किन्तु यह चाक्षुषत्व हेतु पक्ष में न रहने से असिद्ध है यह बात सत्य नहीं है ऐसा मानना चाहिए। अन्यथानुपपत्ति रूप हेतु का लक्षण न होने से यह अनुमान असिद्ध है पक्षधर्मता के अभाव से नहीं। बौद्ध नैयायिकों के अनुसार शब्द अनित्य है क्योंकि चाक्षुष है इस अनुमान में चाक्षुषत्व के शब्द (पक्ष) में न होने के कारण। लिङ्गस्य अनुमेयेसत्त्वमेव' सूत्र से लिंङ्ग को पक्ष में अवश्य ही होना चाहिए। उक्त अनुमान में पक्ष शब्द है, हेतु चाक्षुषत्व है, साध्य है अनित्यत्व। चाक्षुषत्व हेतु शब्द में नहीं है। चाक्षुषत्व चक्षु में होता है। शब्द चक्षु का विषय नहीं है अपितु श्रोतृ का विषय है। शब्द कृतक होता है और यह व्याप्ति सर्वमान्य है यत्र यत्र कृतकत्वं तत्र तत्र अनित्यत्वं अतः अव्यभिचरित अनुमान वाक्य बना, शब्दो अनित्यः श्रावणत्वात्। शब्द में श्रावणत्व है अतः वह अनित्य है। शब्द अनित्य है यह सिद्ध करने के लिए दिया गया 'चाक्षुषत्व' हेतु दोनो, वादी प्रतिवादी के लिए असिद्ध है। बौद्ध नैयायिक इसमें उभयासिद्ध हेत्वाभास मानते हैं। हेमचन्द्राचार्य कहते हैंः अविद्यमान हेतु में अन्यथानुपपत्ति नहीं होती, अत एव जिसकी सत्ता ही सिद्ध नहीं है वह स्वरूपसिद्ध हेत्वाभास कहलाता है।[46] चाक्षुषत्व हेतु का स्वरूप इसलिए असिद्ध है कि वह शब्द (पक्ष) के साथ नहीं पाया

जाता है बिना पक्ष को बीच में लाये अनित्यत्व और चाक्षुषत्व का अव्यभिचरित अन्यथानुपपन्नत्व नहीं ज्ञात कर सकते। त्रैरूप्य का निराकरण करने पर आशंका होती है कि 'अयं प्रसादः धवलः काकस्य कार्षण्यात्' यहाँ पर पक्ष में न रहने वाले काक़ के कार्षण्य से प्रसाद की धवलिमा का अनुमान क्यों नहीं हो जाता? जैनाचार्यो का कहना है कि काक का कार्षण्य प्रासाद की धवलिमा के बिना अन्यथानुपपन्न नहीं है।

वस्तुतः त्रैरूप्य और पंचरूप्य हेतुओं से सम्पन्न अविनाभाव या अन्यथानुपपन्नत्व हेतु सम्यक् अनुमापक होता है।

संदर्भ सूची

1. लिङ्गचते गम्यतेऽनेनेति लिङ्गम् तच्च पञ्चलक्षणम्, कानि पुनः पञ्चलक्षणानि पक्ष-धर्मत्वं, सपक्षधर्मत्वं विपक्षाद्व्यावृत्तिरबाधितविषयत्वमसत्प्रतिपक्षत्वं चेति। न्यायमञ्जरी, प्रमाणप्रकरण; पंचसूत्र की व्याख्या पृ. 101.
2. षड्लक्षणों हेतुरित्यपरे। त्रीणि-चैतानि अबाधितविषयत्वं विवक्षितैकसंख्यत्वं ज्ञातत्वं च।
3. वादिराज ने सप्तलक्षण हेतु का खण्डन किया है।
4. उदाहरणसाधर्म्यात्साध्यसाधनं हेतुः, तथा वैधर्म्यात्, न्यायसूत्र 1.1.34-35.
5. न्यायभाष्य 1.1.34-35.
6. न्यायभाष्य 1.1.34-35.
7. भारतीयन्यायशास्त्र, पृ. 39 पं नीचे से 9 (ले. डा. च.ध. बिजल्वान, उ.प्र.हि.सं.)
8. हेतुस्त्रिरूपः, किं पुनस्त्रैरूप्यम्? पक्षधर्मत्वम्; सपक्षेसत्त्वम्, विपक्षेचासत्वमिति। न्यायप्रवेशसूत्र
9. तत्र 'पक्षः' प्रसिद्धोधर्मी, प्रसिद्धविशेषेण विशिष्टतया स्वयं साध्यत्वेनेप्सितः। वही।
10. साध्यधर्मसामान्येन समानोऽर्थः सपक्षः। तद्यथा अनित्ये शब्दे साध्येघटादिरनित्यः सपक्षः - क्रमशः वही।
11. विपक्षो यत्र साध्यं नास्ति। यन्नित्यं तद्कृतकं दृष्टं, यथाकाशमिति। क्रमशः वही।
12. तत्र कृतकत्वं प्रयत्नानन्तरीयकत्वं वा सपक्षेवास्ति विपक्षेनास्त्येव। क्रमशः वही।
13. आप्तमीमासा, 18 वीं कारिका।
14. हेतोस्तथोपपत्त्या वा स्यातप्रयोगोऽन्यथापि वा

    द्विविधोऽन्यतरेणापि साध्यसिद्धिर्भवेदिति।17। न्यायावतार
15. उपरोक्त कारिका पर सिद्धर्षिगणी की टीका
16. न्यायावतार, कारिका-22.
17. 'तत्त्वसंग्रह' कारिका 1365.
18. न्यायविनिश्चय श्लोक 323, का. 2.154-55.

19. स्याद्वादरत्नाकर पृ. 519, पं. 11.

20. स श्यामस्तस्य पुत्रत्वाद् दृष्टा श्यामा यथेतरे।

    इति त्रिलक्षणो हेतुर्न निश्चित्यै प्रवर्तते। तत्त्वसंग्रह 1369.

21. वही 1363.

22. वहीं 1364.

23. वही 1378.

24. प्रमाणपरीक्षा पृ. 72.

25. यस्यादर्शनमात्रेण व्यतिरेकः प्रदर्श्यते

    तस्य संशयहेतुत्वाच्छेषवत् तदुदाहृतम्

    हेतोस्त्रिष्वपि रूपेषु निश्चयस्तेन वर्णितः

    असिद्धविपरीतार्थव्यभिचारिविपक्षतः। प्रमाणवार्तिक 3.14-15.

26. साध्यविनाभावित्वेन निश्चितो हेतु;; परीक्षामुख 3.15.

27. कार्यकारणभावाद् वा स्वभावाद् वा नियामकात्।

    अविनाभावनियमोऽदर्शनान्न न दर्शनात्। प्रमाणवार्तिक 3.31.

28. तदप्रतिबद्धस्य तदव्यभिचारनियमाभावात्। न्यायबिन्दु द्वि.प. सूत्र 19.

29. स च प्रतिबन्धः साध्येऽर्थे लिङ्गस्य वस्तुतस्तादात्म्यात्साध्यार्थादुत्पत्तेश्च। वही 20.

30. सहक्रमभावनियमोऽविनाभावः

    सहचारिणोः व्याप्य व्यापकयोश्च सहभावः

    पूर्वोत्तरचारिणोः कार्यकारणयोश्च क्रमभावः। परीक्षामुख 3.16, 17, 18.

31. प्रमेयकमलमार्तण्ड 3.15.

32. प्रमेयरत्नमाला 1.11 पृ. 142-44.

33. सन्मतितर्कटीका

34. प्रमाणनयतत्त्वालोक 3.11, 12, 13.

35. प्रमाणमीमांसा 2.12.

36. तदिदं लक्षणं हेतोः किं सामान्येन गम्यते,
जिज्ञासितविशेषे वा धर्मिण्यथ निदर्शने। तत्त्वसंग्रह 1379

37. सामान्येन गते तस्मिन्नेवं चेत् साध्यधर्मिणि,
हेतो सत्त्वं प्रकाश्येत न विवक्षितसिद्धिभाक्। वही 1380

38. तद्यथाचाक्षुषत्वस्य नाशेनाव्यभिचारिता,
सामान्येन गता तच्च ध्वनौ तस्य न साधनम्। वही 1381

39. तस्य धर्मिणि सद्भावः ख्याप्यते चेत् तथा सति,
सैव निरूपताऽऽयाता भवतामपि दर्शने। वही 1382

40. अन्यथानुपपत्त्या हि व्यतिरेकान्वयौ गतौ,
तस्य धर्मिणि सद्भवात् पक्षधर्मत्वसंश्रयः। वही 1383

41. ग्राह्यधर्मस्तदंशेन व्याप्तो हेतुरीदृशम्
आचार्यैरपि निर्दिष्टदृक्क्संक्षेपलक्षणम्।। वही 1384

42. अथेदं लक्षणं हेतोर्धर्मिण्येवावगम्यते
यतः प्रमाणात्तत्सिद्धिः साध्यस्यापि ततो न तु। 1385

43. साध्यस्याप्रतिपत्तौ हि हेतोरभि न निश्चयः
अतो निरर्थको हेतुरन्यतः साध्यसिद्धितः। 1386

44. अन्योन्याश्रय दोषश्च हेतोः साध्यस्य निश्चये
द्वयोरन्यतरासिद्धावन्यस्याप्यविनिश्चितः। 1387

45. निदर्शनेऽपि तत्सिद्धौ न स्याद् धर्मिणि साध्यधीः
न हि सर्वोपसंहारात् तस्य व्याप्तिर्विनिश्चिता। 1388

46. प्रमाणमीमांसा, अध्याय 2, आह्निक 1, स्वोपज्ञवृत्ति सूत्र 17.

जैनप्रमाणमीमांसायां उपमानप्रमाणस्य स्वरूपम्

– के. वी. मेहता

जैनागमग्रन्थेषु स्वतन्त्रतया प्रमाणविचारणा नैव समुपलभ्यते। प्रशापनानन्दीसूत्रादि ग्रन्थेषु ज्ञानपञ्चकस्य जैनदर्शनसम्मतो स्वतन्त्रविचारः प्रवर्तते। मतिश्रुतिभ्यां ज्ञानद्वयी, अवधिमनः पर्यायकेवले ज्ञानत्रयी इत्यनया रीत्या सङ्कलनेन ज्ञानपञ्चकस्य स्वोपशोऽवदातश्च सिद्धान्ते। जैनदर्शने उमास्वातेस्तश्च्चार्थाधिसूत्रे जरीजागर्तीति विदित चरम्। ॥ द्र. तत्त्वार्था. 1.1.9. ॥

तत्र प्रथमा ज्ञानद्वयी न केवलमात्मानं किन्तु इन्द्रियाण्यपेक्षतेऽत एव सा परोक्षज्ञानत्वेनाऽभिधीयते। द्वितीया ज्ञानत्रयी मात्राऽत्मतत्त्वसापेक्षेति कृत्वा प्रत्यक्षत्त्वेनाऽभि धीयते। उपर्युक्ता जैनज्ञानाधिगमस्य द्विधा व्यवस्थाऽपि स्वोपरात्वेनोमास्वातिमनीषायां विद्योतते।

भगवता पूज्यपादेनोमास्वातिसूरिवरण्येनैव कदाचिदिदं प्रथमतयोद्घोषितं यत् जैनसम्मतानि यानि पंचज्ञानानि विभान्ति तान्येव प्रमाणत्वेनाऽपि स्वीकर्तव्यानीति। इत्थं वैदिकवेतरदर्शने समुपलभ्यमानां प्रमाणनिरुपणां प्रति जैनदर्शने समुपलभ्यमानं ज्ञानपच्चकनिरूपणं स्वसाङ्गत्यं सम्यक् साधयतीति। एवं पञ्चसम्यक् ज्ञानस्यैव प्रामाण्यत्वात् तेषामेव प्रमाणत्वेन स्वीकरणस्य स्वेतरदर्शनवैलक्षण्येन जैनप्रमाण-मीमांसायां परिनिष्ठां गतः। इत्थं ''प्रमाकरणं प्रमाणम्'' प्रमीयते (प्रमेयः) अनेनेति प्रमाण 'मिति-सामान्यलक्षणलक्षितेन वैदिकदर्शनस्थेन प्रमाणसिद्धान्ते तादात्म्यतां गतोऽयं जैनतैर्थिकानां ज्ञानपञ्चकात्मकः सिद्धान्तो भगवतोमास्वातिसूरिणा प्रत्यक्षपरोक्षप्रमाणाभ्यां द्विधा विभज्यते।

इत्थं प्रत्यक्षपरोक्षज्ञानाभ्यां द्विधा विभागतां गतस्यास्य जैनदर्शनस्य ज्ञानसिद्धान्तस्य परमं रहस्यं संज्ञापयति कारिकेयं ज्ञानावतारग्रन्थेऽवस्थिता। यथा

"न प्रत्यक्षमपि भ्रान्तं प्रमाणत्वविनिश्चयात्।

भ्रान्तं प्रमाणमित्येतद् विरुद्धवचनं यतः॥ 6 ॥

अनेन श्लोकेन जैनप्रमाणनिरूपणस्योपनिषद्भूतं तत्त्वं समुद्धारयते यत् ज्ञानस्यैव प्रमाणत्वादज्ञानस्याऽथ च विपर्ययज्ञानस्य भ्रान्तज्ञानस्य वा प्रमाणत्वमपि नासित तस्य ज्ञानादन्यत्वरूपभापपदार्थत्वात्।

भगवतोभास्वातिना प्रमाणद्वैविध्यस्य कृतः सङ्केतोऽपि प्रमाणविद्याया जैनतैर्थिकैः सर्वथा स्वीकृत इति।

"प्रमाणं स्वपराभासि ज्ञानं बाधविवर्जितम्।

प्रत्यक्षं च परोक्षं च द्विधामयेविनिश्चयात् ॥ *न्यायावतारः सिद्धसेनदिवाकरप्रणीतः॥*

हरिभद्रसूरिणाऽपि षड्दर्शनसमुच्चये प्रत्यक्षपरोक्षाभ्यां प्रमाणस्य द्विधा विभागः कृतः। यथा।

"प्रत्यक्षं च परोक्षं च द्वे प्रमाणे तथा मते

अनन्तधर्मकं वस्तु प्रमाणविषयसिचह॥ ष.द.स. : 4.55॥

(3) माधवाचार्येण सर्वदर्शनेऽप्युक्तं यत्–

"स्याद्वादस्य प्रमाणे द्वे प्रत्यक्षमुपमायिच।

।माधवः सर्वसंग्रहः : पृ. 153॥

एवं जैनदर्शने प्रमाणद्वयस्य सिद्धान्तः सार्वभौमतां गतः। उपर्युक्तो द्विसंख्यात्मको जैनप्रमाणसिद्धान्तस्तु जिनभद्रसूरिणा कृतं संशोधनं सम्प्राप्यऽन्ततोगत्वाऽधोलिखित-प्रकारेण सम्पूर्णतां गतः।

समाविष्टयोः परोक्षज्ञाने द्वयोर्मतिश्रुतज्ञानयोर्मध्ये वर्तमानस्यैकस्य मतिज्ञानस्य सांव्यवहारिकप्रत्यक्षत्वेनाऽपि व्यवस्था कृता विभाति जैनदर्शने। द्वितीयस्य श्रुतज्ञानस्य शाब्दज्ञानत्वेनाऽर्थात् शब्दप्रमाणात्वेन संकीर्तना कृता परोक्षज्ञानत्वेन, विभात्यर्हदर्शने। पारमार्थिके प्रत्यक्षेऽअवधिमनः पर्यायकेवलज्ञानादित्रितयं समाविष्टं भवति।

पुनश्च परोक्षज्ञानस्य पञ्चधा कृतं विभाजनं जैनतैर्थिकानां मनीषायां सम्प्रकाशते।

तद्यथा-

स्मृतिप्रत्यभिज्ञानतर्कानुमानाऽगमज्ञानपञ्चकैः पञ्चप्रकारकत्वं परोक्षज्ञानं सम्भवति।

तत्र प्रत्यभिज्ञाऽभिधे परोक्षज्ञानप्रकारके वैदिक-दर्शनान्तर्गतस्योपमानप्रमाणस्याऽन्तर्भावं विदधाति, समामनुते च जैनदार्शनिकी प्रमाणनिरूपणपरम्परेति दिक्।

जैन प्रमाणमीमांसा परम्परायामकलङ्काऽभिधेनाचार्यवरेण्येन परोक्षज्ञाने स्मृत्यादिपूर्वोक्तपञ्चज्ञानाज्ञात्मकपरोक्षप्रमाणस्य सिद्धान्तः' प्रतिपादितः। भगवतोमास्वातिसूरिणा मतिज्ञानस्य पर्यायत्वेन यानि पदान्युदीरितानि तानि न केवलानि पर्यायपदानि किन्तु 'प्रत्यर्थं शब्दा भिद्यन्त' इति न्यायेन भिन्नानि पदार्थानीति याथातथ्येनपपद्यि परोक्षज्ञानं स्मृत्यादिपञ्चभेदैः पञ्चधा व्याकृत्य स्मृत्यादिपञ्चप्रमाणत्वेन समाम्नायते।

उपर्युक्त सूरिणाऽकलङ्कपादाचार्यप्रोक्तं मतिसंज्ञकज्ञानपञ्चकात्मकं प्रमाणपञ्चकं सर्वथा स्वीकृत्यैव तस्याऽन्यतमभेदेभूते प्रत्यभिज्ञासंज्ञके परोक्ष-ज्ञानात्मके परोक्षे प्रमाणे 'उपमान' प्रमाणस्य समावेशोऽन्तर्भावो वा समाम्नातो भगवता वादिदेवसूरिणा पूज्यपादेन हेमचन्द्रसूरिणा चेत्यत्र जैनप्रमाणमीमांसा-यामुपमानप्रमाणत्वेन स्वीकृत्य तादृशस्योपमानप्रमाणस्य विभावना तावद वादिदेवसूरिप्रोक्तां हेमचन्द्राचार्यसूरिप्रोक्तामत्यन्तेन संक्षेपेणाऽत्र प्रस्तूयते।

हेमचन्द्राचार्यस्तु, प्रमाणमीमांसायां

"अथ प्रमाणमीमांसा" ॥1.1.1॥ इत्यनेन सूत्रेण प्रमाणमीमांसामरभते। स्वोपज्ञवृत्त्यां हेमचन्द्राचार्यः प्रमाणस्य सामान्यलक्षणमाहेत्युक्त्वा, "सम्यगर्थनिर्णयः प्रमाणम् ॥1.1.2॥ इत्यनेन सूत्रेण प्रमाणस्य सामान्यलक्षणमभिदधाति स्वोपज्ञवृत्त्यां प्रमाणसामान्य- लक्षणप्रवाचकस्य वाक्यस्य पदानां लक्षणघटकीभूतानां पदकृत्यं लक्ष्यलक्षणात्मकं प्रतिपाद्य लक्षणार्थमुपस्थापयति। तद्यथा-"प्रमाणमिति लक्ष्यनिर्देशः। शेषं लक्षणम्। प्रसिद्धानुवादेन ह्यप्रसिद्धस्य विधानं लक्षणार्थः"। अयं वृत्तिसन्दर्भः स्वयमेव निगदव्याख्यानत्वात् न तदिह प्रतन्यते। एवं लक्षणार्थं व्युत्पाद्य ज्ञानात्मकं प्रमाणं तस्य विशेषलक्षणात्मना विभजन्ते तत्रभवन्तो हेमचन्द्राचार्याः।

"प्रत्यक्षं परोक्षं च" ॥1.1.10॥

स्वोपज्ञवृत्तिरूपे भाष्ये, इन्द्रियजमानसात्मसंवेदनयोगिज्ञानानां चतुर्णां प्रत्यक्षेण

प्रमात्मकेन प्रमाणेन संग्रहं करोति स्मृतिप्रत्यभिज्ञानोहानुमानागमानां परोक्षेण संग्रहमभिजानीते। तद्यथा

"तत्र यथा इन्द्रियजमानसात्मसंवेदेनयोगिज्ञानानां प्रत्यक्षेण सङ्ग्रहस्तथा स्मृतिप्रत्यभिज्ञानोहानुमानागमानां परोक्षेण सङ्ग्रहः"॥1.1.10 उपरि.सो.वृ.॥

प्रमाणनयतत्त्वालोके वादिदेवसूरिणाऽपि, प्रायः ज्ञानात्मकस्य प्रत्यक्षपरोक्षादि-भेदप्रत्यभिज्ञादिप्रभेदभिन्नस्य प्रमाणस्य हेमचन्द्राचार्यसदृशी प्रमाणमीमांसा कृता विद्यते, केवलं प्रत्यक्षप्रमाणमधिकृत्य तत्र हेमचन्द्रात् किञ्चित् पृथक् पर्यालोचना दरीदृश्यते। प्रमाणस्य तादृशभिन्नदर्शनसंवलितं प्रतिपादनं तावत् प्रमाणनयतत्त्व-लोकस्थे नसूत्रसन्दर्भेण, तस्य रत्नप्रभाचार्यविरचितायां रत्नाकरावतारिकायां टीकायां संस्थितेन निगदव्याख्यान- स्वरूपेणाऽधोलिखितेन वाक्यसन्दर्भेण तावत् प्रस्तूयते। तद्यथा।

"प्रमाणनयतत्त्वव्यवस्थापनार्थमिदमुपक्रम्यते। ॥ प्र. न. तत्त्वालोकः 1.1॥

"प्रकर्षेण संशयाद्यभावस्वभावेन मीयते परिच्छिद्यते वस्तु येन तत् प्रमाणम् ॥प्र. न. तत्त्वा. 1.1 उपरि रत्ना.॥

"स्वपरव्यवसायिज्ञानं प्रमाणम्" ॥ प्र. न. तत्त्व. 1.2॥

"स्वमात्मज्ञानस्य स्वरूपं। स्वस्मादन्यः - अर्थ। इति यावत् तौ विशेषेण यथावसितस्वरूपेण अवस्यति निश्चिनोतीत्येवं शीलं यत् तत् स्वरूपव्यवसायि तद्विभेदं प्रत्यक्षं परोक्षञ्च॥ प्र. न. त. 2.1॥

अक्षमिन्दियं प्रतिगतं इन्द्रियाधीनतया यदुत्पद्यते तत्प्रत्यक्षमिति तत्पुरुषः॥ प्र. न. त. 2.1 उपरि, रत्नकराव

"स्पष्टं प्रत्यक्षम्"॥ प्र. न. त. 2.2॥

"प्रबलतराज्ञानावरणवीर्यान्तिराययोः क्षेपोपशमात् क्षेपाद् वा स्पष्टताविशिष्टं वैशद्यास्पदीभूतं यत् तत् प्रत्यक्षं प्रत्येयम्॥ प्र. न. त. 2.2 उपरि, रत्नाकरावतारिका॥

" अनुमानाद्याधिक्येन विशेषप्रकाशनं स्पष्टत्वम्। ॥ प्र. न. त. 2.3 ॥" तद् द्विप्रकारकं सांव्यवहारिकं पारमार्थिकं च ॥ प्र. न. त. 2.4॥

संव्यवहारो बाधारहितप्रवृत्तिनिवृत्ती प्रयोजनमस्येति सांव्यवहारिकम्। बाह्येन्द्रिय- सामग्रीसापेक्षत्वाद पारमार्थिकम्। अस्मदादिप्रत्यक्षमित्यर्थः। परमार्थे भवं पारमार्थिकं मुख्यम्। आत्मसन्निधिमात्रापेक्षम्। अवध्यादिप्रत्यक्षमित्यर्थः।

"तत्राद्यं द्विविधमिन्द्रियनिबन्धनमनिन्द्रियनिबन्धनं च॥ प्र. न. त. 2.5॥

प्रत्यक्षानन्तरं परोक्षं लक्षयन्ति॥ रत्नाकरावतारिका पृ. 1. 'अस्पष्टं परोक्षम्'॥ प्र. न. त. 3.1॥

प्राक्सूत्रितस्पष्टताभावभ्राजिष्णु यत् प्रमाणं तत् परोक्षं लक्षितव्यम्। अथैतत् प्रकारतः प्रकटयन्ति स्मरणप्रत्यभिज्ञानतर्कानुमानागमभेदतस्तत् पञ्चप्रकारम्॥ प्र. न. त. 3.2॥ स्मृतिं लक्षयति सूत्रकारः।

तत्र संस्कारप्रबोधसंभूतमनुभूतार्थविषयं तदित्याकारं वेदनं स्मरणम्॥ प्र. न. त. 3.3॥

"तत्रेति प्राक्तनेभ्यः संस्कारप्रबोधसंभूतत्वादिना गुणेन स्मरणं निर्धारयन्ति। संस्कारस्यात्मशक्तिविशेषस्य प्रबोधात् कुलदानाभिमुख्यलक्षणात् स्मृतिप्रत्यभिज्ञानप्रमाणयोः पृथक्विषयता, तयोर्द्वयोरपि प्रमाणत्वेन कृता प्रस्थापना चावलोक्यते। वैदिकदर्शने स्मृतेः प्रत्यभिज्ञायाः प्रमाणत्वेन कृता प्रतिपादना नैव समुपलते। तत्र स्मृतेरनुभवाभ्यत्मकात् ज्ञानादितरज्ञानप्रकारत्वे नैव प्रतिपादना कृता दरीदृश्यते। प्रत्यभिज्ञानस्याऽपि विशिष्टप्रतीतिरूपात्मकज्ञानस्य प्रकारत्वेनोपपादना कृतेति स्पष्टतया दरीदृश्यते।

तत्तीर्थकरबिम्बम् ॥ प्र. न. त. 3.4॥

तदिति यत् प्राक् प्रत्यक्षीकृतम्, स्मृतम्, प्रत्यभिज्ञातम्, वितर्कितम्, अनुमितम्, श्रुतं वा भगवतस्तीर्थकृतो बिम्बं प्रतिकृतिः तस्य परामर्शः इत्येवं प्रकारं तच्छब्दपरामृष्टं यद्विज्ञानं तत् सर्वं स्मरणमित्यर्थः॥ रत्नाकरावतारिका प्र. न. त. 3.4 उपरि, पृ. 3॥

एवं स्मृतेः प्रमाणस्य निदर्शनं प्रस्तूय, वादिदेवसूरिः सूत्रेण रत्नाकरावतारटीकायाः प्रणेता रत्नप्रभाचार्यो वृत्त्या, च प्रत्यभिज्ञालक्षणं सूत्रयति, विशदयति च यथाख्यामिति। संभूतमुत्यन्नमिति कारणनिरूपणम्। अनुभूतः प्रमाणमात्रेण परिच्छिन्नोऽश्चेतनाचेतन रूपो विषयो यस्येति विषयव्यावर्णनम्। 'तत्' इत्याकारं तत् इत्युल्लेखवत्। 'तत्' इत्युल्लेखवता चास्य योग्यतापेक्षयाऽऽख्यायि। यावता स्मरसि चैत्र! 'कश्मीरेषु वत्स्यामस्तत्र द्राक्षा भोक्ष्यामहे' इत्यादि स्मरणे तच्छब्दोल्लेखो नोपलक्ष्यते,

किञ्चिद स्मरणं "तेषु कश्मीरेषु" इति 'ता द्राक्षा' इति। तच्छब्दोल्लेखमर्हत्येव। न चैवं प्रत्यभिज्ञानेऽपि तत्प्रसङ्गः। तस्य "स एवायम्"

इत्युल्लेखत्वात् इति स्वरूपप्रतिपादनम्॥ प्र. न. त. (भा. 2) 3.3 उपरि रत्नाकरावतारिका॥

उपर्युक्तेन प्रमाणतत्त्वालोकसन्दर्भेण तस्य रत्नाकरावतारिकया वृत्त्या निगदव्याख्यानरूपेण समुपलभ्यते यत् तत्शब्दोल्लेखवत् प्रमाणं स्मृतिः स एवायमितिशब्दोल्लेखवत् प्रमाणं प्रत्यभिज्ञानप्रमाणमिति। एवं जैनप्रमाणनिरूपणे प्रत्यभिज्ञानप्रमाणनिरूपणानन्तरं वैदिकन्याय-दर्शनस्य पूर्वमीमांसादर्शनस्य वेदान्तदर्शनस्य चोपमानप्रमाणस्य प्रत्यभिज्ञानरूपे परोक्षज्ञानात्मके प्रमाणेऽन्तर्भावं कुर्वन्ति सूत्रकारा वृत्तिकाराश्च। एवं जैनप्रमाणमीमांसायामुपमानप्रमाणस्य स्वातन्त्र्येणोपपादनात्मकं प्रस्थापनात्मकं निरूपणं नास्तीति सर्वथाऽकलनीयं सुधिभिरिति दिक्।

हेमचन्द्राचार्येण प्रमाणमीमांसायाः प्रथमाऽध्याये प्रस्तावनायामेव प्रतिज्ञातं स्वोपज्ञवृत्त्यां, यत् "**एवं परोक्षस्योपमानस्य प्रत्यभिज्ञाने, अर्थापत्तेरनुमानेऽन्तर्भावोऽभिधास्यते**"॥ हेमचन्द्र : प्र. मी. 1.1.12 उपरि, स्वोपरावृत्तिः॥ उपमानप्रमाणस्य प्रत्यभिज्ञानेऽन्तर्भावनप्रक्रियां वादिदेवसूरिप्रोक्तां रत्नप्रभसूरि-विशदीकृतां च तावत् प्रथमं प्रस्तूयते सूत्रकारवृत्तिकारवचनसन्दर्भेण।

प्रत्यभिज्ञानलक्षणं तावत् सूत्रकारः सूत्रयति। यथा अनुभवस्मृतिहेतुकं तिर्यगूर्ध्वता सामान्यादिगोचरं सङ्कलनात्मकं ज्ञानं प्रत्यभिज्ञानम्॥ प्र. न. त. 3.5॥

उपर्युक्तं प्रत्यभिज्ञानलक्षणं सूत्रकारप्रोक्तं रत्नप्रभाचार्यः स्वस्य रत्ना-करावतारिकाऽभिधेयां टीकायामधोलिखितरीत्या विशदीकरोति। **यथा- अनुभवश्च प्रमाणार्पितः प्रतीतिः, स्मृतिश्चाऽनन्तरोक्तैव, ते हेतुर्यस्येति कारणोपदेशः। तिर्यक् सामान्यं च गवादिषु गोत्वादि-स्वरूपसदृशपरिणामात्मकम्। ऊर्ध्वता सामान्यं च परापरविवर्तव्यापिमृत्स्नादि द्रव्यं, एतदुभयमादिर्यस्य विसदृशपरिणामादेर्धर्मस्तोमस्य स तिर्यगूर्ध्वतासामान्यादि गोचरो यस्येति विषयाख्यानम्। सङ्कलनं विवक्षितधर्मयुक्तत्वेन वस्तुनः प्रत्यवमर्शनमात्मा स्वभावो यस्येति स्वरूपनिरूपणम्**"॥ प्र. न. त. 3.5 उपरि, रत्नाकराव.॥

एवमत्र सूत्रकारप्रोक्तं प्रत्यभिज्ञानसंज्ञकं प्रमाणं लघ्वीटीकायां रत्नप्रभाचार्येण त्रिधा विभाज्य विशदीकृतं विभाति। तत्र प्रत्यभिज्ञानस्य कारणम्अनुभवः स्मृतिश्चेत्युक्तम्। गोपिण्डादिषु गोत्वरूपं तिर्यक्सामान्यं, घटादिद्रव्याणां कपाल-कपालिकादिपूर्वापरपर्यायेषु व्याप्तं मृदादि-द्रव्यरूपमूर्ध्वतासामान्यं चात्र

प्रत्यभिज्ञानस्य विषयत्वरूपेण व्याख्यातम्। प्रत्यभिज्ञानस्य स्वरूपमत्र-सङ्कलनत्वेनोक्तमिति। विवक्षितधर्माणं पूर्वापरत्वेन द्रव्येषु एकत्रमीलनं संकलनत्वेनात्राऽभिधीयते।

प्रत्यभिज्ञानस्योदाहरणानि प्रस्तौति सूत्रकारः। यथा- **तज्जातीय एवायं गोपिण्डः गोसदृशो गवयः, स एवाऽयं जिनदत्त इत्यादि"॥ प्र. न. त. 3.6॥**

उपर्युक्तेषु प्रत्यभिज्ञानस्योदाहरणेषु प्रथमोदाहरणं तिर्यक्सामान्य-स्योदाहरणमिति वृत्तिकारो निर्दिशति। द्वितीयमपि तिर्यक्सामान्यस्यैव निदर्शनं वर्तते किन्तु तत् "गोसदृशो गवयः" इत्यादाहरणं नैयायिककदाग्रहण-निग्रहार्थमुक्तमिति वृत्तिकाराः कथयन्ति। "**स एवायं जिनदत्तः** इत्युदाहरणं वैदिकदर्शनान्तर्गते न्यायादिदर्शने निरूपितस्य प्रत्यभिज्ञाना- रूपस्य ज्ञानस्योदाहरण सदृशं वर्तते तद् यथा स एवाऽयं देवदत' इति।

वैदिकदर्शनान्तर्गते न्यायदर्शने इदं प्रथमतयोपमानप्रमाणस्य निरूपणा पृथक् प्रमाणत्वेन समुपलभ्यते। तदुपमानप्रमाणस्य स्वतन्त्रविभावनामपलाप्य तमुपमानप्रमाणस्य प्रत्यभिज्ञानप्रमाणेऽन्तुर्भावं कर्तु कामयमानो वृत्तिकारो निर्ब्रूते यत्

"अत्र तज्जातीय एवायं गोपिण्ड इत्यस्मिन् तिर्यक्सामान्योदाहरणे दर्शितेऽपि गोसदृशो गवय इति यत् तत्रैवादोहरणान्तरं तद् नैयायिककदाग्रहनिग्रहार्थम्। तस्य खलु 'गोसदृशो गवय इति उपमानमित्यभिमानः। स चायुक्त विधानः। गो विसदृशो महिष इत्यस्य प्रमाणान्तरापत्तेः। अथ गवये गोसदृशो गवय इति विज्ञानं प्रत्यक्षकलमपि संज्ञासंज्ञि-सम्बन्ध प्रतियन्ति रूपे कले प्रमाणन्तराऽप्रसाध्ये साधकतमत्वादुपमानतां प्रतिपद्यते। तर्हि महिषे गोविसदृशे महिषे महिषोपलक्षणं प्रत्यक्षकलमपि तत्रैव तथाविधे कले साधकतमत्वात् प्रमाणान्तरमस्तु। न चैतदुपमानेऽन्तर्भावयितुं शक्यम्, उपमानस्य सादृश्यविषयतया व्यवस्थानात्, प्रस्तुतस्य तु वैसदृश्यव्यवसायात्मकत्वात्। न च वैसदृश्यावसायस्य संज्ञासंज्ञिसम्बन्धप्रतिपत्तिसाधकतमत्त्वं प्रसिद्धम्। यतः स महिषमाहयो मण्डले क्वापि विपिनप्रदेशेऽनच्छा यायां रोमन्थायमाने नारिकेलद्वीपवासी कश्चित् केनचित् प्रेषितः तद्विपिनप्रतिष्ठगोष्ठात् महिषमानय इति, स च तज्ज्ञं समेव पृष्ठवान् किदृग् महिष इति। तेन च गोविसदृशो महिष इत्युक्ते तद् विपिनगोष्ठं प्राप्त आप्ताऽति देशवाक्यार्थस्मरणसहकारि यमेव गोभ्यो विसदृशं पशुं पश्यति तमेव महिषशब्दवाच्यतया प्रतिपद्यत इति कः प्रतिविशेषो द्वयोरपि सङ्केतप्रतिपत्तौ। तदुक्तम्, "**उपमानं प्रसिद्धार्थसाधर्म्यात् साध्यसाधनम्। तद्वैधर्म्या प्रमाणं किं स्यात् संज्ञिप्रतिपादनमिति॥ लधी 3.1.3॥**

यदा वा यादृग् गौ तादृग् गवय इति वाक्याहितसंस्कारः प्रतिपत्ता तुरङ्गं गोविलक्षणमीक्षमाणो गवयसंज्ञासम्बन्ध प्रतिषेधं विधत्ते नाऽयं गवयवाक्वाच्यः पिण्ड इति, तदा गवयसंज्ञासम्बन्ध प्रतिषेध फलं किमतेत् प्रमाणं स्यात्? तत् एवंविधसंवेदनानां संकलनात्मकतया प्रत्यभिज्ञानतैवोपपद्यते, अन्यथा तु प्रमाणेयत्ता प्रलीयेत। यदैव हि यादृग् गौस्तादृग् गवय इति तेन शुश्रुवे तदैवसामान्यश्चेतसि स्फुरति पिण्डे सम्बन्धप्रतिपत्तिरभूत् यथा पृथुबृध्नोदराकारं वृत्तकण्ठं भावं कुम्भं विभावये इत्यादि आकरणात् कुम्भे ततः कान्तारविहारिणोऽस्य गवयसाक्षात्कारे प्राक्तनसामान्याकारसम्बन्धस्मरणे च स एष गवयशब्दवाच्य इति सङ्कलनाज्ञानरूपं प्रत्यभिज्ञानम उन्मज्जति। एवं गोविसदृशो महिष इत्याद्यपि तथा ज्ञेयत्वात् प्रत्यभिज्ञानमेविति "स एवायं जिनदत्त" इति तूर्ध्वतासामान्योदाहरणम्। **आदि शब्दात् "स एवायं वह्निरनुमीयते मया, 'स एवानेनाप्यर्थः कथ्यते' इत्यादि स्मरणसचिवानुमानाऽऽगमादिजन्यम्, तस्माद दीर्घम्, ह्रस्वम्, अणु महद् नेदीयो दवीयो वेदम्, दूरादयं तिग्मस्तनूनपात्, सुरभीदं चन्दनमित्यादि च सङ्कलनमात्रोदाहरण मभाप्यम्"।** ।रत्नाकरावतारिका - 3.6 उपरि मीमासकोऽपि 'अनेन सदृशं गोः' इत्यनधिगतं गवि सादृश्यमपस्यदुपमानं प्रमाणमाचक्षणो "अनेन महिषेण विसदृशः स गौः" इत्यनधिगतमहिषवैसदृश्यव्यवसायकस्य प्रमाणान्तरताप्रसङ्गेन। सादृश्यभावो वैसादृश्यमित्यभाववैसादृश्यमित्वभावप्रमाण-परिच्छेद्यमेवेतदिति चेत्; वैसादृश्यभावसादृश्यमितीदमपि तत्परिच्छेद्यमेव किं न स्यात्? यदि वैसदृश्याभावः सादृश्यं स्यात्, स गौः सदृशो गवयेन "इति विधिमुखेन नाल्लिखेदिति चेत् तदितरत्रापि तुल्यम्"॥ रत्नाकरावतारिका - 3.6. उपरि॥

एवं नैयायिकसम्मतमुपमानप्रमाणं, मीमांसकसम्मतमुपमानप्रमाणं न स्वतन्त्रतया प्रमाणत्वेन स्थातुं शक्यते प्रमाणव्यवहार इति कृत्वा द्वयोस्तयोदार्शनिकयो-रुपमानप्रमाणस्यो परिप्रतिपादितेन नयेन प्रत्यभिज्ञानरूपे ज्ञानात्मके प्रमाणेऽन्र्तभावयन्ति सूत्रकारातानुमोदिना नोदिता वा वृत्तिकाराः।

अत्रेवं विचार्यते यत् नैयायिकानामुपमानप्रमाणं प्रत्यभिज्ञानाऽभिधे जैनप्रमाणेऽना- भावितुं शक्यते न वा। तद्विवारणा सौकर्याय तावदुपमानप्रमाणलक्षणं नैयायिकसम्मतं समुद्ध्रियते।

प्रत्यक्षानुमानोपमानशब्दाः प्रमाणानि॥ न्या. सू. 1.1.3॥

इत्यत्र नैगायिकसम्मतं प्रमाणविभागं चतुर्धा निर्दिश्य समुद्देशक्रमेणोपमानस्य लक्षणं विदधात्यधोलिखितरीत्या।

"प्रसिद्धसाधर्म्यात्साध्यसाधनमुपमानम्"। ॥ न्या. सू. 1.1.6॥

तस्यैव सूत्रात्मकस्योपमानप्रमाणस्य मर्मस्फुरकमधोलिखितं भाष्यं विरचयति वात्स्यायनाचार्यः। तद्यथा–

प्रज्ञातेन सामान्यम् प्रज्ञापनीयस्य प्रज्ञापनमुपनमिति। यथा गौरिव गवय इति। किं पुनरत्रोपमानेन क्रियसे? यदा खल्वयं गवां समानधर्मं प्रतिपद्यत तदा प्रत्यक्षस्तदर्थं प्रतिपद्यत इति? समाख्यासम्बन्ध प्रतिपत्तिरुपमानार्थ इत्याह। यथा गौरेवं गवय इत्युपमाने प्रयुक्ते गवा समानधर्ममर्थमिन्दियार्थसन्निकर्षादुपलभमानोऽस्य गवयशब्दः सञ्ज्ञेति सञ्ज्ञासं संज्ञिसम्बन्धं प्रतिपद्यते इति। यथामुद्गस्तथा मुद्गपर्णी यथा माषस्तथा माषपर्णीत्युपमाने प्रयुक्ते उपमानात् संज्ञासञ्ज्ञिसम्बन्धं प्रतिपद्यमानस्तामौषधीं भैज्याध्यायाऽऽहरति। एवमन्योपमानस्य लोके विषयो बुभुत्सितव्य इति॥ न्या. सू. 1-1.1.6 उपरि व्या. भा॥

अत्र वात्स्यायनमुनिना "उपमानानि सामान्यवन्चनै" ॥2.1.55 - पा. सू.॥ इति पाणिनिसूत्रस्वारस्यमधिकृत्य, "उपमितं व्याघ्रादिभिः सामान्याप्रयोगे"॥ पा. सू. 2.1.56॥ इति पाणिनिसूत्रं चेत्याधिकृत्यो उपमानप्रमाणस्य विमर्शः कृतोति संल्लक्ष्यते।

'घन इव श्यामः' घनश्यामः इह पूर्वपदं तत्सदृशे लाक्षणिकमिति सूचयितुं लोकविग्रह इव शब्दः प्रयुज्यते।

एव सादृश्यसम्बन्धस्य कल्पनं पाणिनिसूत्रतः परिगृह्य सूत्रकारः वात्स्यायनो मुनिः च लोकविदितं व्यवहारं" प्राधान्येन लक्ष्यीकृत्त्योपमानप्रमाणस्य लक्षणं विदधाति विशदयति च।

पुनश्च "अनुभूतविषयासंप्रमोषःस्मृतिः"॥ यो. सू. 1.11॥

इति योगसूत्रस्य स्मृतिवृत्तेरत्रोपमानज्ञानस्योत्पकारणत्वमप्यत्रास्ति।

न्यायदर्शनप्रोक्तं तादृशमुपमानप्रमाणं न खलु याथातथ्येनप्रत्यभिज्ञानामके प्रतीत्यात्मके ज्ञानप्रकारेऽन्तर्भावयितुं न शक्यते, 'तत्तदेन्तावगाहिनीप्रतीतिः प्रत्यभिज्ञा' इति लक्षणलक्षितस्य प्रत्यभिज्ञानात्मकस्य प्रमाणत्वेनाऽङगीकारात्, तस्मिन् संज्ञासञ्ज्ञिसम्बन्ध- ज्ञानस्यानुल्लेखनत्वाच्च।

औत्पत्तिकस्तु शब्दार्थेन सम्बन्ध इति जैमिनिसूत्रभाष्ये शबरमुनिभोपवर्षाचार्यस्यो पमानप्रमाणस्य विभावनं समुद्धियते। तद्यथा–

"उपमानं सादृश्यं, असन्निकृष्टेऽर्थे बुद्धिमुत्पादयति गवयदर्शनगोस्मरणस्य"। उपर्युक्त शबराचार्योद्धृतमुपवर्षाचार्यवचनं पर्यालोच्य कुमारिलभट्टने श्लोकवार्त्तिके,

"न चेदं प्रत्यभिज्ञानं पुनरुत्पद्यतेवने शक्त्यारेतीन्द्रियत्वेन स्मृतेरिव हि सेष्यते॥ श्लो. वा. उपमानपरिच्छेदे-18॥ इति वदता वाच्यवाचकभावरूपात्मकयोः शक्तिद्वयोरतीन्द्रियत्वात् प्रत्यभिज्ञाने उपमानप्रमाणस्यान्तर्भावं कर्त्तुं नैव युज्यत इति सुदृढं प्रतिपादितमिति।

वेदान्तपरिभाषाया उपमानपरिच्छेदे वेदान्तदर्शनसम्मतं "तत्र सादृश्यप्रमाकरणम् उपमान" मिति यदुपमानप्रमाणस्य लक्षणमुक्तं तत् सर्वथा न्यायदर्शनोपमानलक्षण-सदृशमितीति कृत्वा न्यायदर्शनेन सहोक्तेन नयेनैव तस्याऽपि प्रत्यभिज्ञानेनान्तर्भावं कर्तुं पार्यते युज्यते चेत्यलं विस्तरेण॥ एवमस्य शोधपत्रस्य कलितार्थरूपा प्रस्थापनां कृत्वा, द्वितीयेयं प्रस्तूयते। **प्रत्यभिज्ञामानसीप्रतीति इति जयन्तभट्टेन न्यायमञ्जर्यां प्रतिपादितमिति। यथा एवं पूर्वज्ञानविशेषितस्य स्तम्भादेर्विशषणमति तीक्ष्णविषय इति मानसी प्रत्यभिज्ञा (न्या. म. पृ. 46)**

जयन्तभट्टस्योपर्युक्तेन समुद्धरणपरामर्शेन समुपलभ्यते यत् वैदिकदर्शने तावत् प्रत्यक्षरूपैकज्ञानात्मकता प्रत्यभिज्ञानात्मकस्य ज्ञानस्य न तु बौद्धदर्शनसम्मता ज्ञान- द्वयात्मकता प्रत्यभिज्ञानस्य वैदिकदर्शने स्वीकृतेति। बौद्धदर्शने प्रत्यभिज्ञानात्मकं नैकं ज्ञानं किन्तु, स्मरणस्य प्रत्यक्षस्य च याथातथ्येन समुच्चिता ज्ञानद्वयी एव प्रत्यभिज्ञानशब्देनाऽभिधीयते। बौद्धदर्शनस्य प्रत्यभिज्ञानस्य तदेव स्वारस्य जयन्तभट्टाचार्याऽधोलिखिते स्ववचने प्रस्तौति। यथा। **"तस्माद् द्वे एते ज्ञाने स इति स्मरणं अयम् इत्यनुभवः" ॥न्यायमं. पृ. 449॥**

एवं प्रत्यभिज्ञानमधिकृत्य भारतीयदर्शने त्रयः पक्षाः सम्भवन्ति।

(1) एकः पक्षो बौद्धानां पक्षत्वेनाऽभिधीयते। अस्यां बौद्धपरम्परायां प्रत्यभिज्ञानं न प्रमाणत्वेन स्वीकृतं तस्य बौद्धदर्शनस्य क्षणिकवादिता प्रत्यभिज्ञानात्मकं ज्ञानमपि क्षणभङ्गुरयती दिक्। ॥ **द्रष्टव्यम् प्रमाणवा. 3. 501-2॥** अस्मिन्नेव बौद्धदर्शने प्रत्यभिज्ञानात्मकं ज्ञानं प्रत्यक्षस्मरणात्मकाभ्यां द्विधाभिन्नाभ्यां ज्ञानाभ्यां विभावितं विकल्पितं च वर्तते।

"सोऽयं देवदत्तः" इत्यत्र 'से' त्यात्मकोशः अतीतकालत्वेन परोक्षत्वात् स्मरणज्ञानग्राह्यः। "इदमंशस्तु प्रत्यक्षज्ञानग्राह्येतिकृत्वा स्मरणप्रत्यक्षयोर्मध्येऽन्यतमस्यैकस्य ज्ञानस्य सर्वात्मनाऽविषयत्वात्स्य प्रत्यभिज्ञाज्ञानस्य स्मरणप्रत्यक्षोभयज्ञानात्मकस्य

सम्भवतीति वैनाशिकानामिदं मतम्। "तत्तदेन्तावगाहिनी प्रतीतिः प्रत्याभिज्ञेति" प्रत्याभिज्ञायास्तादृशं लक्षणं बौद्धदर्शनस्य प्रत्याभिज्ञाननिदर्शनेषु एव सङ्गमयितुं पार्यते।

(2) द्वितीयः पक्षः वैदिकदर्शनपक्षत्वेनाऽङ्गीक्रियते। अस्मिन् पक्षे वाचस्पत्तिमिश्र जयन्तभट्टादयो मूर्धाभिषिक्ता दार्शनिकाः प्रत्यभिज्ञानात्मकं ज्ञानं 'प्रत्यक्ष-रूपमेकज्ञानात्मकमेवे' ति स्वीकुर्वता।

(3) तृतीयः पक्ष जैनदर्शनत्वेनोपस्थापयितुं पार्यते। जैनमतेनाऽस्मिन् शोधपत्रे सविस्तरेण महतासन्दर्भेण च प्रत्यभिज्ञानात्मकस्य ज्ञानस्य कारणं, तस्य विषयं तस्य स्वरूपञ्चेति त्रिधा निरूपणेन तत्स्वारस्यरूपेण फलति यज् जैनपरम्पराऽस्मिन् ज्ञाने विविधानां ज्ञानानां सङ्कलनां कर्त्तुं वाञ्छति। वादिदेवसूरिवत् हेमचन्द्राचार्योऽयि प्रत्यभिज्ञानात्मकस्य ज्ञानस्य सङ्कलनात्मकत्वेनैव प्राधान्येन निरूपणां करोति। यथा-

1. अविशदं परोक्षम् ॥ प्र. मी. 1.2.1॥

2. स्मृतिप्रत्यभिज्ञानोहानुमानागमस्तद्विधयः ॥ प्र. मी. 1.2.2॥

3. वासनोद्बोधहेतुका तदित्याकाशस्मृतिः ॥ प्र. मी. 1.2.3॥

4. दर्शनस्मरणसम्भवं तदेवेदं तत्ससदृशं तद्विलक्षणं तत्प्रतियोगीत्यादि सङ्कलनं प्रत्याभिज्ञानमिति ॥1.2.4॥

1 अत्र हेमचन्द्राचार्यसूरिणा 'तत्दृशं' इत्यांशेन उपमानप्रमाणस्य प्रत्यभिज्ञायामन्तर्भावः क्रियते "तत्सदृशः गोसदृशः गवयः" ।।स्वोपज्ञ. टी॥ इति तत्सदृश्यस्य प्रदत्तेनोदाहरणेन लभ्यते।

2 "तदेवेदं सामान्यनिर्देशेन नपुंसकत्वं स त्वायं घटः सैवेयं पटी, तदेवेदं कुण्डमिति" ।।स्वोपज्ञटी॥ इत्यनेन वचनेन बौद्धवैदिकदर्शनसम्मतं प्रत्यभिज्ञानस्य स्वरूपं स्वाभिमते प्रत्यभिज्ञानरूपे ज्ञाने सङ्कलयति। 'तद्विलक्षणं' तत्प्रतियोगीत्यादिना लक्षणघटकीभूतेनांशेन प्रत्यभिज्ञानास्मकस्य ज्ञानस्य क्षेत्रविस्तारं प्रसाधयति, कृतेन तेन क्षेत्रविस्तारेणान्यदर्शनपरम्परायामवस्थितानामितरेषां प्रमाणभूतानां पदार्थानां सङ्कलनां कर्त्तुं प्रस्तुत एव प्रत्यभिज्ञाने ज्ञाने याथातथ्येन जैनदार्शनिकैः कर्त्तुं पार्यत्तेति मनसि निधायेति सर्वथाऽऽकलनीयमिति दिक्। एवं द्वितीयां कलितार्थरूपां प्रस्थापनां विधाय तृतीया तावत् प्रस्तूयते।

3 वादिदेवसूरिवत् हेमचन्द्राचार्यः प्रत्यभिज्ञाना त्मकस्य ज्ञानस्य लक्षणे तिर्यक्सामान्यं, ऊर्ध्वतासामान्यमित्युक्त्वा सामान्यं न द्विधा विभजति। हेमचन्द्राचार्यस्तु प्रत्यभिज्ञानलक्षणे सामान्यस्योल्लेखमपलाप्य वा विहाय तत्स्थाने 'तत्सदृशं' मित्यनेन शब्देन सादृश्यस्योल्लेखं करोति।

वादिदेवसूरिना तिर्यक्सामान्यमूर्धता सामान्येति सामान्यस्य द्विधा विभागस्तु स्वप्रोक्ते प्रत्यभिज्ञानलक्षणे कष्टकल्पनात्मकं, नैरर्थक्यात्मकञ्चेति दोषद्वयमवतारयतीति तत्र तत् न प्रयोक्तव्यमिति मया सप्रश्रया निवद्यते। पुनश्च तिर्यक् सामान्यस्य निदर्शने। तज्जातीय एवायं गोपिण्ड इत्यस्मिन्, तथ च "गोसदृशो गवये" तीत्युदाहरणे "ऊर्ध्वतासामा न्यस्यातिव्याप्ति निवारयित्तुम-शक्यमिति। एवं ऊर्ध्वतासामान्यस्योदाहरणभूते" स एवायं जिनदत्तः इत्येतस्मिन्नपि तिर्यक्सामान्यस्यातिव्याप्तिंनिवारयितुं न पार्यतेतिकृत्वाऽपि न तादृशं सामान्यस्य विभागवचनं प्रत्यभिज्ञानलक्षणे प्रयोक्तव्यमिति।

"आकृतिस्तु (पदार्थः) क्रियार्थत्वात्" ।जै. सूत्रम् - 1.3.33॥ इत्येतस्मिन् जैमिनिसूत्रे आकृत्या एव शब्दार्थत्वं स्वीकृतम्। तस्य सूत्रोपरि प्रवर्त्तमाने भाष्ये शबरमुनिना "द्रव्यगुणकर्मणां सामान्यं जातिरिति वचनं यदुक्तं, तमधिकृत्य कुमारिलभट्टेन, जातिमेवाकृतिरित्युक्त्वा" आकृतिशब्देन जातिपदार्थत्वं स्वीकृतम्। यथा- **जातिमेवाकृत्तिं प्राहुः व्यक्तिः व्याक्रियते यया" कु. मा. श्लोक. वा.॥**

एवं भारतीयदर्शने "एकत्वेसति अनेकसमवेतत्वं सामान्यं जातिः" इति सामान्येनाभिन्नत्वस्य जातिरूपपदार्थस्य सर्वतन्त्रसिद्धत्वात्, न तस्य तिर्यगादिभेदादिकमसमुपालभ्यमानत्वात् तादृशे विभागकरणे दर्शनशास्त्रग्रन्थेषु मूलक्षयकारिणी 'अव्यवस्था' समागच्छति कृत्वाऽपि तादृशो विभाग न लक्षणे प्रतोक्तव्यमिति तृतीयो फलितार्थरूपा प्रस्थापना।

(4) प्रमाणप्रत्यक्षपरोक्षादिज्ञानस्वरूपं ज्ञानविभाजनं, परोक्षस्य ज्ञानस्य पञ्चधाविभाजनादिकं सर्वं वैदिकदर्शने न सर्वथाऽनुप्राणितत्वेनैव जैनदर्शने समुपलभ्यते इति न तत्र कस्यचिद् विदुषः विप्रतिपत्तिर्दरीदृश्यत्तेत्युक्त्वा समाप्यते॥

सन्दर्भ सूची

1. NYĀYĀVATARA : SIDDHASENA DIVĀKARA; Abhoy Kumar Burman, Sanskrit Book Depot., First Edition, 1981 (with NYĀYĀVATARAVIVRITI)

2. षड्दर्शनसमुच्चयः : हरिभद्रसूरिः Eastern Book Linkers; Second Edition, 1986.

3. दर्शनसंग्रहः : माधवाचार्यः। हिन्दी भाष्योपेतः उमाशङ्करशर्मा, ''ऋषि''। चौखम्बा विद्याभवन, वाराणसी तृतीयसस्करणं, 1984.

4. Indian Philosophy; Vol. 1st and 2nd : Dr. Radhakrishnan. हिन्दी अनुवाद : नन्दकिशोर गोमिल, राजपाल एण्ड सन्स, दिल्ली 1973.

5. प्रमाणनयतत्वालोकः - वादिश्रीदेवसूरिसूत्रितः

   रत्नाकरावतारिका - रत्नप्रभाचार्यविरचिता टीकासहितः - श्री राजशेखरसूरिकृत-पञ्जिका-पण्डितज्ञानकृतटिप्पणीकाभ्यां समन्विता। पण्डित दलसुखमालवणिया सम्पादितः (मुनि श्रीमलयविजयकुलगुर्जरानुवादसहितः) लालभाई दलपतभाई, भारतीय संस्कृति विद्यामन्दिर, अहमदाबाद

   भाग-1 : द्वितीयं संस्करणम्, 1993

   भाग-2 : प्रथमं संस्करणम्, 1968

   भाग-3 : प्रथमं संस्करणम्, 1969

6. प्रमाणमीमांसा : हेमचन्द्राचार्यविरचितास्वोपज्ञवृत्तिसहिता : दलसुखमालवणिया सम्पादिता सरस्वती पुस्तक भण्डार, अहमदाबाद, द्वितीयं संस्करणम्, 1989.

7. न्यायदर्शनम् गौतममुनिप्रणीतम् : वात्स्यायनभाप्यसहितम् चौखम्बा संस्कृत सीरीज आफिस, वाराणसी, द्वितीयं संस्करणम्, 1970.

8. पातञ्जनलयोगदर्शनम् : तत्त्ववैशारदीयोगवार्तिक विभूषितव्यासभाष्यसमतेम् : भारतीय विद्या प्रकाशन, दिल्ली, (भारत) वाराणसी प्रथमं संस्करणम्, 1992.

9. श्रीमत्सायणा माधवाचार्यप्रणीतः सर्वदर्शनसंग्रह। दर्शनाङ्कुख्यासहितः - प्राच्य विद्या- संशोधन मन्दिर, पूणे, द्वितीया आवृत्तिः, 1951.

10. न्यायकोशः - भीमाचार्यः (भीमाचार्येणरचितः) The Bhandarkar Oriental Research Institute, Poona, 1978.

11. सांख्यकारिका - सांख्यसारकौमुद्या विभूषिता सारबोधिनीव्याख्यासमेता (शिवनारायण शास्त्री) पाण्डुरंग जावजी - निर्णयसागरमुद्रणालयः मुम्बई, प्रथमावृत्तिः 1940.

12. वेदान्तपरिभाषा - श्रीधर्मराजाध्वरीन्द्रविरचिता। चौखम्बा विद्याभवन, वाराणसी, तृतीयसंस्करणम् 1983.

13. केशवमिश्र प्रणीता तर्कभाषा (विश्वेश्वराचार्य - तर्क रहरस्यदीपि का) चौखम्बा संस्कृत सीरीज आफिस, वाराणसी, द्वितीय संस्करणम् 1963.

14. श्री जैमिनिप्रणीतं मीमांसादर्शनम् सशबरभाष्यम्। आनन्दाश्रममुद्रणालयः। 1929.

15. श्लोकवार्तिकम् पार्थसारथिमिश्र विरचितया न्यायरत्नकरव्याख्यया सहितम् तारा पब्लिकेशन, वाराणसी, First Edition, 1978.

जैनदर्शने शब्दप्रमाणस्य स्वरूपम्

कमलेशकुमार छ. चोकसी

प्रस्तावना

विभिन्नेषु दर्शनसम्प्रदायेषु प्रमाणानां सङ्ख्याविषयिणी समानता नास्तीति सुप्रसिद्ध मेव। जैनेतरदर्शनसम्प्रदायेषु मीमांसकाः प्रत्यक्षानुमानशब्दोपमानार्थापत्त्यभावादीनि षड् प्रमाणानि नैयायिकाः प्रत्यक्षानुमानशब्दोपमानानि चत्वारि प्रमाणानि, साङ्ख्याः प्रत्यक्षानुमानशब्दादीनि त्रीणि प्रमाणानि, वैशेषिकाः बौद्धाश्च प्रत्यक्षानुमाने द्वे प्रमाणे चार्वाकादयस्तु प्रत्यक्षैकप्रमाणमिति मन्यन्ते।[1]

जैनसम्प्रदायस्य श्वेताम्बरपरम्परायां सुप्रसिद्धे भगवतीसूत्रे प्रत्यक्षानुमानोपमानागमाश्चेति चत्वारि प्रमाणानि स्वीकृत्य निर्दिष्टानि सन्ति।[2] परन्त्वस्य निर्देशस्य क्रमिको विकासः पूर्वं विचारणीय इतिकृत्वाऽत्र किमपि विकासक्रमवस्तु विमृश्यते।

क्रमिको विकासः

प्रमाणविषयिणीं विचारणामधिकृत्य जैनसाहित्यस्य कृतेनाभ्यासेनैवम्प्रतीयते यत् प्रमाणविषयकस्य खण्डनमण्डनपूर्वकस्य विमर्शस्य दार्शनिकयुगादारम्भो जात इति।[3] अत एव पूर्वजातानां कुन्दकुन्दादिप्रसिद्धदार्शनिकानां विरचितेषु ग्रन्थरत्नेषु ज्ञानज्ञेययोः सम्यग्विचारणा दृग्गोचरीभवति, तथापि तत्र प्रमाण-प्रमेयादिशब्दानाम्प्रयोगो न दृश्यते। अस्मिन्नेव ग्रन्थे ज्ञानस्य द्वौ भेदौ प्रत्यक्षम् परोक्षञ्चेति स्वीकृतौ स्तः।

कालान्तरे सूत्रशैलीप्रणीते तत्त्वार्थसूत्र-नाम्न्युमास्वातिविरचिते ग्रन्थे ज्ञानमेव प्रमाणमस्तीति भणित्वा तस्य प्रमाणस्य प्रत्यक्षम् परोक्षञ्चेति द्वौ भेदौ

प्रदर्शितानुपलभ्येते।[4] जैनदर्शने प्रमाणविषयिण्याः चर्चाया इत एवारम्भो भवतीति मन्यते।

दार्शनिकयुगादूर्ध्वं जैनसिद्धान्ते ज्ञानस्य पञ्चभेदानां मति श्रुतावधिमनः पर्यायकेवलादीनां विचारो दृढ़ीभूय स्थितः प्रतीयते। प्रारम्भिक- जैनसाहित्य-काराणामियमेव मौलिकी परम्परा। अनुगामिनि कालेऽकलङ्कदेवनाम्ना प्रसिद्धैर्दार्शनिकप्रवरैस्तर्कशास्त्रानुसारिणीं दर्शनान्तरेषु प्रसिद्धां शैलीमनुसृत्य लघीयस्त्रये प्रमाणस्य भेदोपभेदलक्षणवती सम्यग् व्यवस्था कृतेति दिक्।

प्रारम्भिके जैनसाहित्ये शब्दप्रमाणचर्चा

जैनागमस्य प्रारम्भिकेषु ग्रन्थेषु तदानीन्तनस्य ज्ञानस्य पश्चाद्वर्तिनः प्रमाणस्य वा पूर्वोक्तभेदद्वयविषये सर्वेषां सम्मतिरेवास्ति। इन्द्रियाणां मनसश्च साहाय्येन विना यज्ज्ञानमात्मना जायते, तत् प्रत्यक्षम्। यच्च ज्ञानमिन्द्रियाणाम्मनसश्च साहाय्येनैव जायते, तत्परोक्षमित्याचक्षते। प्रत्यक्षनामकस्य प्रमाणस्यात्र त्रयो भेदाः सङ्कीर्तिताः। ते च अवधिः मनः पर्यायः केवलश्चेति। परोक्षप्रमाणस्य च मतिज्ञानं श्रुतज्ञानञ्चेति द्वौ भेदौ स्तः।

इन्द्रियाणां मनसश्च साहाय्येन जायमानं प्राथमिकं ज्ञानं तन्मितिज्ञानम्, मतिज्ञानपूर्वकञ्च जायमानं विशिष्टं यज्ज्ञानं तत् 'श्रुतज्ञानम्' कथ्यते। इदमेव श्रुतज्ञानमुत्तरकालिकेषु ग्रन्थेषु शब्दप्रमाणस्यागमप्रमाणस्य वा स्थानापन्नं जातमिति नात्र स्पष्टीकरणस्यावश्यकता।

जैनदर्शने प्रमाणविचारस्येयम्प्राचीनतमा परम्परा। जैनेतरदर्शनेषु प्रत्यक्षानुमान शब्दोपमानार्थापत्तीत्यादीनि प्रमाणानि स्वीकृतानि, परन्तु न तत्र परोक्षनामकं किमपि प्रमाणमस्ति यस्यात्र जैनदर्शने स्वीकारो जातः। अथ चायमपि जैनदर्शनस्य विशेषो यदत्रानुमानादीनि नामान्यपि प्राचीनेषु ग्रन्थेषु नोपलभ्यन्ते।

क्रमशः गच्छति काले जैनसाहित्यं यथा यथा विकासपथमारूढं तथा तथा जैनेतरदर्शने प्रचलितानां प्रमाणानामनुसारिणी कापि व्यवस्था विचारणीयेति जैनदार्शनिकैरावश्यकतानुभूता। परिणामतः जैनेतरदर्शनसम्प्रदायेषु शब्दप्रमाणत्वेन यत् स्वतन्त्रप्रमाणमासीत्तस्यैवात्र श्रुतप्रमाणरूपेण स्वीकारो जातः। तस्मिन्नेव परोक्षप्रमाणे प्रत्यक्षप्रमाणे वा दर्शनान्तरे प्रसिद्धान्यर्थापत्यनुमानोपमानादिप्रमाणान्यन्तर्भावितानि।

एवं रीत्या स्पष्टमिदं प्रतिभाति यदागमकाले प्रमाणविषये स्वतन्त्रतया कृतो विचारः नोपलभ्यते, परन्तु तद्विषयकः संग्रह एव दर्शनान्तरेभ्य सङ्गृहीत इति।

श्रुतप्रमाणम्

जैनदर्शने प्रसिद्धोऽयं श्रुतशब्दः श्रवणार्थकाद्धातोः निष्पन्नः, अतः श्रुतशब्देनानेन भूतकालिकी श्रवणक्रियावगम्यते; परन्तु ज्ञानविशषेऽत्र जैनदर्शने रूढोऽयं शब्दः मतिज्ञानपूर्वकं यज्ज्ञानं भवति तदर्थे प्रयुज्यते।[5] जैनेतरदर्शनेषु यच्छब्दप्रमाणं प्रमाणतया स्वीक्रियते, तदेवात्र जैनदर्शने श्रुतप्रमाणरूपेण जरीगृह्यते।

श्रुतज्ञानं मतिज्ञानपूर्वकं भवतीति सिद्धान्तः। पूर्वं मतिज्ञानं जायते तदनन्तरं श्रुतज्ञानम्। इत्यत एव श्रुतज्ञानस्य मतिज्ञानं कारणमपि मन्यते। एतन्मतिज्ञानं श्रुतज्ञानञ्च सर्वेषां प्राणिनां सञ्जायते।

मतिज्ञानेन जातेषु पदार्थेषु मनसः साहाय्येन जायमानं विशिष्टं ज्ञानं श्रुतज्ञानमाचक्षते। मतिज्ञानं पञ्चेन्द्रियैः मनसा चोत्पन्नं भवतीत्यतः तत्साहाय्येन ज्ञातस्य विषयस्यैवाश्रयमाश्रित्य श्रुतज्ञानस्य व्यापारः प्रवर्तते। अस्य श्रुतज्ञानस्य भेदद्वयमस्ति - अनक्षरात्मकम्, अक्षरात्मकञ्चेति। श्रोत्रेन्द्रियेतराणामिन्द्रियाणां मनसश्च साहाय्येन जायमानं मतिज्ञानपूर्वकंयच्छ्रुतज्ञानन्तद् अनक्षरात्मकमिति कथ्यते। अथ च श्रोतेन्द्रियजन्यं मतिज्ञानपूर्वकं यच्छ्रुतज्ञानन्तद् अक्षरात्मकमिति कथ्यते। अनक्षरात्मकश्रुतज्ञानं केचन तार्किकाः लिङ्गजं श्रुतज्ञानमप्याचक्षन्ते।

अकलङ्काचार्यानुसारन्तु खल्वेकमेव श्रुतज्ञानम् अक्षरात्मकमनक्षरात्मकञ्च भवति। लघीयस्त्रयनामके ग्रन्थेऽमी दार्शनिकाः कथयन्ति यत् - शब्दानां योजनायाः पूर्वं यन्मतिस्मृतिप्रत्यभिज्ञानतर्कानुमानादिकं ज्ञानं भवति, तन्मतिज्ञानमस्ति। अथ च शब्दानां योजनातः तदेव श्रुतज्ञानम्भवति। इदञ्च श्रुतज्ञानमन्यैः प्रमाणैः यदा ज्ञाता स्वयं जानाति, तदा तदनक्षरश्रुतमिति कथ्यते; तद्द्वारा च तदन्येषां कृते ज्ञानं कारयति, तदा तदक्षरश्रुतमिति कथ्यते।[6]

श्वेताम्बरसम्प्रदायेऽपि श्रुतज्ञानविषये कृतो विस्तृतो विमर्शः समुपलभ्यते। तत्र जिनभद्रगणिमहाभागानां विशेषावश्यकभाष्यनामकः ग्रन्थः ध्यानपात्रमस्ति। तैस्तत्र श्रुतज्ञानं मतिज्ञानस्यैवैको भेद इति प्रतिपादितम्।[7] इन्द्रियमनोनिमित्तेन जायमानं सर्वप्रकारकं ज्ञानं ते मतिज्ञानत्वेनैव स्वीकुर्वन्ति। परन्तु परोपदेशवचनैः आगमवचनैश्चोत्पन्नं ज्ञानविशेषं श्रुतज्ञानमस्तीत्यपि ते स्वीकुर्वन्ति।

मतिश्रुतयोर्भेदस्य कारणानि प्रदर्शयन् विशेषावश्यकभाष्ये निगदितं यत् - मतेः श्रुतस्य च लक्षणं भिन्नमस्ति; मतिः कारणं श्रुतञ्च कार्यमस्ति, मतिभेदाः श्रुतभेदाश्च पृथक् पृथक् सन्ति, श्रुतज्ञानस्येन्द्रियं श्रोत्रमेवास्ति, मतिज्ञानस्य च पुनः

सर्वाणीन्द्रियाणि; मतिज्ञानं मूकमस्ति श्रुतञ्च वाचालम्। एवं मतिश्रुतयोः विविधः भेदः।[8]

इन्द्रियमनसोः साहाय्येन शब्दानुसारि यज्ज्ञानं जायते, तत् स्वस्मिन् प्रतिभासमानस्यार्थस्य प्रतिपादने समर्थं भवति; तदेव श्रुतज्ञानं कथ्यते।[9] तद्यथा- 'घट' इति शब्दं श्रुत्वा घटार्थेन सह तस्य सङ्गतिः क्रियमाणे घट-घट-घट इत्यादिना शब्दोल्लेखेन सहान्तरङ्गे उत्पन्नं ज्ञानं स्वस्मिन् प्रतिभासमानस्यार्थस्य श्रुतिपारकं शब्दं जनयति, अतः तस्मादन्यं श्रोतारं बोधः सञ्जायते। अर्थात् श्रुतज्ञानद्वारा ज्ञाता स्वयमपि जानाति अन्यान् च ज्ञानं कारयति। मतिज्ञानं पुनरिन्द्रियमनसोः निमित्तेनोत्पन्नं भवति; शब्दानुसारि च तन्न भवत्येष एवोभयोः भेदः।

एवञ्च कथनीयार्थमेव विषयीकरोत्यतः यादृशमपि श्रुतज्ञानमस्ति, तत्सर्वं शब्दस्यैव परिणामः प्रतीयते। शब्देनात्र परोपदेशरूपः शब्दः ग्रन्थरूपश्च शब्दः संगृहीतो भवति। ताभ्यामुभाभ्यां जायमानञ्ज्ञानं शब्दस्यैव परिमाणरूपं भवतीति स्पष्टमेव।

एतादृशीं श्वेताम्बरमान्यतां प्रति दिगम्बरमान्यता न किमपि विरोधं सन्दधाति। यतोहि दिगम्बरमान्यतायामपि श्रुतज्ञानं पदार्थपरप्रबोधकमस्ति। तत्र च तस्य परार्थत्वे श्रुतज्ञानस्य वचनात्मकत्वं वा शब्दात्मकं वा कारणमिति प्राहुः।

श्वेताम्बरसम्प्रदाये श्रुतज्ञानस्याक्षररूपानक्षररूपौ च द्वौ भेदौ स्वीकृतौ स्तः। तथाप्युभावपि शब्दजावेव। तयोस्त्वियानेव भेदो यदक्षररूपं श्रुतज्ञानमक्षरात्मकेन शब्देनैवोत्पन्नं भवति, अनक्षररूपं श्रुतज्ञानं चानक्षररूपेण शब्देनोत्पन्नं भवति। परन्तु दिगम्बरपरम्परायां शब्दजं श्रुतज्ञानमक्षरात्मकश्रुतम्, लिङ्गजश्रुत-ज्ञानञ्चानक्षरात्मकं श्रुतज्ञानमिति मन्यते। परन्त्वत्र सुस्पष्टमेव यच्छ्रुतज्ञाने शब्दस्यैव प्रधानता वरीवर्ति-इति दिगम्बर सम्प्रदायेऽपीष्टमेवास्ति।

श्रीगोमट्टसारस्य जीवकाण्डे श्रुतज्ञानमित्थं वर्णितमस्ति - नियमेणिह सङ्कजं पमुहं॥ अस्य व्याख्यानावसरे कथितमस्ति यत् - "श्रुतज्ञानस्य प्रकरणे शब्द-जाक्षरात्मकाल्लिङ्गजानक्षरात्मकाद्भेदाच्च वर्णपदवाक्यात्मकशब्दाज्जनितस्य श्रुतज्ञानस्य प्रधानता वर्तते; यतोहि आदानप्रदाने, पठन-पाठने वा सर्वत्र व्यवहारे वेदमेव मूलम्। यद्यपि लिङ्गजमनक्षरात्मकं श्रुतज्ञानमेकेन्द्रियाणां पञ्चेन्द्रियाणां च जीवानां भवति तथापि व्यवहारे तदनुपयोगित्वाद् प्रधानमस्ति।

अथ च श्रोत्रेन्द्रियेणास्य ग्रहणं भवतीत्यतः एवेदं श्रुतम् कथ्यते।

शब्दाच्चोत्पन्नमर्थज्ञानं श्रुतज्ञानं कथ्यते - इत्यतोऽपि अक्षरात्मकस्य श्रुतज्ञानस्यैव प्राधान्यम्प्रतीयत इति॥

दार्शनिकयुगस्य शब्दप्रमाणविमर्शः

अस्य दार्शनिकयुगस्यारम्भकाले जैनदार्शनिकेषु मूर्धन्येनाकलङ्कनामकेन दार्शनिकप्रवरेण परम्परया प्राप्तानि मतानि दर्शनान्तरसम्प्रदायगतविचारसरणिं यथानुकूलं स्यात्तथा प्रदर्शितानि। प्रमाणसङ्ग्रहे प्रथमे प्रस्तावेऽमी आचार्याः-

"प्रत्यक्षं विशदज्ञानं त्रिधा श्रुतमविप्लवम्।

परोक्षं प्रत्यभिज्ञादि प्रमाणे इति सङ्ग्रहः॥

प्रत्यक्षं विशदज्ञानं तत्त्वज्ञानं विशदम्, इन्द्रियप्रत्यक्षमनिन्द्रियप्रत्यक्ष-मतीन्द्रियप्रत्यक्षं त्रिधा। श्रुतमविप्लवम् प्रत्यक्षानुमानागमनिमित्तम्। परोक्षं प्रत्यभिज्ञादिस्मरणपूर्वकम्।" - इत्यादिभिर्वचोभिः स्वमतानुसारिणो भेदाः प्रदर्शितवन्तः। परन्तु तदनन्तरं परम्परया प्राप्तौ। प्रत्यक्षं परोक्षञ्चेति द्वौ भेदौ प्रमाणस्य स्वीकृत्यान्यैराचार्यैः तयोरूपभेदप्रदर्शनमित्थमकारि-

1. प्रमाणस्य प्रत्यक्षम्परोक्षञ्चेति द्वौ भेदौ।
2. प्रत्यक्षप्रमाणस्य च सांव्यावहारिकं पारमार्थिकञ्चेति द्वावेवान्तर्भेदौ।
3. सांव्यावहारिकस्य प्रत्यक्षस्य - अवग्रहः, ईहा, अवायः, धारणा चेति चत्वारो भेदाः।
4. परोक्षप्रमाणस्य स्मृतिः, प्रत्यभिज्ञानम्, तर्कः, अनुमानम् आगमश्चेति पञ्च भेदाः।

उत्तरकालिकैः सर्वैः दार्शनिकैः परोक्षप्रमाणस्यैते भेदाः स्वीकृताः। अत्र यदन्तिमो भेदस्स आगमप्रमाणम् जैनेतरदर्शनसम्प्रदायेषु शब्दप्रमाणत्वेन स्वीकृतं प्रमाणमस्ति तद्वर्तते।

न्यायादिषु दर्शनेषु 'आप्तोपदेशः शब्दः।'[12] इत्युक्त्वा शब्दप्रमाणस्य लक्षणं लक्षितमस्ति। आप्तश्चात्र "आप्तः खलु साक्षत्कृत धर्मा यथादृष्टस्यार्थस्य चिख्यापयिषया प्रयुक्त उपदेष्टा।"[13] इत्यादिना कश्चित्पुरुषविशेषो गृह्यते।[14]

एतत्सर्वं मनसि निधाय जैनदर्शनेऽपि 'आगमप्रमाणंस्य' शब्दप्रमाणस्य वा लक्षणं लक्षितम्। तद्यथा-

1. न्यायावतारे सिद्धसेनदिवाकराः प्रोचुः-

हृष्टेष्टाव्याहताद्वाक्यात् परमार्थभिधायिनः।
तत्त्वग्राहितयोत्पन्नं मानं शाब्दं प्रकीर्तितम्॥

आप्तोपज्ञमनुल्लङ्ध्यमहृष्टेष्टविरोधकम्।
तत्त्वोपदेशकृत्सार्वं शास्त्रं कापथघट्टनम्॥[15]

अर्थात् प्रमाणतः निश्चितार्थात् अबाधितम्, परमस्य विशिष्टस्य वाऽर्थस्याभिध ाायिनो वाक्यात् तत्त्वग्राहिरूपेण यत्प्रमाणमुत्पद्यते, तच्छब्दप्रमाणम्।

तच्च लौकिशास्त्रजभेदाद् द्विविधम्।[16] लौकिकम् अविप्रतारकस्य वचनादुत्पन्नं भवति, शास्त्रजञ्चाप्तोपज्ञम्, अनुलङ्घ्यम् न केनापि खण्डयितुं शक्यमिति यावत्; अहृष्टेष्टविरोधकम्, जीवादिसप्ततत्त्वानां स्वरूपस्य प्रकाशकम्, सर्वेभ्यो हितं करोति तत् तीर्थान्तरस्य च यत् निराकर्तृं तच्छास्त्रं शब्दप्रमाणं कथ्यते॥

अस्य न्यायावतारस्य वार्तिककाराः श्रीशान्त्याचार्या आगममित्थं व्याचक्षुः -

तापच्छेदकाषैः शुद्धं वचनं त्वागमं विदुः।
तापो लाप्तप्रणीतत्वमाप्ता रागादिसंक्षयात्॥[17]

अत्र स्पष्टमेवास्ति यच्छुद्धं वचनमेवागमप्रमाणमस्ति।

2. इत उत्तरं सर्वैरपि जैनतार्किकैः न्यायादिदर्शनमनुसरद्भिः प्रमाणस्यास्य लक्षणं लक्षितमस्ति। तत्रादौ परीक्षामुखनामके स्वग्रन्थे माणिक्यनन्दिनः प्रसिद्धाः जैनतार्किकाः शब्दप्रमाण मागमप्रमाणत्वेन लक्षयन्त एवमाहुः-

आप्तवचनादिनिबन्धनमर्थज्ञानमागमः इति[18] न्यायदीपिकायामपि धर्मभूषणाः इत्थमेव प्रोचुः।[19]

3. राजवार्तिककारास्तु - 'तदुपदिष्टं बुद्धयतिशयर्द्धियुक्तगणधरावधारितं श्रुतम्।' - इत्यादौ श्रुतप्रमाणं श्रुतमेव' इत्यादिवचनैः पर्यायत्वमाहुरुभयोः।[20] अत्रायमाशयः- केवलिभिः भगवत्पादैः कथितम्, अतिशयबुद्धि-ऋद्धिमद्भिः गणधरैरवधारितञ्च वचनं शब्दप्रमाणम्मन्यत इति।

यद्यप्युपर्युक्तानुसारम्भगवत्पादनान्तीर्थङ्कराणां वचांसि, तेषां संग्राहकानां साक्षाच्छिष्याणां गणधराणां वचांसि चागमत्वेन, श्रुतत्वेन शब्दप्रमाणत्वेन वा स्वीकर्तव्यानि सन्ति, तथापि नैतदात्यन्तिकम्, अन्याऽपि वाचः सन्ति येषामत्र

समावेशो भवति। जैनदर्शनस्याग्रजैः दार्शनिकैः श्रीमद्भिरकलङ्काचार्यैः आप्तवचनमेव शब्दप्रमाण- मित्यायशम्प्रकटपित्वाप्तलक्षणमित्थं व्याचक्षुः – "यो यत्राविसंवादकः स तत्राप्तः, ततः परोऽनाप्तः। तत्त्वप्रतिपादनमविसंवादः, तदर्थ-ज्ञानात्" इत्यादि।[21]

अनेन यः कश्चिदपि यस्मिन् कस्मिन् विषयेऽविसंवादको भवति, स तस्मिन् विषये आप्त इत्यवगन्तव्यम्। अर्थादाप्तत्वनिर्णयार्थन्तद्विवयकं ज्ञानं तद्विषयिकी चाविसंवादकता अवंचकता वा स्यादित्येव प्रमुखतयापेक्षते। अतो व्यवहारेऽपि शब्दजन्यार्थ-बोधमप्यत्रागमप्रमाणे समावेष्टुं शक्यते। तच्च येन केनापि अविसंवादिनावञ्चकेनोच्चार्यमाणानि वचनान्यप्याप्तवचनानीति यावत्।

आगप्रमाणस्य भेदाः

अनुयोगद्वारनामके ग्रन्थे आगमप्रमाणस्य द्वौ भेदौ व्यवस्थितौ लौकिकम् लोकोत्तरञ्च। अलौकिकञ्चेति। लौकिकागमे जैनेतरशास्त्राणां समावेशो भवति। तद्यथा- महाभारतम्, रामायणम्, वेदाः इत्यादयोऽपि ग्रन्थाः। लोकोत्तरागमे जैनशास्त्राणां समावेशो भवति।

आगमप्रमाणमेकेनान्येन प्रकारेणापि विभाजितमस्ति। तद्यथा- आत्मागमः, अनन्तरागमः परम्परागमश्चेति त्रिधा। एतद्विभाजनं सूत्रार्थयोरपेक्षातः कृतं वर्तते। जैनसम्प्रदाये मान्यतेयमस्ति यत्तीर्थङ्कराः 'अर्थम्' उपदिशन्ति, गणधराश्च तानाश्रित्य सूत्राणि विरचयन्ति। अतोऽर्थरुप आगमः तीर्थङ्करेभ्य आत्मागमः, सूत्ररूपेण च ग्रथित आगमः गणधरेभ्य आत्मागमोऽस्ति। अर्थस्य मूलतयोपदेशस्तीर्थङ्कराणा- मस्तीतिकृत्वा गणधरेभ्यो न स आत्मागमः, परन्तु तेभ्यस्तु अनन्तरागमः, तेभ्य एवोपदिष्टत्वात्।

गणधराणां ये शिष्यास्सन्ति तेभ्योऽर्थरूपागमः परम्परागमो वर्तते। यतोहि तीर्थङ्करेभ्यो गणधरैः गणधरेभ्यश्च शिष्यैश्चायमागमो लब्धः। सूत्ररूपागमस्तु गणधरशिष्येभ्योऽनन्तरागम एव; सूत्राणामुपदेशस्तु गणधरेभ्यः साक्षात्प्राप्त इत्यतः। गणधरशिष्यानन्तरभाविभ्य आचार्येभ्यः सूत्रार्थोभयरूपागमः परम्परागम एवास्ति।

जैनेतरदर्शनसम्प्रदायानाम्मतानि तन्निरासश्च

जैनतार्किकैः स्वकीयदर्शनसम्प्रदाये पूर्वोक्तदिशा यदागमप्रमाणस्य विमर्शः कृतः, तत्र जैनेतरदर्शनसम्प्रदायस्य विविधानि मतानि पूर्वपक्षत्वेन संस्थाप्य खण्डितानि सन्ति। तानि च प्राधान्येनैतानि सन्ति।

1. बौद्धादयो, ये खल्विदं शाब्दप्रमाणमेव न स्वीकुर्वन्ति, तेऽत्र प्राथम्यं लभन्ते। एतेषाम्मते तु शब्दप्रमाणम्प्रमाणमेव नास्ति, शब्दस्यार्थेन सहासम्बन्धात्। अथ च शब्दस्यार्थस्तु न विधिरूपः परन्तु अन्यापोहरूपो शब्दार्थः। अतः शाब्दं प्रमाणत्वेन स्वीकर्तुमेते नोत्सहन्ते॥

अत्र जैनदार्शनिकाः - "शब्दार्थयोरसत्यपि तादात्म्यसम्बंन्धे तदुत्पत्तिसम्बन्धे च, योग्यतारूपसम्बन्धस्य सद्भावाच्छाब्दप्रमाणमस्त्येव" इत्यादिना स्वमतस्थापनपरविमर्शं कृतवन्तः।[22]

2. वैशेषिकादयोऽन्ये शब्दप्रमाणं स्वीकुर्वन्ति, परन्तु तस्यानुमान-प्रमाणेऽन्तर्भावमनुभावयन्ति, न तु स्वतन्त्रप्रमाणत्वेन॥

अत्र शब्दानुमानयोरैक्यमस्तीति न, उभयोर्विषयान्यत्वात्। शब्दस्य केवलमर्थ एव विषयः, अनुमानस्य तु साध्यधर्मेण युक्तः धर्मी इति जैनदार्शनिकाः॥[23]

3. मीमांसकादयोऽप्यत्र जैनदर्शने पूर्वपक्षीयाः सन्तस्तिष्ठन्तीति। यतोहि शब्दप्रमाणस्यैते स्वीकारङ्कुर्वन्ति; तदंशे च जैनदर्शनानुकूल्यमत्र; परन्तु मीमांसकानां शाब्दप्रमाणविषयिकी या मान्यता अस्ति तामेते न स्वीकुर्वन्तीति। तद्यथा-

(क) मीमांसकाः शब्दार्थयोः सम्बन्धम् नित्यम् मन्यन्ते।

जैनतार्किकाणाम्मते शब्दार्थयोः नित्यसम्बन्धः नास्ति।

(ख) मीमांसकानाम्मते शब्दोऽपि नित्यः। जैनाः शब्दमनित्यम्मन्यन्ते।

(ग) वेदाः अनादयोऽपौरुषेयाश्चेति मीमांसकानाम्मतम्।

जैनदर्शनसम्प्रदायानुसारन्तु वेदाः अपौरुषेयाः अनादयश्च न सन्ति।

(घ) शब्दस्यार्थः सामान्यम्, इत्येतन्मतम् मीमांसकानाम्। तद्यथा- गोशब्दः गोत्वम् सामान्यञ्जातिं वाऽभिदधति न तु गोव्यक्तिम्।

अत्रैषः जैनानाम्पक्षः[24] - सामान्यमात्रमेव शब्दस्य विषय इति न, यतोहि सङ्केतानुसारमेव शब्दो वाचको भवति। संकेतश्च सामान्यविशिष्टे विशेष एव क्रियते, न तु सामान्यमात्रे। यथा 'दण्डी' इत्यनेन शब्देन दण्डविशिष्टस्य पुरुषस्य प्रतीतिर्भवति, तथैव गोशब्देन गोत्वविशिष्टस्य गोपिण्डस्य प्रतीतिर्भवतीति।

4. वैयाकरणानां कानिचिन्मतान्यप्यत्र पूर्वपक्षत्वम्भजन्ति। तेषामपि स्वमतस्थापनपुरस्सरो निरासोऽत्र कृतो वर्तते। तद्यथा-

(अ) केचन वैयाकरणाः संस्कृतशब्देष्वेवार्थबोधस्य शक्तिवर्तते इति मन्यन्ते; न तु पाली-प्राकृतादिदेशभाषाशब्देषु।

जैनदार्शनिकास्तु देशभाषाशब्देष्वपि अर्थबोधस्य शक्तिं मन्यन्ते।[25]

(आ) वैयाकरणाः शब्दाद्वैतवादिनस्सन्ति। शब्दं विना ज्ञानं न संभवतीति मतमेतेषाम्।

परन्तु जैनतार्किकास्तु शब्दसंसर्गं विनापि ज्ञानं सम्पद्यत इति स्वीकुर्वन्त उपर्युक्तस्य मतस्य निराकरणं कुर्वन्ति।

उपसंहारः

एवम्प्रकारेण जैनसाहित्यस्य दार्शनिकानां विविधानां ग्रन्थानां कृतेनाभ्यासेनैवं प्रतिभासते यत् जैनसाहित्यस्य प्रारम्भिके काले प्रथमं श्रुतज्ञानरूपेण; दार्शनिकाद्युगाच्चागमप्रमाणरूपेण दर्शनान्तरेषु प्रसिद्धस्य शब्दप्रमाणस्य विषये ऊहापोहपूर्वको विचारः समुपलभ्यते। अत्रायमेव सारः यद् दर्शनान्तरेषु न्यायमीमांसादिषु शब्दप्रमाणस्य यादृशो विमर्शः (विभावना वा) प्राप्यते, तादृशोऽत्रापि प्रवर्तत एव। तथाप्यत्र जैनागमग्रन्थानुसारिणो दार्शनिकाः स्वमतमनुसरन्तोऽनुकूलानि मतानि दर्शनान्तरेभ्यो गृहीतवन्तः प्रतिकूलानि च मतानि स्वसिद्धान्तविरोधात् खण्डनपूर्वकं व्यक्तवन्त इत्यलं बुद्धिमद्वर्य्येषु॥

सन्दर्भ सूची

* सेन्टर ऑफ एडवांस स्टडी इन संस्कृत, पूना युनिवर्सिटी, पूना द्वारा समायोजिते जैन लोजिक एन्ड एपिस्टोमोलोजी-परिसंवादे (दि. 27-28-29 मार्च, 1995) पठितो निबन्धः।

1. तौलनीयोऽत्रायं श्लोकः

जैमिनेः षट् प्रमाणानि चत्वारि न्यायवादिनः।

साङ्ख्यस्य त्रीणि वाक्यानि द्वे वैशेषिकबौद्धयोः।।

प्रमेयरत्न 2.2 इत्यत्र टिप्पण्यामुद्धतः।

प्र. चौखम्बा, वाराणसी, वि.सं. 2020; पृ. 43.

2. "अहवा हेऊ चउब्विहे पण्णत्ते, तं जहापच्चक्खे अणुमाणे औवम्मे आगमे।" - स्थानाङ्ग-सूत्र, सं. मुनि कनैयालाल, प्र. धनपतिसिंह, कलकत्ता, सूत्र-338.

3. निखिलमपि जैनसाहित्यन्तज्ज्ञाः चतुर्षु विभागेषु विभजन्ति। तद्यथा- 1. सिद्धान्तागम-कालः - 600 वि. सं. यावत्। 2. अनेकान्तस्थापनाकालः - 300 तः 800 वि. सं. यावत्। 3. प्रमाणव्यवस्थायुगः - 800 वि. सं. तः 1700 वि. सं. यावत्। अयमेव दार्शनिकयुगः। 4. नवीनन्याययुगः - प्रारम्भादद्ययावत्। - *जैनदर्शन*, ले. डा. महेन्द्रकुमार जैन, काशी, द्वितीय सं., सन् 1966, पृ. 14.

4. 'मतिश्रुताऽवधिमनः पर्यायकेवलानि ज्ञानम्।।9।। इत्यनेन सूत्रेण सम्यग्ज्ञानस्य पञ्चभेदान् व्याख्याय

   तत्प्रमाणे।।10।। आद्ये परोक्षम्।।11।। प्रत्यक्षमन्यत्।।13।। इति त्रिभिः सूत्रैः सम्यग्ज्ञानस्य प्रमाणत्वं तद्भेदौ च कथितौ वर्तेते। - तत्वार्थसूत्र, सं. पं. सुखलाल संघवी, प्रकाशकः - जैनसंस्कृति संशोधन मंडल, बनारस, सन्-1952, द्वितीयसंस्करण; पृ. 18.

5. श्रुतशब्दोऽयं श्रवणमुपादाय व्युत्पादितोऽपि रूढ़िवशात् कस्मिंश्चिज्ज्ञानविशेषे वर्तते. .. कः पुनरसौ ज्ञानविशेषः इति। अत आह - श्रुतं मतिपूर्वमिति। - *सर्वार्थसिद्धिः*, प्रकाशक भारतीय ज्ञान पीठ, वाराणसी; 1-10.

6. "ज्ञानमाद्यं मतिः संज्ञा चिन्ता चाभिनिबोधिकम्।।10।। प्राङ्नामयोजनाच्छेषं श्रुतं शब्दानुयोजनात्।।" - *लघीयस्त्रय*, सं. महेन्द्रकुमार शास्त्री, प्रका. सिन्धी जैन ग्रन्थमाला, अहमदावाद, सन्-1939, कारिका- 10-11.

7. 'मइभेओ चेव सुयं।' - विशेषावश्यकभाष्य, सं. प्रका. यशोविजयग्रन्थमाला, काशी, गाथा-86.

8. द्रष्टव्यः विशेषावश्यकभाष्य, गाथा-17.

9. इंदियमणोनिमित्तं जं बिण्णाणं सुयाणुसारेणं।

नियमत्थुत्तिसमत्थं तं भावसुयं मई सेसं।।

तत्रैव; गाथा-100.

10. *प्रमाणसङ्ग्रहः*; सं.- महेन्द्रकुमार शास्त्री, प्रका. सिन्धी जैनग्रन्थमाला, अमदावाद, सन् 1939; पृ. 97.

11. तुलना कार्या- 'स्मरणप्रत्यभिज्ञानतर्कानुमानागमभेदतस्तत् पञ्चप्रकारकम्।। - *प्रमाणनयतत्त्वालोकः*, (रत्नाकरावतारिकया सहितः), सम्पा. पण्डित दलसुख मालवणिया, प्रका. ला.द. विद्यामंदिर, अमदावाद, सन् 1968, भा. 2; तृतीयपरिच्छेद, सू. 2.

12. न्यायदर्शनम् - 1.1.7.

13. उपर्युक्तस्य न्यायसूत्रस्य वात्स्यायनभाष्यम्।

14. जैनदर्शने तदितरदर्शनस्थानि प्रमाणानि कदा केन च प्रकारेण प्रविष्टानि; प्रवेशकश्चेति मात्रैतिह्यप्रधानविमर्शे श्रीमतां सुखलालसंधवी महाभागानां वचांसीमानि ध्यातव्यानि प्रतीयन्ते। तद्यथा- जान पड़ता है सबसे पहिले आर्यरक्षित ने, जो जन्म से ब्राह्मण थे और वैदिक-शास्त्रों का अभयास करने के बाद ही जैन साधु हुए थे, अपने ग्रन्थ अनुयोगद्वार में प्रत्यक्ष, अनुमानादि चार प्रमाणों का विभाग जो गौतम दर्शन (न्याय सू. 1.1.3) में प्रसिद्ध है, उसको दाखिल किया।'' - *प्रमाणमीमांसा*, भाषा टिप्पणानि, सं. पण्डित सुखलाल जी संघवी, अमदावाद, पुनर्मुदण, सन् 1989; पृ. 20.

15. *न्यायावतारः* - सं. विजयमूर्ति शास्त्राचार्य, प्रका. श्री परमश्रुतप्रभावक मंडल; बम्बई, सन् 1950, पृ. 59 (कारिका-8, 9)।

16. अन्यत्राप्तभेदरुपेणैतौ भेदौ किञ्चित्परिवर्तनं विधायेत्थं प्रदर्शितौ - ''स च द्वेधा लौकिको, लोकोत्तरश्च।।6।। लौकिको जनकादिर्लोकोत्तरस्तु तीर्थङ्करादि।।7।। - प्रमाणनयतत्त्वालोकः; भा. 2, 4-6, 7.

17. न्यायवतारसूत्रवार्तिकम् - कारिका-54; न्यायवतारसूत्रवार्तिकवृत्तौ; संपा. दलसुख मालवणिया, मुंबई, सन् 1949.

18. परीक्षामुखम्, 3.94.

19. न्यायदीपिका, 3.73-112.

20. राजवार्तिक, 6.13.2.52.3-29. 1.20.25.7.8-18.

21. अष्टशती, अष्टसह. पृ. 236.

22. द्रष्टव्यम् - न्यायकुमुदचन्द्रे। पृ. 538.

23. द्रष्टव्यम् - न्यायकुमुदचन्द्रः, पृ. 532-536.

24. द्रष्टव्यमत्र 'न्यायकुमुदचन्द्रः', पृ. 568 (प्रका. माणिक्यचन्द्र ग्रन्थमाला, बम्बई)

25. द्रष्टव्यम् - तदेव, पृ. 762 अथ च प्रमेयकमलमार्तण्डेऽपि पृ. 668 (निर्णयसागर प्रेस, मुंबई)

Jaina Concept of Meaning and Referent

Vinayaka P. Bhatta

Introduction

The Jainas have admitted right knowledge (*pramāṇa*) to be of two kinds: (i) direct valid knowledge (or perception) (*pratyakṣa*) and indirect valid knowledge (*parokṣa*). Verbal testimony (*śabda* or *āgama*), which is one of the two kinds of indirect valid knowledge, is the knowledge derived from the words of reliable including knowledge from scripture (*āptopajñam, Nyāyāvatāra*, 9); or is a method of correct nominclature (*yathārthābhidhāna*, Tattvārthādhigama sūtra, P. 32). However, according to the Jainas (Laghīyastraya, 44), the verbal testimony, while denoting its objects (referents), becomes of three kinds; (1) the suitable or conventional (*sāmprata*) such as 'enemy' (*śatru*), the etymological (*samabhirūḍha*) such as 'strong' (*śakra*), and the such like or actual (*evambhūta*) such as 'doer' (*kartā*). Now the modern linguists (Moravcsik, 1974) have distinguished meaning or sense from referent. While the object intended to be spoken of are the referents, the ideas that are associated with the objects and to be conveyed by means of words are the meanings or senses. For instance, in the expressions such as 'the morning star' and 'the evening star' the planet Venus, which is intended to be denoted, is the referent, whereas the senses of the rising and the setting stars seen at East and the West are the meanings or the senses (Frege 1960).

Indian epistemologists including the Jaina epistemologists too can be said to have distinguished the senses or meanings from the referents. Since the Indian epistemologists were primarily concerned with the words (*śabda* or *āgama*) as the direct or indirect means of valid knowledge (*pramāṇa*), the cognition or awareness of the objects created by words (*padārthadhī*) can be considered as the sense or meaning and the objects denoted by the words can be considered as the referents (*artha*). Thus, the Indian analysis of word-meanings is essentially the analysis of senses and the analysis of ontological aspects of objects is the analysis of referents.

Problem

However, the Jaina epistemologists differed from other epistemologists in India regarding what exactly constitute word-referents. While the Hindu logicians held that generic property (*jāti*), form (*ākṛti*) and individual (*Vyakti*) constitute word-referents, the Classical Sanskrit grammarians held that universal and individuals constitute word-referents, and also the ritualists held that only generic property constitutes word-referents. On the other hand, the Jaina epistemologists have admitted that an entity consisting of both general and particular is the object of knowledge (*vastu* or *viṣaya*) or word-referent (*artha*). Also the Jainas have held that the functional relation of words (*śabdasambandha* is eternal (*nitya*) with the referents. In the present article, we shall present the position of all these epistemologists so that a critical study of Jaina concept of meaning and referent is possible.

Logicians' theory

When a word such as 'cow' (*go*) denotes an object such as the cow, three distinct things can be considered as being conveyed. They are: (1) the universal (*jāti*) such as the cowness (*gotvajāti*) so that the cow in general is understood, (ii) the distinguishing form (*ākṛti*) such as the dewlap (*sāsnādimattva*) so that an animal such as the cow with its distinguishing characteristics can be identified and the individual (*vyakti*) such as the cow so that the particular animal can be understood as qualified. Thus, Akṣapāda Gautama (Nyāyasūtra, ii.2.68) has held that universal (generic property), form and individual constitute word-referents (*jātyākṛtivyaktayaḥ padārthaḥ*).

It should be noted that word-referent is generally what is denoted by word (*padābhidheya*). And since a non-polysemous word such as 'cow' cannot be admitted to have three separate denotations in generic property, form and individual, the Prācya logicians (Śaktivāda, 1) have held that generic property form, and individual constitute a single word-meaning; and therefore have a single denotation of word. However, to overcome such a difficulty, some Navya logicians (Gautamasūtravṛtti, on ii.2.68) have proposed that individual as qualified by generic property constitutes single word-referent, whereas form is merely the relation of generic property with individual. On the other hand, Gadādhara (Śaktivāda, 3) has proposed that individual as qualified by both generic property and form constitutes a single word-referent; and therefore, a single denotation of word can be admitted in such qualified individual. This view is justified on the ground that generic property and form are two sides of individual and hence do not constitute separate word-referents.

However, the most important contribution of the logicians (Śaktivāda, 1) to the analysis of word-referent is their concept of cause or basis of word-usage (*padapravṛttinimitta*). While admitting that generic property, form, and individual constitute word-referents, they have proposed the out of three, only generic property is the cause or basis of word-usage. They have done so on the ground that, of the three referents, only generic property is permanent and non-deviating and hence helps to recognize the item denoted without fail, whereas form and individual being non-permanent and deviating do not help in recognizing the same. Thus, they have held that words such as 'cow' (*go*) are used keeping only the universals such as the cowness in mind, and hence have only the same cowness as the basis of the word-usage such as 'cow'.

Grammarians' theory

The grammarians such as Vājapyāsna and Vyādi, both contemporaries of Pāṇini (Vār. on P. i.2.64), have proposed two divergent theories that the generic property and the individuals are the word-referents. While Vājapyāna maintains that the generic property such as the cowness which qualifies the individual such as the cow is the word-referent, Vyādi maintains that the individual such as the cow which is qualified by the generic property such as the cowness is the word-referent. On the other hand, Pāṇini can be said to have upheld the theory that both the generic property and the individual constitute the word-referents as his rule *jātyākhyāyām ekasmin bahuvacanam anyatarasyām* (P. i.2.58) amply implies. Thus, the early grammarians can be held to have admitted the views that only the generic property qualifying the individual, or only the individual qualified by the generic property, or both the generic property and the individual as the word-referents.

Kātyāyana (under P. v.1.119) has stated that the abstract suffixes such as '*tā*', '*tva*' are added to the nouns for expressing the qualities (*guṇa*) of the things which function as the cause or basis of word-usage (*padapravṛttinimitta*). Now since only the generic property such as the cowness is the basis of word-usage, only the same generic property can be held to be the meaning of the word 'quality' (*guṇa*). However, Kaiyaṭa, while commenting on the explanation of Kātyāyana, states that (Matilal, 1990) the word 'quality' may be taken to include both the generic property and the action as only then a moving cow individual as qualified by the cowness can be understood from the word 'cow'. Thus, according to Kātyāyana, both the generic property and the action can be held to be the word-referents.

Patañjali was aware of the theories proposed by both the logicians and Kātyāyana. However, he does not recognize either of the two theories; and hence does not admit any of the five entities, the generic property, the form, the individual, the quality, and the action separately as the word-referents. According to him, all the five entities put together constitute the word-referents. Thus, while rising the question what is in fact the word 'cow'? (*gauriti kaḥ śabdaḥ,* Śivasūtras). Patañjali states that it is neither the property of the cowness, nor the form dewlap, nor the individual cow, nor the quality of white colour, nor the action of moving, but rather it is all the things put together which are conducive to the comprehension of all the things put together. Thus, according to Patañjali, a number of things such as the generic property etc. taken together constitute the word-referents.

Bhartṛhari's theory

Bhartṛhari (Vākyapadīya, iii.1.9) who has formulated the theory of word-essence or meaningful linguistic unit (*sphoṭa*) has proposed that words essentially refer to the word-universals (*śabdajāti*) which are superimposed on the objective meaning-universals (*arthajāti*). According to him, words such as 'cow' cannot be distinguished from the referents such as the cow and the generic properties such as the cowness cannot be distinguished from the individuals such as the cow. While the generic properties refer to the permanent nature of things, the individuals refer to the ever changing nature of things. Thus, the external phenominal objects, which can be identified with the meaningful linguistic units and at the same time not distinguished from the generic properties, may be held as the word-referents.

Diṅnāga's theory

Diṅnāga (Pramāṇasamuccaya, V), however, totally denies the existence of the external phenominal or thing-meant universals and holds that only the exclusion from what is other than what it is (*apoha*) is the word-referent. While the Naiyāyikas have proposed that external phenominal or thing-meant universals are real and hence constitute the basis of word-usage (*padapravṛttinimitta*), Diṅnāga proposes that exclusion from what is other than what it is (*apoha*) can itself function as the basis of word-usage, by referring to the individuals such as the cows etc. negatively as what are other than the non-cows etc. and hence can be considered as the word-referents. Thus, according to him, there is no need that universals, forms and individuals should be considered as word-referents.

Ritualists' theory

The ritualists such as the Prābhākaras and the Bhāṭṭas (Nyāyamañjari, 4.6) admit only the generic property as the word-referent. They hold so because the denotation of words (*abhidhā*) is to be admitted only in the economical generic property, whereas the idea of the individuals (and forms) can be obtained through implication (*ākṣepa*). That is to say that since the generic property such as the cowness is not tenable without its abode, i.e. the individual such as the cow, the same generic property implies the individual, whereas since the individual such as the cow is tenable to be perceived even without perceiving the generic property such as the cowness, the same individual does not imply the generic property. Also they hold that the word (*śabda*) being permanent and evers present, the referent being referred to should also be permanent and ever present. And only the generic property between the generic property and the individual is permanent and ever present. Thus, according to them, only the generic property which is permanent and non-deviating, and not the individuals which are non-permanent and deviating, must be admitted to constitute the word-referent.

Jains' theory

The Jains do not openly admit any word-meanings or word-referents as such. However, it is abundantly clear that the objects of valid knowledge (*viṣaya*) which are dealt with immediately after a detailed account of verbal testimony (*āgama*) are meant to be word-referents as well.

According to the Jains (Pramāṇanayatattvāloka, 5.1), the object of valid knowledge (*viṣaya*) or word-referent is an entity (*vastu*) of the nature of any form consisting of both general and particular (*Sāmānyaviśeṣādyanekāntātmaka*). Thus neither only general (*sāmānya*) nor only particular (*viśeṣa*), nor both general and particular can be admitted as word-referents. According to them, such an entity consisting of both general and particular must be admitted to be the word referent because the same is the object of the knowledge of commonality (such as this is a cow and this is a cow) and also is the object of the knowledge of exclusivity (such as this cow is *śabala*, this cow is *khamba*) (*anugataviśiṣṭākārapratītiviṣaya*). Also, according to them, the entity consisting of both general and particular must be admitted to be the object or word-referent because the same has the efficaciousness by assuming the transformation of the nature such as the abandoning of the earlier form and the assumption of the later form.

Here the general (*sāmānya*) is of two kinds: (i) homogeneous (*tiryak*) and (ii) heterogeneous (*ūrdhvatā*). The homogeneous general is a general notion such as the cowness continuing in many individuals of like nature such as the cow which signifies many individuals of like nature such as Śabala cow, Khamba cow. Whereas the heterogeneous general is a general notion continuing in many individuals of dissimilar nature such as the gold which signifies many individuals of dissimilar nature such as the gold bracelet, the gold necklace etc.

The particular (*viśeṣa*) is also of two kinds (i) coherent quality (*guṇa*) and successive quality (*paryāya*). The coherent qualities are the particular properties such as the knowledge, the power, the happiness etc. found together in the self; whereas the successive qualities are the particular properties such as the happiness, the sorrow etc. found successively one after another in the same self etc.

Permanency of word-relation (function)

Since the Jains have admitted the objects of knowledge or word-referents to be the entities consisting of both general and particular, they have maintained (pramāṇasaṁgraha, 74) an eternal or permanent relationship between words and their referents (*nityaḥ śabdārthasambandhaḥ*). According to them, the word-relation must be permanent because otherwise the same cannot be perceived in the entities consisting of general and particular. However, the question is how to account for the conventional senses which are not permanent. Thus, the Jains need to concede that the conventional relaton of a word which is not permanent is found in a conventional sense after obtaining the permanent word-relation in the established sense.

Resume

Words are admitted as the means of communication since they communicate certain ideas or knowledges of objects to our mind. While the objects intended to be denoted by words are the word-referents (*padṝtha* or *śabdārtha*), the ideas or the cognitions (awareness) of objects are the word-meanings or senses (*padārthadhī*). For instance, consider the expressions *'śaśaḥ, śṛṅgaśca staḥ' 'kimtu śaśaśṛngaḥ nāsti'*. Here while the objects denoted such as the hare and the horn are the referents of the words '*śaśaḥ*' and '*śṛṅgaḥ*', the idea or the cognition of the non-existing horn of a hare created by the expression '*śaśaśṛṅgaḥ*' is the meaning or sense.

Indian epistemologists although the Jain epistemologists cannot be singled out, have maintained a clear distinction between the sense or meaning and the referent. Thus, while the Indian analysis of word-meaning is essentially the analysis of sense or meaning, the Indian analysis of various ontological aspects of objects is the analysis of referents. And Indian epistemologists have presented a systematic account of referents.

Akṣapāda Gautama recognized the fact that the universals (generic properties) such as the cowness, the forms such as the dewlap and the individuals such as the cow are understood from the words such as 'cow'; and therefore held that the generic properties, the forms and the individuals are the word-referents (*jātyākṛtivyaktayaḥ padārthaḥ*). However, since Gautama used a singular ending after the word '*padārtha*' (word-referent), the Prācya logicians have held that the generic property, the form and the individual together constitute a single word-referent. On the other hand, the Navya logicians perceived the generic property such as the cowness and the form such as the dewlap to be the qualifiers of the individuals such as the cow, and hence held that the individual as qualified by both the generic property and the form constitute word-referent. However, the single most significant contribution of the Navyas to the analysis of word-referent is their recognition of the role of the permanent generic property in recognizing and identifying the word-referents, and therefore conferring of the status of the basis of word-usage (*padapravṛttinimitta*) to the generic property.

Now as regards the grammarians' theory of word-referent. While the earlier contemporaries of Pāṇini, i.e. Vājapāyana and Vyādi, and Pāṇini have held that either the generic property, or the individual or both constitute the word-meanings, Kātyāyana has introduced a new-element that the quality which includes even the action is the word-referent. Patañjali was aware of these earlier grammarians' theories; however he recognized the linguistic fact that no one of the five things such as the generic property etc. can be held to constitute the word-referent separately as one without the others is incomplete, and impossible to congize and hence held that all the five things put together constitute word-referents.

It should be observed here that while the Bhartṛhari's theory of superimposition of the word-universals (*śabdajāti*) on the objective phenominal thing (meant)-universals (*arthajāti*) implies the identification of the words with the things-meant on the one hand, and that of the universals with the individuals on the other, Diṅnga's theory of the exclusion from what is other than what it is (*apoha*) as the word-referent opposes the logicians' theory of the reality of the phenominal thing (menat)-universals and thereby the reality of the word-referents. Thus, the two theories, right as they are in their own way, introduce metaphysical and negative characteristics to the Indian concept of word-referents.

Now as regards the ritualists' theory. The significance of the ritualists theory of word-referents lies in its admittance of merely the universal (generic property) as the word-referent. The ritualists have admitted so on the ground that only the generic property out of the generic property, the form and the individual, is economical and non-deviating; and hence deserves to be the word-referent. However, it should be noted that this theory betrays an uncanny resemblance to the logicians' theory of the generic property as the basis of word-usage.

Finally, as regards the Jains theory of word-referents. The Jains were clearly aware of Gautama's basic theory that the generic property, the form, and the individual constitute the word-referent. However, they have modified Gautama's theory and proposed that the entity (to be identified with the individual) consisting of the general and the particular is the object of knowledge or word-referent as no entity such as the cow without its general and particular properties can be viable. Thus, the Jains theory could be held to have provided the very basis for the Navyas' theory that the individual as qualified by the generic property and the form constitute the word-referent.

Notes and References

Bhattā-kalaṅka : (i) Pramāṇasaṁgraha, (Akalaṅka granthatraya), Singhi Jain Granthamala, Ahmedabad, 1939.

(ii) Laghīyastraya, see Akalaṅkagranthatraya

Bhatta, V.P. : Gadādhara's Śaktivada, EBL, Delhi - 1994.

Bhartṛhari : Vākyapadīya, with comm. of Helārāja, KSS 124, Banaras, 1937.

Gautama : Nyāyasūtras, ASS, 91, Poona, 1922.

Jayantabhaṭṭa : Nyāyamañjari, KSS, 106, 1936.

Matilal, B.K. : The World and the Word, Oxford University. Oxford, 1990.

Moravcsik, J.M.E. : Logic and Philosophy for Linguists, Houton Publishers, The Hague, Paris, 1974.

Pāṇini : Aṣṭādhyāyī, NSP, Bombay, 1900.

Patanjali : Mahābhāṣya with Kātyāyana's Vārtika, ed. F. Keilharn, Bombay, BSS, 1892.

Umāswāmi : Tattvarthasūtram, Ed. by J.L. Jaini, BCR Jain Trust, Delhi, 1956.

Vādidevasūri : Pramāṇyanayatattvāloka, Ed. by Pt. D. Malavaniya, LDBS Mandir, Ahmedabad, 1968.

Vidyabhusan S.C. : A History of Indian Logic, Motilal Banarasidas, Delhi, 1971.

"न सिद्धं पौरूषेयत्वं नयचक्रसमीहितम्"

श्रीराम शर्मा

सुविदितमेवैतत् दर्शनेषु प्रतितन्त्रसिद्धान्ताः पृथक्पृथक् वर्तन्ते। तेषां च विषये तत्तद्दार्शनिकाः प्रदर्शितमहाग्रहाः स्वाभिमतस्थापनाय महान्तं प्रयत्नं कुर्वन्तो दृश्यन्ते। वस्तुतस्तु यत्र विषयभेदः परिदृश्यते तत्र अन्यदर्शनविषयकविचारः दर्शनान्तरेषु प्रतिपादितोपि न प्रयोजनकारी। तथा हिअस्तिकदर्शनेषु नास्तिकदर्शनेषु च यत्र मौलिकोभेदः वेदप्रामाव्यादौ – तादृशेषु केवलं बुद्धिप्रभावमूलक एव विचारः प्रवर्तयितुं शक्यः – न तु प्रमाणमुखेन इति एतादृशेषु स्वस्वनयमार्गानुसारेण नयान्तरविषयविचारे क्रियमाणे वादिदोर्बल्यम् पराजयहेतुः न वाददौर्बल्यम्। अथवा-यद्यपि सिद्धान्तः संसाधितः स्यात् तथापि तद्दर्शनीयाः एतं मार्गम् एतद्दर्शनीया वातं मार्ग न स्वीकुर्वन्तीति-प्रयोजनं शून्यमेव। अतएवेति विभाव्यते यत् मीमांसाग्रन्थेषु आदृत-प्रतिपादितवेदापौरुषेयत्वादिकं पूर्वपक्षत्वेनापि न स्वीकृतम् – अपौरुषेयत्वे सधितेपि नास्ति येषां तत्र प्रमाणबुद्धिः तत्र किं साधितं स्यात्? यत्र उभाभ्यां प्रमाणीकृतोर्थः तत्र वादः शोभते अन्यथा केवलं जल्पो वितण्डा वा प्रवर्तते। भवतु नाम – तथापि प्रकृतसंसदि – यत्र द्वादशारनयचक्राख्ये ग्रन्थे वेदविषयको विचारः परिदृष्टः तमधिकृत्य किञ्चित् परिशीलनं प्रदर्श्यते विदुषां मोदाय। तथाहि–

"क्रियोपदेशन्याय्यत्वाभ्युपगमोपि चैवं विघटेत, संसेव्यविषयस्वतत्त्वानुपाति-परिणामविज्ञानविरहितत्वात् – अज्ञातवैविध्यवस्तुतत्त्वपरिणामवदवैद्यौषधोपदेश-वदग्निहोत्रं जुहुयात् स्वर्गकाम इत्याद्युप देशो बालकादिग्रहणवत्" –(द्वा. नयचक्रम्. पृ. 136) इति। अयं भावः "अग्निहोत्रं जुहुयात् स्वर्गकामः" इतिवचनस्य

क्रियोपदेशकत्वं सिद्धम्। स क्रियोपदेशो न युक्तः। आसेव्यमानस्य वस्तुनः - तत्क्रियात एव स्वरूपानुपातेन यः विपाकपरिणामः - तद्विज्ञानविरहितत्वं - स इत्थं विपाकः सुखाय दुःखाय वा इत्येतद्विज्ञानं हिताहितप्राप्तिपरिहारार्थम् इति तादृशज्ञानविरहितत्वात्' अग्निहोत्रं जुहुयात् इत्यादिवाक्यं प्रामाण्यं न भजते। तत्र दृष्टान्तः अविज्ञातरसवीर्यविपाकप्रभावद्रव्यगुणविशेषभागाभागसंयोगस्य देशकालातुरप्रकृतिसाम्यबलाबलवद्रोगसमुत्थनिदानादिलक्षणानभिज्ञस्य वैद्यस्य औषधोपदेशः यथा न घटते तथा इति।

अत्रोच्यते तादृशज्ञानाभावः उपदेशकस्य इति कथं निर्धार्यते इति विवेचनीयम्। वस्तुतः कस्यापि वचनस्य प्रामाण्यं वोत अप्रामाण्यम्? इति विषये लोके तावत् अनुभवः प्रमाणम्। तादृशानुभवमूलकप्रामाण्ये सम्पादनीये लोकस्थितविषयाः चेत् शक्यते। यथा 'नद्यास्तीरे फलानि सन्ति' इतिश्रुत्वा गत्वा दृष्ट्वा- यदि स्युः तत् वाक्यं सत्यम् इति जानाति यदि न असत्यमिति। अत्रापि- तदाशया तत्र गमनं यत् तत् प्रामाण्यज्ञाननिश्चयमूलकम् इति प्रामाण्यं स्वतः सिध्यति- सतिबाधके अप्रामाण्यज्ञानं पश्चात् उदेति इत्यादिविषयः स्वतः-प्रामाण्य परतःप्रामाण्यवादविषयकः इति नात्र प्रस्तूयते। परन्तु अलौकिके अतीन्द्रिये च विषये स्वतःप्रामाण्यसिद्धौ नास्ति विप्रतिपत्तिः। यैः प्रामाण्यं परत एवेति तत्र विप्रतिपत्तिः ईदृशी इदं प्रमाणं नवेति। तत्र प्रामाण्यग्रहणे लौकिकदृष्टया परिशील्यमाने विश्वासः कारणमिति वक्तव्यम्। अनुभवः न वक्तुं पार्यते। जैनप्रणाल्यां च सर्वज्ञं जिनं स्वीकृत्य तद्वचनं प्रमाणयन्ति। तत्रापि परलोकः अङ्गीकृतः - "अहो सति जगत्पूज्ये लोकद्वयविशुद्धिदे" (ज्ञानार्णव 1-25) इति वचनात्। एवं मोक्षोपि - "अयं जागर्ति मोक्षाय वेत्तिविद्यां" (ज्ञा. 1-20) इति वचनात्।

तर्हि तादृशविषये च यदि सर्वज्ञवचनं प्रमाणं तत्रायं प्रश्नः - स विश्वासपूर्वकः अनुभवपूर्वको वेति। स्वानुभवपूर्वक इति वक्तुं न युक्तम्। उक्तस्य पुनः अयुक्तजीवत्वापत्तेः। अंगीकारे च उक्तेः निष्प्रयोजनत्वापत्तेः। अथ न स्वानुभवः, सर्वज्ञानुभवः इति चेत् सच तदवस्थ एव। यदा सर्वज्ञः उक्तः तस्य पुनरिहलोके जन्म नास्तीति तस्य अनुभव- पूर्वकोपदेशकत्वं न सिद्धम्। अनुभवात् प्राक् एतादृश्या क्रियया आचरणेन वा उक्तिः भविष्यति इत्युपदिश्य ततो उक्त इति चेत् एतदपि न युक्तम्। अनुभवात् प्रागुक्तस्य वचनस्य अनुभवपूर्वकत्वाभावात् एकान्ततया तादृशक्रियायाः तद्धेतुत्वासिद्धेः। एवं च अनुभवपूर्वकत्वं न सिद्ध्यतीति अस्माकं विश्वासः कारणमिति वक्तव्यम्। एवं दृष्टान्तेऽपिरुग्णस्यानुभवः वैद्यवचने

प्रामाण्यसम्पादनाय न कारणतामश्नुते। नापि च वैद्यस्यानुभवः। परन्तु वैद्यस्य ज्ञानम्। तन्निश्चयोपि विश्वासमूलकएव पूर्वं मयि रूग्णे अनेन औषधं दत्तम् अहं नीरोगः सम्पन्नः। इदानीं पुनः रूग्णः अतः तेन औषधं दीयते चेत् नीरोगो भविष्यामि इति। परन्तु यदि तेन औषधं सम्यग्दत्तमपि कदाचन सफलं न स्यात्। कर्मजानां औषधनाश्यत्वं वैद्यशास्त्रेपि तिरस्कृतमिति - तदर्थं तत्रापि शान्त्यादिकमुक्तमिति च। अपि च पुराकृतकर्मवशात् अर्धायुष्के अल्पायुष्के वा तदौषधं नहि स्वकार्य जनयतीति च। एवं सर्वज्ञवचनेपि। अपि चात्रायं प्रश्नः उदेति यत् - जिनस्य सर्वज्ञत्वं यदि स्वीकृतं, तर्हि मन्वादेरपि सर्वज्ञत्वं कुतो वा न स्यात् उपदेशकत्वसामान्यात्। यथा यद्यद्वचनं, तत्तत् उपदेशकज्ञानपूर्वकं इति सामान्यात् वेदे पौरुषेयत्वं सम्पायितुमिच्छता प्रोच्यते। नास्माभिः स्वीक्रियते मन्वादेः सर्वज्ञत्वं इति केवलं प्रतिज्ञामात्रनिर्बाध्यतां सूचयति इति न विचारितरमणीयम् सर्वज्ञत्वस्यैव विश्वासमात्रालम्बनत्वात्। अथ यदि सर्वज्ञत्वं तद्वचनपरिशीलनवेद्यमिति - तदपि न क्षोदक्षयम्। तेषां अस्मदवेक्षया अधिकज्ञानवत्त्वात्। अधिकज्ञानवतो विषये न्यूनज्ञानवतः पुरुषस्य परिशीलनायोगात्। तेषां अधिकज्ञानवत्वं च, विना आचार्यादिव्याख्यानं अस्माकं तद्वचनज्ञानोदयाभावात् इति नास्मासु परिशीलकत्वं अर्हति। एवञ्च सर्वज्ञत्वं उतासार्वज्ञ्यं न सिद्धान्तरूपेण अस्मदादिभिः निश्चेतुं शक्यम्। अपिचात्रायमधिकोविशेषः यत् स्याद्वादिनां सप्तभङ्गीनयानुसारेण न कस्यचन वस्तुनः पाकान्तत्वासिद्धे सर्वज्ञे सर्वज्ञत्वमपि तादृगवस्थमेवेति न सर्वज्ञतायाः साधकं प्रमाणमन्यत् विद्यते ऋते प्रतिज्ञायाः। तच्चपरेषामपि समानमेवेति नैकसर्वज्ञसिद्धिः।

अपिच - प्रकृते स्वसंसेव्यविषयस्वतत्त्वानुपरिणामविज्ञानविरहितत्वं यत् हेतुत्वेन प्रोक्तम् - तत् ज्ञानविरहितत्वं कस्येति वक्तव्यम्। उपदेशकस्येति चेत् तत्तु वेदे न घटते। शब्दराशेः वेदस्य स्वर्गक्रियान्यतरस्यापि सेव्यविषयत्वायोगात्। ननु शब्दस्य तादृक्त्वे तदुच्चरयितुः तदुपदेशकस्य तज्ज्ञानविरहितत्वं अस्माभिः प्रतिपाद्यते इति चेत्तदपि न वेदस्यापौरुषेयत्वात्। यदि पुनरुच्येत वेदः पौरुषेयः - वाक्यत्वात् - यद्यत् - वाक्यं - तत्तत् पौरुषेयं - कालिदासादिवाक्यवत् इति। तत्र ब्रूमः। यत्र यत्र कर्तृस्मरणं तत्र तथा। यत्र कर्तृस्मरणं सनातनादपि कालात् न - तत्र कर्त्रनुपलब्धेः अपौरुषेयमिति। ननूच्चारयित्रभावे कथं शब्दोत्पत्तिः - येन अपौरुषेयत्वं सिध्येत् इति चेन्न। न वयं उच्चारयित्रभावं प्रतिपादयामः किन्तु कर्तृत्वं उच्चारयिता भगवानेव। सच एकरूपो वा भिन्नरुपो वा इत्यन्यदेतत्। परन्तु उच्चारयितृत्वं न कर्तृत्वं अन्यथा

कण्ठस्थीकृतग्रन्थस्य पाठेपि कर्तृत्वप्रसङ्गात्। सनातनो भगवान् सनातनं वेदं सृष्ट्यादौ ब्रह्मणे उपदिशति सच ऋषिभ्यः - तथापि न स्वयं विरच्य - यतो हि वेदोपि ईश्वर इव नित्यः - अनादिश्च। अतो भगवतः वेदकर्तृत्वं न सिद्धम्।

अपिच यदि कर्तृत्वं स्वीक्रियते तर्हीदं वक्तव्यम् तैः - कर्तृत्वं द्विविधं लोके प्रमाणान्तरज्ञातार्थप्रतिपादनम् स्वानुभवसिद्धवस्तुप्रतिपादनम्। प्रथमन्तु तत्तत्प्रमाणज्ञ-साधारणम्-द्वितीयं पुनः तन्मात्रमितम्। वेदविषयेच नाद्यम्। 'तद्धेतोरेव तद्धेतुत्त्वे मध्येकिन्तेनेतिन्यायेन तादृशप्रमाणभूतस्यैव स्वीकरणसामञ्जस्यात्। तद्धेतुकवेद-स्वीकरणे कारणाभावाच्च। अपिच- तादृशमूलभूतवचनस्य वा अन्यस्य वा प्रामाण्यं केन सिद्धम् किं तस्य स्वरूपमित्यादीनां निरुपयितव्यप्रसङ्गाच्च। तस्य च असम्भवेन अशक्यत्वाच्च। न द्वितीयम्-वेदप्रतिपाद्यवस्तुनः स्वानुभवपूर्वक प्रतिपादनाशक्यत्वात्। पारलौकिक-जन्मान्तरीय-फलस्थले कार्यकारणज्ञानाभावप्रसंगाच्च। विशिष्यप्रायश्चित्तप्रकरणगतवस्तुपरिज्ञाने तदशक्यत्वं स्पष्टतया भासते। अपिच सकर्तृकत्वस्वीकारे सादित्वप्रसंगाच्च। जगन्नित्यत्व-मभ्युपगच्छतां वेदरहितकालसत्तायाः अङ्गीकार्यत्वापत्तिरपि। अतः अपौरुषेत्वं नित्यत्वमित्यादिः मीमांसकैरुच्यते। पावञ्च यदुक्तं स्वसंसेव्यविषयस्वतत्त्वानुपातिपरिणाम-विज्ञानविरहितत्वं स वेदः अपौरुषेयेन घटते इति 'क्रियोपदेशन्याय्यत्वविघटनं' - हेतुत्वेन यत् प्रोक्तं तदेव विघटत इति हेतोः दार्ष्टान्तिके असिद्धेः।

एतेनैव "उपदेशादेव न ज्ञानयोगः - इति भेदयुक्तम् उभयथापि पौरुषेयत्वादित्यपि (द्वा. न. पृ. 137) निरस्तम्। उपदेशकस्य वेदस्य सर्वज्ञासर्वज्ञान्यतरपुरुषत्वाभावात् तत्र च पूर्वविज्ञानकारणावश्यम्भावाभावात्, यैश्च पौरुषेयः स्वीक्रियते वेदः तैर्वक्तव्यं यत्प्रमाणमूलकत्वेन स उपदिष्ट इति तादृशोपदेशायुक्तता च निरूपिता पूर्वमेव। यैश्च परतः प्रामाण्यमङ्गीक्रियते तैः वक्तव्यम् - सर्वस्यापि परतः प्रामाण्याङ्गीकारे न कस्यापि स्वतः प्रमाण्यानङ्गीकारे न कस्यापि प्रामाण्यसिद्धिः इति - केषांचन स्वतः केषाञ्चन परतः इति चेत् वैरूप्यदोषः कथं वार्येतेति च। एवञ्च पूर्वोक्तदोषवारणायैव प्रोक्तं सेश्वरमीमांसकेन तत्र भवता आपदेवेन "ईश्वरो गतकल्वीयं वेदं अस्मिन् कल्पे स्मृत्वा उपदिशतीत्येतावतैव उपपत्तौ प्रमाणान्तरेणार्थमुपलभ्यरचितत्वकल्पनानुपपत्तेश्च।" इति यत्र कारणं युक्त्यधीनं तत्र लाघवस्यैव स्वीक्रियमाणत्वात् अपौरूषेयात्वकल्पनाया एव लाघवम्। अथवा

अस्तु तर्कनयसिद्धान्ताभ्युपगमः यैः जिनानुयायिभिः ईश्वरोप्यङ्गीक्रियते -

तेषां ईश्वरे सार्वज्ञ्यमभ्युगम्यते न वा? यद्यभिमतं तदुक्तवचने किं सर्वज्ञवचनवत् प्रामाण्यं स्वीक्रियते न वा? यदि न तर्हि किं तस्य सर्वज्ञतया? यदि सर्वज्ञत्वमपि नाङ्गीक्रियते किं तर्हि प्रयोजनं तेन ईश्वरेण? इत्युभयतःपाशारज्जुः। यदीश्वरः सर्वज्ञः तद्वचनत्वात् वेदस्य प्रामाण्यं अङ्गीकार्यमेवापतति। यदि न ईश्वरः सर्वज्ञः तर्हि तदुपासकतीर्थंकराणां तदुपासने प्रयोजनाभावात् ईश्वरतिरस्कारमात्र सिद्धयेत्। यदि ईश्वरवचनत्वं अपि निराक्रियते तर्हि कस्येदं वचनमित्यपि वक्तव्यम् - ईश्वरवचनत्वाभावेऽत्र हेतुरपि वक्तव्यः। एवञ्च जिनानुयायिक्रियमाणं वेदप्रामाव्यतिरस्करणं निर्मूलकमेवेति बोध्यम्।

अपि च यदि स्वीयागमः सर्वज्ञवचनं तर्हि वेदस्यापि स्वीयसर्वज्ञेनापि उपास्यमानस्य ईश्वरस्य वचनत्वेन कुतो वा न ग्रहणमित्यदि वक्तव्यमापतेत्। यत् पूर्वोक्तवचनस्थले अस्मिन् प्रसङ्गे न्यायागमानुसारिण्यां व्याख्यायां "तथा असर्वज्ञोपदेशस्य उपदिष्टज्ञानस्य" इत्याद्युक्तौ-तत्र वक्तव्यम्। कथमयं असर्वज्ञोपदेशः इति। कर्ता लब्धोवा? यस्य असर्वज्ञता प्रतिपाद्यते, यस्य कर्तैव नोपलभ्यते तस्मिन् कर्तरि असर्वज्ञताप्रतिपादनं वन्ध्यापुत्रे दण्डापातः इव असम्भवमेव।

अथ यदुक्तम् - "वानरमूलिकादिपरिज्ञानवत्तद्विषयं तज्ज्ञानं स्यात् सर्वौषधादि-विषयकैकपुरुषविज्ञानवदतीन्द्रियग्राह्यसर्वविषयकैकपुरुषविज्ञानाभ्युपगमो वा अवश्यम्भावी, वेदवचनयोरन्यथानुपपत्तेः"। पृ. 37, द्वा. न. इति।

अर्थात्- लोके वानरादिजातिषु यत्किंचिदौषधिज्ञानं वर्तते सहजसिद्धम्। तद्वत् वैद्यस्यापि यत्किंचिद्विषयकमेव भवति। न तु सर्वौषिधिविषयकविज्ञानम् एकस्य पुरुषस्य। सत्येवमतीन्द्रियसर्वपदार्थविषयकं पुरुषज्ञानमित्यङ्गीकारे तादृशपुरुषेण उपदिष्टो वेदः इत्यङ्गीकर्तव्य एवेति पौरुषेयता आयाता - इति - तस्य भावः। अत्रोच्यते।

वानरादौ पूर्वविज्ञानाभावेपि यत्किञ्चिज्ज्ञानं दृश्यते। तत्र उपदेशकत्वं नास्ति। यत्र वैद्यादौ उपदेशकत्वं दृश्यते - तत्र पूर्वविज्ञानाभावे ज्ञानं नास्ति। परन्तु अतीन्द्रियज्ञानस्यैतदुदाहरणं दृष्टान्तो वा कथं भवतीति चिन्तनीयम्। यदतीन्द्रियं ज्ञानं तत्तु पूर्वज्ञानवता प्रतिपाद्यं न भवति। तादृशज्ञानस्य पूर्व ज्ञानवता प्रतिपादनविषयतायोग्यत्वमेवनास्तीति पूर्वमेवोक्तम् अथ अभ्युपगमे वा - यथा वानरादेः पूर्वविज्ञानाभावेपि सहजसिद्धं विज्ञानं एवं कुत्रचिन्मन्नुष्यादौ च सहजसिद्धं ज्ञानं दृश्यते च। तादृशाः योगि-मुनि-प्रभृतिशब्दैः उच्यन्ते लोके। तादृशेष्वपि ज्ञाने तरतमभावः दरीदृश्यते च एवञ्च यत्र वेदे सर्वविषयकविज्ञानं प्रतिपादितं दृश्यते -

तस्य सामान्य-विशिष्टमनुष्या-साध्यत्वात् परिदृश्यमानसर्वविषयकज्ञानान्यथानुपपत्या – अयमुपदेशः न पौरुषेयः सर्वविषयकज्ञानरूपत्वात् – यन्नैवं तन्नैवं यथा इतरोपदेशः। इति व्यतिरेकदृष्टान्तवता केवलान्वयिना अनुमानेन अपौरुषेयत्वं सिध्यत्येव पौरुषेयत्वसाधने तत्प्रतिपादितज्ञानस्य सर्वविषयकत्वं अभ्युपेतमिति पूर्वपक्षिणापीति – अतः तेनापि पौरुषेयत्वं न सिध्यति च। वस्तुतः ये तावत् आप्तवाक्यत्वेन वेदस्य प्रामाण्यमिच्छन्ति, तैः ईश्वरोक्तत्वात् वेदस्य प्रामाण्यम् वेदप्रतिपादितत्वात् ईश्वरस्य प्रामाण्यमित्याकारकान्योन्याश्रयदोषपरिहरणाय – प्रथमतः ईश्वरसाधनाय यदनुमानमुपन्यस्यते 'क्षित्यङ्कुरादिकं सकर्तृकं कार्यत्वात् घटवत्'' इत्यादि, तदपि क्षित्यङ्कुरादेः कर्तुः साधनमात्रं तस्य पुनः ईश्वरत्वसाधनाय च पुनः पुनः अनुमानकल्पनेति अनुमानपरम्पराकल्पनातो वरं अपौरुषेयत्वकल्पनं लाघवात्। यो य उपदेशः स स पुरुषमूलकः इति यदुच्यते तदपि न चारु। अतएव लौकिकोपदेशभिन्नता श्रुतिविषये स्वीकृता। अतीन्द्रियविषय-बोधकत्वात्। तर्हि यद्यदतीन्द्रियविषयबोधकं तस्य अपौरुषेयत्वं भवेदिति चेत् – ओमिति ब्रूमः। परन्तु तत्र प्रमाणान्तरनिरपेक्षं इति विशेषणं देयम्। यत्र स्मृत्यादौ अतीन्द्रियविषयबोधकत्वेपि प्रमाणान्तरसापेक्षता कर्तृभिरेव स्वीकृतेति तादृशातीन्द्रियविषयबोधकग्रन्थजातस्य नापौरुषेयत्वं कर्त्रृपलब्धेः। यत्र प्रमाणान्तरनिरपेक्षं तत्र अपौरुषेयत्वम्। अत एवोच्यते-

''प्रत्यक्षेणानुमित्या वा यस्तूपायो न बुध्यते।
मानं विदन्ति वेदेन तस्माद्वेदस्य वेदता॥'' इति।

एवञ्च वानरमूलिकादिपरिज्ञानदृष्टान्तसाधितं न सेत्स्यतीति स्वाभिमत-साधन इति बोध्यम्।

अपिच लौकिकदृष्टया परिशीलिते च वेदे न केवलम् अतीन्द्रियज्ञानं लौकिकमपि विज्ञानं दृष्टान्तादिमुखेन प्रतिपादितम्। प्रतिपादितालौकिकवचनसत्यत्वं परीक्षकैः शक्यत्वात् अनुभूते – तत्सादृश्यात् अतीन्द्रियज्ञानस्य च परीक्षणायोग्यत्वेपि सत्यत्वमङ्गीकरणीयमेव स्यात्। बाधकाभावाच्च। तादृशज्ञानस्य उपदेशक-अनुभवमूलकत्वं न युज्यत इति पूर्वमेवास्माभिः प्रतिपादितत्वात् अपौरुषेयत्वमेव वक्तव्यमापतति इति च अपौरुषेयत्वसिद्धिः।

अथ यदुक्तं ''अग्निहोत्रं जुहुयात् स्वर्गकाम इति। इदन्तु पुनः किं विधिः अनुवादः अर्थवादः? उच्यते विधिः। अप्रसिद्धार्थविषयविधायित्वात्, अत्रे

अप्रसिद्धमग्निसम्प्रदानं हवनं विधीयते इत्युपायस्य अपूर्वत्वात् तदभिव्यङ्ग्यापूर्वाभावः त्वन्मतादेवोक्तवत्" इति। अस्यायमभिप्रायः 'अग्निहोत्रं जुहुयात्' इति वाक्यं लोके अप्रसिद्धं कञ्चनविषयं विधत्ते इति तस्य अप्रसिद्धत्वात् तदभिव्यङ्ग्यपूर्वस्य अर्थात् फलस्यापि अभाव एव वक्तव्यः इति। तत्रायं प्रश्नः। का नाम अप्रसिद्धिः लोकसिद्धा इति प्रतिज्ञायते आयुष्मता। अग्निः अप्रसिद्धो वा उत हवनं? अथ अग्निसम्प्रदानकं हवनम्? अग्निः लोकसिद्धः एव यथा घटादिः। एवं हवनशब्दार्थोपि लोकसिद्ध एव अथ अग्निसम्प्रदानकं हवनम् अप्रसिद्धमिति चेत् तदेवखलु विधीयते। लोके यथा व्रीहिमात्रभोजनाभ्यासवति प्रदेशे वर्तमानानां जनानां कृते यवा अपि भोक्तव्याः इति उपदेशे क्रियमाणे अप्रसिद्धिः स्वीक्रियते वा? तत्र यवाः अपि ज्ञाता एव व्रीहय इव - भोजनं च ज्ञातमेव परन्तु यवभोजनसम्बन्धः न ज्ञातः - स एव विधीयते - यद्येतादृशापूर्वस्य विधेयत्वं न स्वीक्रियते तर्हि व्रीहिमात्रभोजनाभ्यासवतां 'यवाः अपि भोक्तव्याः' इति उपदेशश्रवणसमनन्तर- क्रियमाणयवभोजनेन क्षुधानिवृत्तिरपि न भविष्यतीत्येव वक्तव्यम्। तथा च लोकविशेषः। अपि च यदि एतादृशा-पूर्वविधेयत्वं न स्वीक्रियते लोकसिद्धमात्रस्यैव स्वीक्रियते तर्हि प्रमाणान्तरप्राप्तार्थ-बोधकत्वात् अनुवादत्वमेव न विधायकत्वमिति-अन्ततोविधिस्वरूपहानिः अङ्गीकर्तव्या। यद्योमित्युच्येत तर्हि सर्वज्ञोक्तागमस्यापि तदवस्थत्वात् तस्यापि वैयर्थ्यमापततीति स्वमतस्यापि स्वादेनैव उच्छेदः। अपिच वस्तुतः 'अप्रसिद्धार्थविषयविधायित्वात्' इति हेतुप्रदर्शनं न युक्तम्। तत्र एतद्वाक्यभिन्नप्रमाणान्तराज्ञातार्थविधायित्वं प्रोक्तम् मीमांसकैः। अपिच " अग्निसम्प्रदानं हवनं विधीयते' इति यदुक्तं तदपि न चारु। अनेन वाक्येन अग्निः सम्प्रदानभूत इति न विधीयते। अपिच यत्र प्रातरग्निहोत्रादौ अग्निर्देवता नास्ति तत्र अग्निहोत्रशब्दो वाचको न स्यात्। वस्तुतस्तु अत्र अग्निहोत्रनायकः होमः केवलो विधीयते नत्वग्निः सम्प्रदानभूतत्वेन अधिकरणत्वेन वा विधीयते तत्प्रख्यन्याय-विरोधात् एवञ्च - अत्र एतद्वचनव्याख्यायां न्यायागमानुसारिण्यां (शाबर) भाष्यन्यायसुधाकारादिमतानि उदाहृतानि अथवा अनूदितानि तानि न सिद्धान्तभूतानि - अन्ततोगत्वा "अत्राप्रसिद्धमिति - अत्राग्नये होत्रमिति चतुर्थीतत्पुरुषमाश्रित्य अग्निसम्प्रदानकहवनविधिरुक्तः" इति व्याख्यातम् तदपि अयुक्तमेव अग्नेः सम्प्रदानभूतस्य प्रतिपादकं नैतद्वाक्यम्। तादृशार्थस्य प्रमाणान्तरसिद्धत्वं तत्राप्युदाहृतमवेति एतादृशार्थस्वीकारे अयुक्तत्वं स्पष्टीभवति।

अपि च मूले "अतश्च विधेरसंव्यवहार्यत्वात् तद्विहित क्रियाफलसम्बन्धा-

भावः - आरोग्यार्थिडित्थभक्षणादिवत्'' इत्यत्र भाष्ये ''अतश्च तर्कोत्थापित-लोकतत्त्वज्ञानानपेक्षत्वात्'' इति 'असंव्यवहार्यत्वात्' इत्यस्य अर्थो वर्णितः। अत्रोच्यते 'असंव्यवहार्यत्वं' नाम 'लोकतत्त्वज्ञानानपेक्षत्वं' इति विवृतम्। लोकतत्त्वज्ञानानपेक्षत्वं च किं इति चेत् ''अतो न तस्य घटपरमाण्वादिकार्यकारणसामान्यविशेषादिस्वरूप-विचारापेक्षा वर्तत इति भावः।'' इति न्यायागमानुसारिणी व्याख्याच। तत्रायं प्रश्नः। यत्र यत्र घटपरमाण्वादिकार्यकारणसामान्य- विशेषादिस्वरूपविचारानपेक्षत्वं - तत्र तत्र क्रियाफलसम्बन्धाभावः वर्णनीयः ईति यदुच्येत तर्हि

''विरम विरम सङ्गान्मुञ्च मुञ्च प्रपञ्चम् विसृज विसृज मोहं विद्धि विद्धि स्वतत्त्वम्।

कलय कलय वृत्तम् पश्य पश्य स्वरूपम् कुरु कुरु पुरुषार्थं निर्वृतानन्दहेतोः॥''

इति (ज्ञानार्णवे 15 सर्गे 41 श्लोके) वर्तमानेषु विधिषु ब्रह्मचर्यादिप्रतिपादकेषु आयुष्मता घटपरमाण्वादिकार्यकारणसामान्यविशेषणादिस्वरूपविचारसापेक्षत्वं कीदृशं स्वीकृतमिति वक्तव्यम्। न केवलं तत्र अत्रवा, यत्र यत्र क्रियाविधिः तत्र तत्र अयं दोषः प्रसज्यत एव। ''प्रत्यक्षसिद्धमपि वस्तु अनुमानेन बुभुत्सन्ते तर्करसिकाः'' इतिवत् क्रियायामपि घटपरमाणुप्रभृति कार्यकारणसामान्यविशेषविचारापेक्षां इच्छन्तः तादृश- कार्यकारणैकविचारप्रवणाः सन्तः ग्रन्थलेखनादीनादिक्रियां उपदेशक्रियां च परित्यजन्तु इति वक्तव्यम्। क्रियाया निष्फलत्वप्रतिपादनात्।

अपिच- ''ननु चैतमग्निहोत्रादिविषयकर्तव्यताप्रतिपत्तिः प्रतिपत्तित्वात् लौकिककर्तव्यताद्यर्थतत्त्वानुसृतेरेव भवितुमर्हति, अन्यथा नारिकेलद्वीपजातवृद्धस्य धेनुप्रतिपत्त्यर्थवत् सा स्यात्। कर्तव्यताविधानानन्तरं च इतिकर्तव्यतावसरः तदुभयं अलौकिकत्वात् अग्निहोत्रसामान्यस्य अग्निष्टोमादिविशिष्टस्य द्रव्यमन्त्रदेवताग्नि-यमाद्यात्मनः च अप्रसिद्धेरयुक्तम्। यथा घटादिकर्तव्यतायां विहितायां घटं कुर्विति, ततः पुनः इतिकर्तव्यताक्रमः, एवं मृत्पिण्डं चक्रमूर्धनि संस्थाप्य दण्डेन भ्रामयित्वा द्वाभ्यां पाणिभ्यां शिवकाद्याकारविशेषान् क्रमेण निर्वर्तयेत् इति प्रसिद्धकर्तव्यता-विधानोत्तरकालं प्रसिद्धेति- कर्तव्यताविधानं घटादिविषयमुपपन्नम्, प्रसिद्धार्थत्वात्, नत्वग्निहोत्रकर्तव्यतायाः पशुवधादीतिकर्तव्यतायाश्च प्रसिद्धिः अप्रसिद्धार्थत्वादग्नि-होत्रशब्दस्य, न तु घटवदग्निहोत्रशब्दः कांचिदपि कर्तव्यतां ब्रवीति'' इति यदुक्तम् अत्र ब्रूमः येयमप्रसिद्धिः अग्निहोत्रस्थले वर्णिता येयं प्रसिद्धिः घटस्थले च वर्णिता - सा किं निरूपिता? यः कुलालादिः स घटकरणे प्रवृत्त इति घटो वा तत्करणं वा, तेन ज्ञायत इति तन्मात्रप्रसिद्धिः। यो हि घटं तत्करणं वा सर्वात्मना न जानाति तस्य

विषये घटादेरपि प्रसिद्धयभाव एव - यथा नारिकेलद्वीपजातस्य वृद्धस्य धेनुप्रतिपत्यभावः स्वयमेव उदाहृतः तद्वत्।

एवं ये अनादिकालात् परम्परानुगतं अग्निहोत्रादिकं कर्म अनुतिष्ठन्तो वर्तन्ते तेषां अग्निहोत्र - तत्करणं च प्रसिद्धमेवेति न सिध्यत्यप्रसिद्धिः। तस्य चाप्रसिद्धिवर्णनं स्वीयाज्ञानमूलकमात्रमेव। अपि च अग्निहोत्रादौ पशुवधादीतिकर्तव्यतां प्रतिपादयतः - स्वाप्रसिद्धिं प्रकटयतीति च युक्तमेव। यतोहि अग्निहोत्रकर्मणि न कदापि न कस्मिंश्चित् प्रयोगे पशुर्द्रव्यं भवितुमर्हतीति। अपिच - यद्यपि तत्क्रियां न जानाति - तथापि शब्दार्थज्ञानवतः तत्र घटस्थले इव अग्निहोत्रस्थलेपि अग्निप्रणयनस-मिन्धनादिक्रियाजातं ज्ञायत एवेति न द्वयोः भिन्नरूपता। अतः 'अप्रसिद्धेरयुक्तं' इति कथनं अविचारितरमणीयमेव। यद्येवं तर्हि 'ओदनं पचे' त्यस्यापि अप्रसिद्धत्वमेव वर्णनीयमापतेत्।

अपिच ''जुहुयादित्ययं, तर्हि'' इत्यारभ्य ''अथ तदेव तदिति एतत्तावदनयोः ऐकार्थ्यं प्रसिद्धिविरुद्धम्-पौनरुक्त्यपरिहारार्थं जुहुयादित्येवास्तु किमग्निहोत्रमित्यनेन'' इति यदुक्तम् तत् एतत्प्रश्नकर्तुः नामधेयप्रयोजनज्ञानाभावं प्रदर्शयति। यत्र यत्र जुहुयात् इति दृश्यते तत्र तत्र होमः इति सामान्यरूपेण अर्थः। तत्र अग्निहोत्रप्रभृतिशब्दैः अर्थात् नामधेयेन विशेषसंज्ञकेन अतिदेशसंकल्पकरणफलसम्बन्धकथनादौ तस्य अनुवादः फलमिति नामधेयप्रयोजनमभिहितम्। तादृशज्ञानमलब्ध्वा खलु अयं प्रश्नः क्रियते - ''जुहुयादित्येवास्तु किमग्निहोत्रमित्यनेन'' इति।

अपिच- ''तत एवं वचनव्यक्तिः भवति अग्निहोत्राख्यं हवनं कुर्यात् घटवदिति'' (पृ. 143) इति पक्षखण्डनाय यदुक्तं'' एतदयुक्तं, दृष्टान्तवैषम्यादर्थभेदासिद्धेः, नहि किञ्चिदग्निहोत्रं नाम घटवत् प्रसिद्धं यदनूद्य उच्येत। नहि साधर्म्येण यदग्निहोत्रसंज्ञकं हवनं तत्कुर्यादिति अग्निहोत्रहवनयोः ऐक्येन तद्विषयं करणमनुविधीयेत, नापि वैधर्म्येण हवनं कुर्यादिति हवनक्रियामनूद्य तदग्निहोत्राख्यमित्येकेन विधानं युज्येत, परेण अग्निहोत्रस्य हवनस्य वा अविहितत्वात्, अत एव तूभयमप्यशक्यम्, विशेषणं विशेष्यञ्च, प्रधानमुपसर्जनं च, विधिरनुवादश्च, शेषः शेषीच, उत्सर्गोपवादश्च, अन्यतरस्याप्यर्थाप्रतीतेः, यदि विशेष्येणैव विशेषणीयं हवनं कुर्यात्तच्चाग्निहोत्रसंज्ञकं इति, अग्निहोत्रं वा हवनमिति, तच्च नैवं शक्यमप्रसिद्धार्थत्वादिति (पृ. 144) - तत्रोच्यते। यदुक्तमप्रसिद्धत्वं तत्पूर्वमेवनिरस्तम्। - अत्र तु वाक्यार्थः एवं-यदग्निहोत्रसंज्ञकं हवनं तेन भावयेत्

इति। एवञ्च अग्निहोत्रहवनयोरेकत्वेन तद्विषयं करणमनुविधीयते। साधर्म्येणैव (सामानाधि- करण्येन) परन्तु हवनक्रियामनूद्य तदग्निहोत्राख्यं इति तु नात्र विधेयम्। यदि प्रामाण्यं स्वीक्रियते तदा सिद्धवस्तुसमन्वयाय असिद्धवस्त्वाक्षेपः क्रियते। येषां वेदे प्रामाण्यं सिद्धं – ते आक्षिपन्ति अत्र उभयस्याप्यनेनैव बोधाङ्गीकारे वाक्यभेदः इति दोषः प्रदर्श्यते प्रतिपक्षिभिः। परन्तु एतादृशो दोषः स्वग्रन्थेपि परिदृश्यत एव। यथा अस्य ग्रन्थस्य नयचक्रमिति नाम। इतः पूर्वमस्य ग्रन्थस्य अभावात् अप्रसिद्धमेव। अवस्थायामस्यां" अस्य चार्थस्य पूर्वमहोदधि-समुत्थितनयप्रभूततरङ्गागमप्रभ्रष्टशिलभष्टार्थकणिकामात्रस्य प्रतिपादकस्य नयचक्रस्य शास्त्रस्य संक्षिप्तार्थं गाथासूत्रम्" इति वाक्ये तत्पदं प्रयुक्तम्। अयं ग्रन्थः एतन्नामको भवतु इति ग्रन्थ- कर्तुः अभिप्रायः न प्रमाणान्तरवेद्यः। न केवलं अत्रैव। "बालानां सुखबोधाय क्रियते तर्क- संग्रहः।" "वैयाकरण सिद्धान्तकौमुदीयं विरच्यते" इत्यादौ च। यदि तस्य वाक्यस्य प्रामाण्यं स्वीक्रियते तदा ग्रन्थस्यास्य ग्रन्थकर्त्ता एतादृशं नाम भवतु इत्यभिप्रायेण एवं निर्देशः कृतः इति एतन्निर्देशान्यथानुपपत्या तस्य ग्रन्थस्य तन्नामेति स्वीक्रियते। यदि न तत्प्रामाण्यं स्वीकृतं तर्हि अनुपपन्नमेव दृश्यते। एतन्यायेनैव पूर्वोक्तेपि समन्वयः। परन्तु तत्र कल्पितश्रुत्या। यथा लिङ्गवाक्यप्रकरणादौ श्रुतिं कल्पयित्वा कल्पितश्रुत्या अनुष्ठानं एवमत्रापि कल्पितश्रुत्या तादृशक्तियाजातस्य अग्निहोत्राख्यत्वं सिध्यति एतत्सर्वं पूर्वोक्तदृशा प्रामाण्यसिद्धेः अपौरुषेयत्वसिद्धेश्च – निरस्तप्रायमेवेति च ग्रन्थविस्तरदृष्ट्या विरम्यते। एवञ्च तत्तद्ग्रन्थप्रतिपादितपूर्वपक्षयुक्तिप्रदर्शनमात्रेण अनादित्वमपौरुषेयत्वं तिरस्कर्तुं न शक्यत इति दिक्।

Dharmabhūṣaṇa's Treatment of Pramāṇa

Itaru Wakiryo

Introduction

The question : "What is *pramāṇa*", "What is its nature" and "What are its varieties etc.", are answered differently by various schools of Indian philosophy. Occasion was made to discuss about these view-points, and this mutual discussion contributed to rise up many new theories in the process of eliminations, additions and modifications.

In the present paper, it is proposed to study the treatement of the concept of *pramāṇa* by Dharmabhūṣaṇa (15th Century), one of the later philosophers of Jaina Digambara Sect, in his Nyāya Dīpikā. Attempt will be made to study the historical development of the concept, in the text tradition of Indian philosophical systems.

I)

Before proceeding to discuss Dharmabhūṣaṇa's treatement of *pramāṇa*, it is worth to see the historical development of the concept with reference to its definition in Indian logic, in general and Jaina logic, in particular. The word *pramāṇa* is derived generally from the root *mā* with a prefix *pra* - and sufix - *lyuṭ* and stands for 'knowledge' as well as 'means of knowledge' in a loose sense. In most of the cases, it is understood in the sense of *karaṇa*, that is, instrument. We notice striking differences of views among the philosophers on the nature of *pramāṇa*.

In the history of epistemological tradition, Kaṇāda (B.C. 2c) occupies the first place to give a general definition of *pramāṇa*. According to him, the general definition of *pramāṇa* should be based on the principle that the cause of cognition should be free from defects.[1] In the Bhāṣya of Vaiśeṣika Sūtra, we don't find any clear definition of *pramāṇa*. Among the Vaiśeṣika Philosophers, it is only Śaṅkara-miśra who asserts that the *pramāṇa* is that which produces knowledge.[2]

Coming to Nyāya system, we don't find any definitions of *pramāṇa* in Nyāya Sūtra. Gautama only enumerated four means of valid knowledge. It is only Vātsyāyana who provided the definition of *pramāṇa*. According to him, *pramāṇa* is instrument of valid knowledge[3]. Uddyotakara repeated the same view of Vāstyāyana. The later text book writers have accepted *pramāṇa* as the instrument of valid knowledge with exception to Jayanta who proposes *pramāṇa* to be the collection of all causal factors.[4] Thus, according to Jayanta, *pramāṇa* is the collection of 'conscious' as well as 'unconscious' factor which produces apprehension of objects that is different from illusion and doubt. The later writers like Śivādityamiśra and Varadarāja have been influenced by Jayanta and corroborate this sāmagrī in their definitions of *pramāṇa*.[5] This notion of instrument as *pramāṇa* is seen to have been accepted by all other schools of Indian philosophy.

It is necessary to note that Udayanācarya in his Nyāyakusumañjalī has defined *pramāṇa* to be the knowledge and not the means of knowledge. There is no basic difference on this idea of instrument, though there is difference on the nature of the *pramāṇa*.

II

There is difference of opinion amongst the Buddhist philosphers on the definition of *pramāṇa*. The *Sautrāntika* and *Vaibhāṣika* maintained that *pramāṇa* is that which generates true knowledge of objects. The Prābhākaras defined pramāṇa as to be immediate experience.[6]

The definition of Prabhākara is ambiguous in the sense that the meaning of the term '*anubhūti*' is not clear. The Bhāṭṭas defined *pramāṇa* as to be a definite and assured cognition of object and does not need confirmation by other cognition.[7] Commenting on this Umbeka notes that the word 'dṛddha' and '*avisaṁvādi*' would exclude the 'doubt' and 'error' from the valid knowledge respectively.[8]

III

We may now turn to the discussion of *pramāṇa*, according to Jaina logicians, particularly, Dharmabhūṣaṇa. Dharmabhūṣaṇa in his Nyāya Dīpikā has quoted the definition of pramāṇa of the Buddhist, the Bhāṭṭas, the Prabhākaras, and the Naiyāyikas as well. After a critical examination, he has rejected all those definitions of *pramāṇa*.

He has also quoted some definitions of some early Jaina logicians and has refuted them. We present here a detail analysis of his treatment.

According to Dharmabhūṣaṇa, *pramāṇa* is right knowledge, "*Samyak jñānam pramāṇam*". He states that the word '*samyak*' is given in order to exclude doubtful, erroneous and indefinite knowledge from becoming *pramāṇa*. By the word '*jñāṇa*', the knower and the knowledge are excluded from *pramāṇa*.

It may be observed that in Jaina tradition, *pramāṇa* is taken as identical with *pra-mā* (the valid knowledge) and not the means unlike the other systems of Indian philosophy. Vidyānanda in his Pramāṇa-parīkṣā has given the same definition like Nyāya Dīpikā. Let us now see the definition of *pramāṇa* as given by other Jaina logicians. Siddhasena Divākara defines *pramāṇa* as the knowledge which illuminates its self and others and which is not sublated experience.[10]

It must be noticed here that the word, '*bādha-varjita*' of Siddhasena Divākara is the same as '*bādha-varjita*' of the Mīmāṁsākas and '*avisamvādi*' of Dharmakīrti.

Akalaṅka refers to 'novelty and un-cotradictory-ness' along with 'Sva-parāvabhāsaka' as the definition of pramāṇa. In Māṇikyanandin, we have the combination of the view of Siddhasena and Akalaṅka. According to him, pramāṇa is valid knowledge of its self and of things not proved before.[11] Vidyānanda follows Siddhasena with some modification. In the Jaina tradition, the credit of introducing the term '*vyavasāyātmaka*' goes to Vidyānanda. Hemacandra's definition seems to be an improvement on the earlier definitions. The word '*sva*' is discarded and in place of '*avabhāsa*', he takes *nirnīti* and introduced the word '*samyak*'.[12] It may be observed that Siddhasena's definition was influenced by *Vijñāna-vādi* sect of the Buddhist, and the definition of Akalaṅka and Māṇikyanandin have borrowed from the Mīmāṁsākas.

IV

Let us now see how Dharmabhūṣaṇa refutes the definition of pramāṇa as given by the Buddhist and others. As noted earlier, the Buddhist define *pramāṇa* as *avisaṁvādi jñāna*[13] - an unfailing knowledge. Dharmabhūṣaṇa thinks that the two pramāṇas, namely, perception and inference are not unfailing.

To him, perception being non-determinate cannot be unfailing. Same is the case with inference. Against the Bhāṭṭas' definition of *pramāṇa*, Dharmabhūṣaṇa comments.

The Bhāṭṭas want *pramāṇa* to be that which determines the object which is not already known[14]. The same Bhāṭṭas accept repeated or continuous knowledge (*dhārāvāhika jñāna*) as *pramāṇa*. As matter of fact, according to their theory of *pramāṇa*, the repeated knowledge should not be *pramāṇa*. Hence a case of contradiction. In other words, the Bhāṭṭas' definition of *pramāṇa* suffers from the fault of 'too-narrowness', that is *avyāpati*, and is not applicable to continuous repeated knowledge which is valid according to them.

On the Prābhākaras' definition of *pramāṇa*, namely, "*anubhūtiḥ pramāṇaṁ* - *pramāṇa* is direct experience, Dharmabhūṣaṇa raises the following objections. Whether the word '*anubhūti*' in the definition of *pramāṇa* has an 'action-derivative-structure' or an '*instrumental-derivative-structure*'.[15]

In either case, the definition of *pramāṇa* will be defective. Let us make the point bit more clear. The word '*anubhūti*' may mean *karaṇa*, that is instrument, of '*phala*', that is knowledge, whereas *pramāṇa* includes both; means and knowledge. Thus, if '*anubhūti*' is understood in the sense of instrument on the basis of 'instrumental-derivative-structure', it would exclude the other sense, namely, the sense of knowledge on the basis of 'action-derivative-structure', and vice-versa. Thus, the definition of *pramāṇa* of Prabhākara is defective, as thinks Dharmabhūṣaṇa.

On the Naiyāyikas' definition of *pramāṇa* Dharmabhūṣaṇa observes - *tadāpi pramādakṛt* - defective. He quotes from Nyāyakusumāñjalī where it is stated that God is *pramāṇa* and the Naiyayikas accept God as the instrumental cause. In reality, God is the abode or '*adhikaraṇa*' of *pramāṇa* and not identical with *pramāṇa* as desired by the logicians. Thus, the definition of *pramāṇa* as *pramākaraṇa* is not correct. Dharmabhūṣaṇa gives his view on *dhārāvāhika-jñāna*, that is, repeated knowledge and *nir-vikalapa jñanam* (non-determinate knowledge).

It seems that Dharmabhūṣana does not want the repeated knowledge to be *pramāṇa*. It is possible that his refutation of repeated knowledge is grounded on the Bhāṭṭas' definition of *pramāna*.

Similarly, he does not want the undeterminate knowledge to be *pramāna* unlike the logicians. To him, the non-determinate knowledge is mere sensation and the knowledge having forms is *pramāṇa*. In favour of his view, he quotes from Sarvārtha-siddhi or Pūjyapāda.[16]

A point which needs special mention is the derivation of the word *pramāna* by Dharmabhūṣana. Dharmabhūṣaṇa proposes that *pramāna* may be derived from the sense of *bhāva* (action) and *karana* (instrument). When the word *pramāṇa* has an 'action-derivative-structure', it refers to knowledge and when it has an 'instrumental-derivative-structure', it refers to means of knowledge. Similarly, the word '*jñāna*' may mean knowledge or the means of knowledge, basing on the fact of its derivation.[17] It is interesting to note that it is only in the tradition of Jaina philosophy that the word '*jñāna*' is derived from *karaṇa* to mean, means of knowledge and *pramāṇa* as knowledge. In most cases, the word *jñāna* means knowledge and *pramāṇa*, the means.

V

We may now summarize our discussion by making the following observation in the form of conclusion:

1. In Jaina tradition, *pramāṇa* is understood in the sense

of jñāna, unlike the other system of philosophy.

2. Siddhasena Divākara defines *pramāṇa* as the knowledge which illuminates its self and others and which is not sublated experience. The word hādavarjita of Siddhasena is same.

3. Akalaṅka introduces new factors in his definition, namely, novelty and un-contradictory-ness, and in the *Parīkṣāmukha* of Māṇikyanandin, there is combination of the definition of Siddhasena and Akalaṅka.

4. Dharmabhūṣaṇa defines *pramāṇa* as 'right knowledge' which is same as given by Vidyānanda.

5. We have a synthesis of the early definition of *pramāṇa* in the definition of Hemacandra.

6. Dharmabhūṣaṇa's refutations of definitions of *pramāna* of the Buddhist and others are not convincing. To be impartial, Dharmabhūṣaṇa's refutation is based on his mispresentation of fact. For example, the Naiyāyikas lightly postulate God as one of the causes and the abode of knowledge. There is no contradiction in holding so. In one case, it is instrument and in the other, it is knowledge.

7. On the Bhāṭṭas: he says that, their definition is not applicable in the case of the repeated knowledge. As a matter of fact, the Bhāṭṭas' definition of *pramāṇa* is well-applicable to repeated knowledge, and, there is no harm for them in accepting repeated knowledge as *pramāṇa*. Because, according to the Bhāṭṭa, the repeated knowledge are distinct knowledges distinguished by time. The story is same, in the case of the Prābhākaras as well.

Footnotes

1. Vaiśeṣika Sūtra 9, 2, 12.
2. Vasīkara on Vaiśeṣika Sūtra p. 224 (Chowkhamba)
3. Vātsyāyana's Bhāṣya, on N.S. 1.1.2.
4. Nyāya-mañjalī 'Sāmagrī pramāṇaṁ'.
5. Śaptapadārthī & Tārkikarakṣā.
6. Anubhūtiḥ pramāṇa sā smṛttir anya etc. Prakaraṇa Pañjikā p. 127.
7. Tasmāt dṛdhamaṁ yad utpannaṁ nāpi samvādaṁ rucchate jñānantarena vijñānam tad pramāṇam pramīyatāṁ ś'lokavārttika, II.80.
8. Tattrayatika on S'lokavarttika II.80.
9. Nyāya Dīpikā p. 9 etd. Daravarīlal Kottiyā.
10. Pramāṇaṁ Sva-para-bādha varjītam, Nyāyāvatāra.
11. Svā-pūrvārtha-vyavasāyātmakam jñānam pramāṇam Parīkṣāmukha sūtra - 1.1.1.
12. Samyak artha nirnayaḥ pramāṇaṁ, Pramāṇa Mīmāṁsā 1.1.2.
13. Avisaṁvādi jñānam pramāṅaṁ Pramāṇa-Vārttika II,1 also cf. Nyāya Dīpikā p.18.
14. anādhigata tathābhūtārtha niścāyakaṁ pramāṇaṁ, Śāmstra Dīpikā p. 123.
15. anubhūti-śabdasya bhāva-sādhanatve karaṇa-lakṣaṇa-pramāṇāvyāpteḥ, karaṇa-sādhanatre tu bhāva-lakṣaṇa-pramāṇāvyāpteḥ, karaṇa-bhāvayor ubayor api tanmate, prāmāṇyābhyupagamāt, Nyāya Dīpikā p. 19.
16. Nirakāraṁ darśanaṁ sākāraṁ jñānam - Nyāya Dīpikā p. 14.
17. bhāvasādhanaṃ tu jñānapadaṁ pramitim āha - evameva pramāṇapadamapi pramīyate anena iti karaṇa sādhanaṁ kartavyam, Nyāya Dīpikā p. 11.

जैनदर्शन में मिथ्या और अप्रमाण

धर्मचन्द जैन

जैन दर्शन में मिथ्याज्ञान के दो रूप दिखाई देते हैं। एक रूप वह जो आगमों में निरूपित है तथा दूसरा वह जो प्रमाणमीमांसीय ग्रन्थों में प्रतिपादित है। आगमों में मिथ्याज्ञान का पारमार्थिक रूप तथा प्रमाणमीमांसीय ग्रन्थों में सांव्यवहारिक रूप प्रस्तुत हुआ है।

मिथ्याज्ञान का प्रथम रूप : अज्ञान

जैनागमों में एवं तत्त्वार्थसूत्र में जो सम्यग्दर्शन, सम्यग्ज्ञान एवं सम्यक्चारित्र को मोक्ष का मार्ग कहा गया है[1] वहां सम्यग्ज्ञान का सम्यग्दर्शन के साथ गहरा सम्बन्ध है। जब दर्शन सम्यक् होता है तभी ज्ञान सम्यक् होता है। यदि दर्शन किं वा दृष्टि मिथ्या है तो ज्ञान सम्यक् नहीं होता। इस दृष्टि से मिथ्यात्व अथवा मिथ्यादर्शन युक्त जीव का समस्त ज्ञान मिथ्या होता है तथा सम्यक्त्व अथवा सम्यग्दर्शन युक्त जीव का सारा ज्ञान सम्यक् होता है।[2] 'तत्त्वार्थश्रद्धानं सम्यग्दर्शनम्' के अनुसार तत्त्वों पर यथार्थ श्रद्धा करना सम्यग्दर्शन है। यह दर्शन सम्यक् कब होता है इसके लिए आगमों में उल्लेख मिलता है कि जब किसी जीव के आठ कर्मों में प्रमुख मोहनीय कर्म की सात प्रकृतियों (अनन्तानुबन्धी क्रोध, मान, माया एवं लोभ तथा मिथ्यात्व मोह, सम्यक्त्व मोह एवं मिश्रमोह) का क्षय (सम्पूर्ण नाश), उपशम या क्षयोपशम होता है तो उस जीव के सम्यग्दर्शन प्रकट होता है।[3] यह सम्यग्दर्शन उक्त सात कर्मप्रकृतियों का क्षय होने पर क्षायिक, उपशम होने पर औपाशमिक एवं क्षयोपशम होने

पर क्षायोपशमिक कहलाता है। सम्यक्त्व का कोई भी प्रकार प्रकट हो, किन्तु उसके प्र.कट होते ही जीव का विद्यमान समस्त मिथ्याज्ञान सम्यग्ज्ञान में परिणत हो जाता है।

इस प्रकार आगमिक-सरणि के अनुसार मिथ्यादृष्टि युक्त जीव का समस्त ज्ञान मिथ्याज्ञान है। इस मिथ्याज्ञान को अज्ञान अथवा विपर्यय भी कहा गया है। अज्ञान शब्द का दो अर्थों में प्रयोग हुआ है- एक तो ज्ञान की कोटि के अभाव में एवं दूसरा मिथ्याज्ञान के अर्थ में। आगम-सरणि में प्रायः 'अज्ञान' शब्द इसी मिथ्याज्ञान के अर्थ में प्रयुक्त होता है। ज्ञान के जहां पांच भेद निरूपित हैं- मतिज्ञान (आभिनिबोधिक ज्ञान), श्रुतज्ञान, अवधिज्ञान, मनः पर्याय ज्ञान एवं केवलज्ञान[4], वहां अज्ञान तीन ही प्रकार का मान्य है, यथा- मति-अज्ञान, श्रुत-अज्ञान एवं विभङ्गज्ञान।[5] ये तीनों अज्ञान प्रथम तीन ज्ञानों के विपर्यय रूप हैं, जैसा कि तत्त्वार्थसूत्रकार कहते हैं- **मतिश्रुतावधयो विपर्ययश्च** (1.31) अर्थात् मति, श्रुत एवं अवधि ज्ञानों का विपर्यय रूप भी होता है। मनः पर्याय एवं केवलज्ञान मिथ्यात्वी को नहीं होते, इसलिए इनका विपर्यय रूप नहीं पाया जाता।

मति आदि तीन ज्ञानों के विपर्यय रूप मिथ्याज्ञान अथवा अज्ञान से युक्त जीव को भी बाह्य दृष्टि से सम्यग्ज्ञानी की भांति ही टेबिल, कुर्सी, पंखा आदि वस्तुओं का ज्ञान होता हैं दोनों के इन्द्रिय जन्य ज्ञान में कोई भेद नहीं होता है।[6] ऐसा नहीं है कि मतिज्ञान से युक्त जीव सीप को सीप जानता हो एवं मति-अज्ञान से युक्त जीव उसे रजत समझ लेता हो। दोनों ही सीप को सीप समझते हैं, किन्तु सम्यग्दृष्टि से युक्त जीव का ज्ञान मोक्षाभिमुख दृष्टि के कारण सम्यक् एवं मिथ्यादृष्टि से युक्त जीव का ज्ञान संसाराभिमुख दृष्टि के कारण मिथ्या माना जाता है।[7] यही मिथ्याज्ञान का पारमार्थिक रूप है।

तत्त्वार्थसूत्र में उमास्वाति ने सत् एवं असत् में भेद नहीं करने के कारण मिथ्याज्ञानी को उन्मत्त पुरुष की भांति बतलाया है।[8] जिस प्रकार उन्मत्त पुरुष इन्द्रिय एवं बुद्धि के उपहत होने से कदाचित् अश्व को गौ समझ लेता है, लोष्ठ को सुवर्ण समझ लेता है, उसी प्रकार मिथ्याज्ञानी सत् एवं असत् में भेद नहीं कर पाता है। वह तत्त्वज्ञान से दूर ही रहता है। सवार्थसिद्धि में पूज्यपाद देवनन्दी एवं तत्त्वार्थवार्त्तिक में अकलङ्क ने मिथ्यादृष्टि जीव के मिथ्याज्ञान को कड़वे तुम्बे में रखे दूध की उपमा दी है। जिस प्रकार कड़वे तुम्बे में रखा

दूध दूषित हो जाता है उसी प्रकार मिथ्यादृष्टि जीव का ज्ञान भी दूषित होने से मिथ्या हो जाता है।[9]

पूज्यपाद देवनन्दी ने कारण विपर्यास, भेदाभेद विपर्यास एवं स्वरूप विपर्यास के रूप में मिथ्याज्ञान किंवा अज्ञान का निरूपण करते हुए जैनेतर दर्शनों का मिथ्याज्ञान में समावेश किया है।[10] कारणविपर्यास के अन्तर्गत वे रूप आदि का एक अमूर्त एवं नित्य कारण मानने वाले सांख्यों तथा पृथिवी आदि जाति से भिन्न परमाणुओं को तुल्य जातीय कार्यों के आरम्भक मानने वाले वैशषिकों का समावेश करते हैं। इसी प्रकार बौद्धों एवं लौकायतिकों की मान्यताओं को भी उन्होंने कारण विपर्यास में सम्मिलित किया है। भेदाभेद विपर्यास के अन्तर्गत कारण से कार्य को भिन्न मानने वाले नैयायिकों एवं अभिन्न मानने वाले सांख्यों का समावेश किया है। स्वरूपविपर्यास के अन्तर्गत बाह्यार्थ को अस्वीकार करने वाले बौद्धों आदि का समावेश किया है।

इस प्रकार जैनदर्शन से भिन्न मान्यता रखने वाले दर्शनों के ज्ञान को पूज्यपाद ने मिथ्याज्ञान अथवा विपर्यय ज्ञान की श्रेणी में रख दिया है, क्योंकि उनके अनुसार जैनेतर दार्शनिक मिथ्यादर्शन से युक्त हैं।

यहां पर यह भी उल्लेख करना उचित होगा कि जैन दार्शनिक अपने अनेकान्त एवं नय-सिद्धान्त के अनुसार अपर दर्शनों के द्वारा प्रतिपादित सिद्धान्तों को कथञ्चित् अथवा किसी अपेक्षा से या किसी अंश में सत्य भी स्वीकार करते हैं।

मिथ्याज्ञान का द्वितीय रूप : अप्रमाण

सम्यग्ज्ञान के विरोधी मिथ्याज्ञान का दूसरा रूप प्रमाणमीमांसीय ग्रन्थों में मिलता है। इसके अनुसार संशय, विपर्यय एवं अनध्यवसायात्मक ज्ञान को मिथ्याज्ञान कहा जा सकता है। इसे जैनाचार्यों ने समारोप एवं अप्रमाण शब्द से अभिहित किया है। यह मिथ्याज्ञान सम्यग्दृष्टि एवं मिथ्यादृष्टि जीवों को समानरूप से हो सकता है, क्योंकि मिथ्याज्ञान का यह स्वरूप सांव्यवहारिक है। जैन दार्शनिकों ने स्व एवं अर्थ के निश्चायक ज्ञान को प्रमाण प्रतिपादित करते हुए उसे सम्यग्ज्ञान भी कहा है। आचार्य **विद्यानन्द** ने तो सम्यग्ज्ञान को प्रमाण कहकर उसे स्वपर-व्यवसायात्मक प्रतिपादित किया है तथा उसे संशय,

विपर्यय एवं अनध्यवसाय से रहित कहा है।[11] **प्रभाचन्द्र** एवं **हेमचन्द्र सूरि** ने प्रमाण का व्युत्पत्तिपरक लक्षण इस प्रकार दिया है- **प्रकर्षेण संशयादिव्यवच्छेदेन मीयते परिच्छिद्यते वस्तुतत्त्वं येन तत् प्रमाणं प्रमायां साधकतमम्**।[12] अर्थात् संशयादि से रहित जो ज्ञान वस्तुतत्त्वं को जानने में साधकतम होता है वह प्रमाण है। आशय यह है कि 'प्रमाण' संशयादि अप्रमाणभूत ज्ञानों से रहित होता है।

अकलङ्क, विद्यानन्द, माणिक्यनन्दी, प्रभाचन्द्र, वादिदेवसूरि, हेमचन्द्र आदि आचार्यों के प्रमाण-लक्षणों के अनुसार प्रमाण की जैन दर्शन में निम्नाङ्कित विशेषताएं स्वीकार की गई हैं- (1) वह ज्ञानात्मक होता है। इसलिए स्व-पर प्रकाशक भी होता है।[13] (2) वह स्व एवं अर्थ का निश्चायक होता है।[14] (3) वह निश्चयात्मक होने से सविकल्पक होता है। (4) वह संवादक होता है।[15] अर्थात् प्रमाण के द्वारा अर्थ जैसा जाना गया है वह वैसा ही प्राप्त होता है। (5) वह संशय, विपर्यय एवं अनध्यवसाय से रहित होता है।

इसके विपरीत अन्य दर्शनों को मान्य प्रमाण का स्वरूप जैन दार्शनिकों के अनुसार अप्रमाण है।

जैन दार्शनिकों के मत में नैयायिकों के द्वारा मान्य कारकसाकल्य, इन्द्रिय एवं इन्द्रियार्थसन्निकर्ष प्रमाण नहीं हैं, क्योंकि ये अज्ञानात्मक हैं।[16] इनमें ज्ञान का ही अभाव है। जबकि प्रमाण ज्ञानात्मक होता है। जैन दार्शनिक 'प्रमाकरणं प्रमाणम्' वाक्य को स्वीकार करते हुए भी प्रमा का करण ज्ञान को अंगीकार करते हैं। जैन दार्शनिकों के अनुसार सांख्य सम्मत इन्द्रियवृत्ति या बुद्धिवृत्ति भी प्रमाण नहीं है, क्योंकि वह अचेतनात्मक है। सांख्यों ने ज्ञान को अचेतन बुद्धि का धर्म माना है जबकि जैनों के अनुसार वह चेतन आत्मा का गुण है। मीमांसकों का ज्ञातृव्यापार भी जैन दर्शन में प्रमाण नहीं है, क्योंकि वह स्वप्रकाशक नहीं होता। न्याय-वैशेषिकों के द्वारा मान्य सविकल्पक ज्ञान भी जैन दार्शनिकों के अनुसार प्रमाण नहीं है, क्योंकि वह मात्र परप्रकाशक होता है, स्वप्रकाशक नहीं होता। बाह्यार्थप्रलापी विज्ञानवादी बौद्ध ज्ञान को स्वसंवेदी ही स्वीकार करते हैं उसे पर-प्रकाशक नहीं मानते, इसलिए जैन मत में उनका ज्ञान भी प्रमाण नहीं है।[17] जैन दार्शनिकों के अनुसार तो वही ज्ञान प्रमाण हो सकता है जो स्व एवं अर्थ दोनों का व्यवसायक हो।

जैनाचार्यों ने बौद्धों द्वारा मान्य चतुर्विध निर्विकल्पक प्रत्यक्ष को भी अप्रमाण माना है, क्योंकि वह निर्विकल्पक होने से व्यवसायात्मक नहीं होता। व्यवसायात्मकता के साथ सविकल्पकता की व्याप्ति है, निर्विकल्पकता की नहीं। जैन दार्शनिकों ने अपने ही मत में प्रतिपादित 'दर्शन' को जो कि ज्ञान के पूर्व अनिवार्य रूप से होता है, उसे भी व्यवहार का अंग नहीं होने के कारण एवं ज्ञान की कोटि से बहिर्भूत होने के कारण प्रमाण नहीं माना है।

यहां हम अप्रमाणभूत संशय, विपर्यय एवं अनध्यवसाय के स्वरूप पर कुछ विचार करेंगें। जैन दार्शनिक इन तीनों को 'समारोप' संज्ञा प्रदान करते हैं। समारोप का लक्षण (अतस्मिंस्तदध्यवसाय : समारोपः) तो यद्यपि मुख्यतः विपर्ययज्ञान में ही घटित होता है, तथापि संशय एवं अनध्यवसाय को भी उपचार से उसी कोटि में लिया गया है।

संशयज्ञान

संशयज्ञान को जैन एवं जैनेतर प्रायः सभी दार्शनिक अप्रमाण मानते हैं। जैन दाशनिक वादिदेवसूरि ने इस संशयज्ञान का लक्षण देते हुए प्रतिपादित किया है कि जो ज्ञान साधक एवं बाधक प्रमाणों के अभाव से अनेक कोटि को स्पर्श करते हुए निर्णयात्मकता को प्राप्त न हो, वह संशय ज्ञान है।[18] जैसे दूर से प्रत्यक्ष गोचर वस्तु में स्थाणु एवं पुरुष दोनों के समानधर्म दिखाई देने पर किसी एक का निर्णय न हो सके तो वहां संशयज्ञान होता है। इसमें प्रतिपत्ता को यह पुरुष ही है, या यह स्थाणु ही है, ऐसा निश्चित ज्ञान नहीं होता, अपितु वह दोनों ओर दोलायमान रहता है। ऐसा संशय ज्ञान प्रत्यक्ष की भांति परोक्ष ज्ञान में भी संभव है। जैसे सींग मात्र को देखकर 'यह गवय है या गौ', यह संशय परोक्षज्ञान के अन्तर्गत समाहित होगा।

विपर्यय ज्ञान (विपरीतार्थख्याति)

भ्रमज्ञान अथवा विपर्ययज्ञान (Erroneous cognition) को संकुचित अर्थ में मिथ्याज्ञान का तृतीय रूप कहा जा सकता है। भ्रमज्ञान अथवा विपर्यय ज्ञान को अप्रमाण मानने के संबंध में भारतीय दार्शनिक एकमत हैं, किन्तु उसके स्वरूप की व्याख्या को लेकर वे परस्पर मतभेद रखते हैं। विपर्ययज्ञान के सम्बन्ध में ख्यातिपञ्चक प्रसिद्ध है, जिसके अनुसार विज्ञानवादी बौद्ध आत्मख्याति के रूप में, शून्यवादी बौद्ध असत्ख्याति के रूप में, प्राभाकर मीमांसक विवेकाख्याति के रूप में, नैयायिक एवं भाट्टमीमांसक विपरीत

ख्याति अथवा अन्यथाख्याति के रूप में तथा वेदान्ती अनिर्वचनीयख्याति के रूप में विपर्यय की व्याख्या करते हैं। जैन दार्शनिक इनमें नैयायिकों की विपरीतख्याति अथवा अन्यथाख्याति को स्वीकार करते है। **प्रमेयकमलमार्तण्ड** के रचयिता जैन दार्शनिक **प्रभाचन्द्र** ने अख्यातिवाद को संभवतः चार्वाककृत व्याख्या मानकर मीमांसकों की ओर से स्मृतिप्रमोष सिद्धान्त निरूपित किया है। सांख्यों की ओर से उन्होंने प्रसिद्धार्थख्याति का निरूपण किया है तथा इन सबका खण्डन करते हुए विपरीतार्थख्याति को जैनदृष्टि से मान्यता प्रदान की है।[19]

वादिदेवसूरि के **स्याद्वादरत्नाकर** का अवलोकन करने पर ज्ञात होता है कि उन्होंने विपर्ययज्ञान के सम्बन्ध में उस समय तक (12 वीं शती तक) प्रचलित सभी मान्यताओं को पूर्वपक्ष में उपस्थापित कर उनका खण्डन किया है तथा अन्त में वृद्ध नैयायिकों की विपरीतार्थख्याति का समर्थन करते हुए उसे प्रतिष्ठित किया है। **वादिदेवसूरि** ने प्राभाकरों की विवेकाख्याति, चार्वाक की अख्याति, शून्यवादी बौद्धों की असत्ख्याति, सांख्यों की प्रसिद्धार्थख्याति, विज्ञानवादी बौद्धों की आत्मख्याति, वेदान्तियों की अनिर्वचनीयख्याति एवं नव्यनैयायिकों की अलौकिकख्याति की विशद चर्चा की है।[20]

प्राभाकरों की विवेकाख्याति के अनुसार सीप में रजत का भ्रम प्रत्यक्ष एवं स्मरण में भेद नहीं करने के कारण होता है। चार्वाक के अनुसार ख्याति ही नहीं है। शुक्ति में रजत का भ्रम होने में न रजत कारण है, न रजत का अभाव कारण है और न ही शुक्ति कारण है इसलिए इसमें भ्रम को स्वीकार करना उचित नहीं है। शून्यवादी बौद्धों की असत्ख्याति के अनुसार सीप में रजत के भ्रम में न तो ज्ञान ही कारण है। और न अर्थ इसलिए असत् की प्रतीति होने से यह असत्ख्याति है। सांख्यों की प्रसिद्धार्थख्याति के अनुसार प्रतीतिसिद्ध अर्थ ही विपर्ययज्ञान में प्रकाशित होता है। विज्ञानवादी बौद्धों की आत्मख्याति में अनादिवासना के कारण ज्ञानात्मा को ही बाह्य अर्थ के आकार में भ्रान्ति उत्पन्न करने वाला माना गया है। वेदान्तियों के मत में शुक्ति में प्रतिभासित रजत न सत् है, न असत् और न ही सत्-असत् उभयरूप है, इसलिए इसे अनिर्वचनीयख्याति कहा गया है। नव्यनैयायिकों की अलौकिकख्याति के अनुसार सीप में रजत का ग्रहण अलौकिकसन्निकर्ष से होता है।

जैनदर्शन सम्मत विपरीतख्याति को स्पष्ट करते हुए **वादिदेवसूरि** कहते हैं कि सीप का जब रजत के रूप में ग्रहण होता है, तो वस्तुतः सीप एवं रजत के समान धर्म के कारण ही यह भ्रान्ति उत्पन्न होती है। सीप का जो त्रिकोणादि विशेषधर्म है, वह तो दुष्टिगोचर होता नहीं है तथा चाकचिक्य आदि समान धर्म को देखने से रजत का स्मरण होता है एवं वह सीप रजत के आकार को ही ग्रहण करती हुई प्रतीत होती है। इस प्रकार सीप से भिन्न रजत का ज्ञान होने से यह विपरीत ख्याति है। वादिदेवसूरि के शब्दो में-

'संवृतस्वाकारा समुपात्तकलधौताकारा च शुक्तिकैवालम्बनमिति तु वृद्धाः। वस्तुस्थित्या हि शुक्तिरेव सा त्रिकोणत्वादिविशेषग्रहणाभावात्तु संवृतस्वाकारा चाकचिक्यादिसमानधर्म दर्शनोपजनितरूपस्मणारोपितरूप्याकारत्वाच्च समुपात्तरूप्याकारेत्यभिधीयते।[21]

अनध्यवसाय

अनध्यवसाय को जैन दार्शनिकों ने अप्रमाण घोषित कर अपने मत में प्रतिपादित निर्विकल्पक दर्शन एवं बौद्धदर्शन में प्रतिपादित निर्विकल्पक प्रत्यक्ष को प्रमाणकोटि से बहिष्कृत कर दिया है। अनध्यवसाय का लक्षण वादिदेवसूरि ने इस प्रकार दिया गया है- '**किमित्यालोचनमात्रमनध्यवसायः**[22] अर्थात् जब यह क्या है, इस प्रकार का जो आलोचनमात्र ज्ञान है उसे अनध्यवसाय कहा गया है। इस अनध्यवसाय में किसी प्रमेय के सम्बन्ध में कोई निर्णयात्मक बोध नहीं होता। जैसे कोई चलता हुआ पुरुष तृण को स्पर्श करते समय यह भान नहीं कर सके कि क्या छुआ है, तो यह अनध्यवसायात्मक ज्ञान है। चित्त के अन्यत्र आसक्त होने से भी ऐसा संभव है। यह संशय ज्ञान की पूर्वावस्था है एवं संशय से भिन्न है, क्योकि संशय में तो अनेककोटि को स्पर्श करने वाला अनिर्णयात्मक ज्ञान होता है जबकि अनध्यवसाय में ज्ञान किसी भी कोटि को स्पर्श नहीं करने कारण अनिर्णयात्मक होता है। इस अनध्यवसायात्मक ज्ञान को अप्रमाण मानने का जैन प्रमाणमीमांसा में जो कारण दृष्टिगोचर होता है वह है उसके द्वारा हान-उपादान का बोध न होना। प्रमाण को जैन दार्शनिक हान-उपादान के बोध में समर्थ मानते हैं।[23] बौद्ध दर्शन में प्रतिपादित निर्विकल्पक प्रत्यक्ष एवं अपने ही दर्शन में प्रतिपादित निर्विकल्पक दर्शन भी जैन दार्शनिक मत में इसीलिए अप्रमाण माने गये हैं।

प्रश्न यह होता है कि जैन दर्शन में ही मतिज्ञान के चार भेदों (अवग्रह, ईहा, अवाय एवं धारणा) के अन्तर्गत मान्य अवग्रह एवं ईहाज्ञान भी प्रमाण हैं या नहीं? क्योंकि प्रमाण का व्यवसायात्मक लक्षण तो पूर्णतः अवाय ज्ञान में ही घटि होता है,[24] अवग्रह एवं ईहाज्ञान को निर्णयात्मक ज्ञान मानने के सम्बन्ध में जैन दर्शन में मान्यता भेद है। आगम-परम्परा के **जिनभद्र क्षमाश्रमण, सिद्धसेनगणि, यशोविजय** आदि दार्शनिक अवायज्ञान को ही निश्चयात्मक मानते हैं, अवग्रह एवं ईहा को नहीं। दूसरी परम्परा प्रमाणमीमांसीय आचार्यों की है जिसके अनुसार अवग्रह एवं ईहाज्ञान में भी निर्णयात्मकता अङ्गीकार की गई है। आचार्य **विद्यानन्द** के अनुसार अवग्रह ज्ञान प्रमाण है, क्योंकि वह संवादक है, साधकतम है, अनिश्चित अर्थ का निश्चायक है और प्रतिपत्ता को उसकी अपेक्षा होती है।[25]

अवग्रह ज्ञान प्रमाण है या नहीं, इसके सम्बन्ध में हम संक्षेप में यह कहना चाहेंगें कि अवग्रह के दो भेद हैं- व्यञ्जनावग्रह एवं अर्थावग्रह। इनमें से व्यञ्जनावग्रह ज्ञान प्रमाण नहीं है, किन्तु अर्थावग्रह ज्ञान प्रमाण है। **अकलङ्क, विद्यानन्द, प्रभाचन्द्र, वादिदेवसूरि** आदि प्रमाणमीमांसीय आचार्यों के मत में तो इसका प्रामाण्य स्वीकृत है ही, किन्तु **जिनभद्र गणि** के द्वारा निरूपित उपचरितअर्थावग्रह[26] एवं **वीरसेनाचार्य** के द्वारा निरूपित विशदावग्रह[27] को प्रमाण स्वीकृत करने में कोई बाधा नहीं है, क्योंकि उसमें प्रमाण का व्यवसायात्मक लक्षण घटित हो जाता है।

गृहीतग्राही ज्ञान को प्रमाण या अप्रमाण मानने के सम्बन्ध में जैन दार्शनिकों में मान्यता भेद है। अकलङ्क, माणिक्यनन्दी, प्रभाचन्द्र आदि दिगम्बर आचार्य अपूर्व अर्थ के व्यवसायात्मक ज्ञान को प्रमाण मानने के कारण गृहीतग्राही ज्ञान को अप्रमाण मानते हैं, जबकि हेमचन्द्र, वादिदेवसूरि आदि श्वेताम्बर दार्शनिक ग्रहीष्यमाण ग्राही ज्ञान की भांति गृहीतग्राही ज्ञान को भी प्रमाण मानते हैं।[28] जैन तत्त्वमीमांसा में प्रमेय वस्तु को द्रव्यपर्यायात्मक एवं नित्यानित्यात्मक स्वीकार किया गया है। इसलिए उसमें पर्याय की अपेक्षा कथञ्चित् अगृहीग्राहिता तथा द्रव्य की अपेक्षा कथञ्चित् गृहीतग्राहिता घटित होती है। दिगम्बर दार्शनिक विद्यानन्द ने इसीलिए प्रमाणलक्षण में अपूर्व विशेषण को व्यर्थ बतलाया है।[29]

प्रामाण्य एवं अप्रामाण्य के सम्बन्ध में भी जैन दार्शनिकों ने विचार

किया है। वादिदेवसूरि ने प्रामाण्य का लक्षण देते हुए कहा है जब कोई ज्ञान या प्रमाण प्रमेय अर्थ से अव्यभिचरित होता है, तो यही उसका प्रामाण्य है। यदि प्रमाण में प्रमेय अर्थ की अपेक्षा कोई व्यभिचार पाया जाता है तो वह उसके अप्रामाण्य का द्योतक होता है।[30] प्रामाण्य एवं अप्रामाण्य की उत्पत्ति वादिदेवसूरि ने 'परतः' स्वीकार की है। किन्तु उनका ज्ञान अभ्यास दशा में स्वतः एवं अनभ्यासदशा में परतः अंगीकार किया है।[31]

संदर्भ सूची

1. (क) उत्तराध्ययन सूत्र, 28.30

(ख) सम्यग्दर्शनज्ञानचारित्राणि मोक्षमार्गः। तत्त्वार्थसूत्र, 1.1

2. (क) यदा तु सम्यग्दर्शनं प्रादुर्भूतं तदा मिथ्यापरिणाम दर्शनाऽभावात् तेषां मत्यादीनां सम्यक्त्वम्।-तत्त्वार्थवार्तिक 1.31 पृ. 92

(ख) मिथ्यादर्शनोपहतेन्द्रियमतेर्मतिश्रुतावधयोऽप्यज्ञानमेव भवन्तीति। -तत्त्वार्थवार्तिक 1.32 पृ. 92

(ग) सम्मदिट्ठिस्स मई मइनाणं मिच्ददिट्ठिस्स मई मइ-अन्णाणं।-नन्दीसूत्र, 46

3. देवेन्द्रसूरि, कर्मग्रन्थ भाग 2

4. (क) नाणं पंचविहं पण्णत्तं तंजहा-आभिणिबोहियनाणं सुयनाणं ओहिनाणं मणपज्जवनाणं केवलनाणं।-नन्दीसूत्र

(ख) मतिश्रुतावधिमन- पर्यायकेवलानि ज्ञानम्।-तत्त्वार्थसूत्र 1.9

5. स्थानांग सूत्र, स्थान 3 उद्देशक 3

6. सम्यग्दृष्टिर्यथा चक्षुरादिभी रूपादीनुपलभते तथा मिथ्यादृष्टिरपि मत्यज्ञानेन। यथा च सम्यगदृष्टिः श्रुतेन रूपादीन् जानाति निरूपयति च तथा मिथ्यादृष्टिरपि श्रुताज्ञानेन। यथा चावधिज्ञानेन सम्यग्दृष्टिः रूपिणोऽर्थानवगच्छति तथा मिथ्यादृष्टिर्विभङ्गज्ञानेनेति।- सर्वार्थसिद्धि 1.31

7. द्रष्टव्य, समयसार गाथा 280 आदि

8. सदसतोरविशेषाद्यदृच्छोपलब्धेरुन्मत्तवत्।-तत्त्वार्थसूत्र ।.32

9. (क) मिथ्यादर्शनेन सहैकार्थसमवायात् सरजस्कटुकालाबुगतदुग्धवत्।-सर्वार्थसिद्धि 1.31 पृ. 98

(ख) तत्त्वार्थवार्तिक 1.31 पृ. 92

10. द्रष्टव्य, सर्वार्थसिद्धि, 1.32

11. (क) सम्यग्ज्ञानं प्रमाणम्। प्रमाणपरीक्षा, पृ. 1

(ख) किं पुनः सम्यग्ज्ञानम्। समभिधीयते-स्वार्थव्यवसायात्मकं सम्यग्ज्ञानम्। सम्यग्ज्ञानत्वात्। यत्तु न स्वार्थव्यवसायात्मकं तन्न सम्यग्ज्ञानम्, यथा संशयविपर्ययानध्यवसायाः।-प्रमाणपरीक्षा, पृ. 5

12. न्यायकुमुदचन्द्र भाग-1, पृ. 48.10 एवं प्रमाणमीमांसावृत्ति 1.1.1

13. यत्पुनः स्वपरप्रकाशात्मकं न भवति न तद् ज्ञानम्।-प्रमेयकमलमार्तण्ड, भाग-1 पृ. 364

14. स्वपरव्यवसायि ज्ञानं प्रमाणम्।-प्रमाणनयतत्त्वालोक, 1.2

15. अविसंवादकं प्रमाणम्।-लघीयस्त्रयवृत्ति, 22 अकलङ्कग्रन्थत्रय, पृ. 8.10

16. सन्निकर्षादेरज्ञानस्य प्रामाण्यमनुपपन्नम् अर्थान्तरवत्।-लघीयस्त्रयवृत्ति 1.3

17. जैनेतर दर्शनों की प्रमाण सम्बन्धी मान्यताओं के खण्डन के लिए द्रष्टव्य-अकलङ्क, विद्यानन्द, प्रभाचन्द्र एवं वादिदेवसूरि के ग्रन्थ।

18. साधकबाधकप्रमाणाभावादनवस्थितानेककोटिसंस्पर्शिज्ञानं संशयः।-प्रमाणनयतत्त्वालोक 1.11

19. द्रष्टव्य, प्रमेयकमलमार्तण्ड भाग-1 (वीर ज्ञानोदय ग्रन्थमाला, दिल्ली पुष्प, 23)

20. द्रष्टव्य, स्याद्वादरत्नाकर, 1.11

21. स्याद्वादरत्नाकर, 1.11 पृ. 138 (भारतीय बुक कार्पोरेशन, दिल्ली)

22. प्रमाणनयतत्त्वालोक, 1.13

23. हिताहितप्राप्तिपरिहारसमर्थं हि प्रमाणं ततो ज्ञानमेव तत्।- परीक्षामुख 1.2

24. ईहितविशेषनिर्णयोऽवायः।-प्रमाणनयतत्त्वालोक 2.9

25. तत्त्वार्थश्लोकवार्तिक 1.15

26. विशेषावश्यकभाष्य, 282-284

27. धवलापुस्तक, 9

28. ग्रहीष्यमाणग्राहिण इव गृहीतग्राहिणोऽपि नाप्रामाण्यम्।-प्रमाणमीमांसा, 1.1.4

29. तत्स्वार्थव्यवसायात्मज्ञानं मानमितीयता। लक्षणेन गतार्थत्वाद् व्यर्थमन्यद् विशेषणम्।। तत्त्वार्थश्लोकवार्तिक, 1.10.78

30. ज्ञानस्य प्रमेयाव्यभिचारित्वं प्रामाण्यम्। तदितरत्वप्रामाण्यम्।-प्रमाणनयतत्त्वालोक 1.18

31. तदुभयमुत्पत्तौ परत एव ज्ञप्तौ तु स्वतः परतश्चेति।-प्रमाणनयतत्त्वालोक, 1.21

Jaina Critique of the Metaphysical Doctrines of the Heretics with Special Reference to the Doctrine of 'Self' as Presented in the Sūtrakṛtāṅga

V.V.S. Saibaba

I

Date, Authorship and importance of the Sūtrakṛtāṅga in the Jaina Canonical Literature

The *Sūtrakṛtāṅga* is the second among the eleven extant Jain Aṅgas which belong to the Aṅga Pravista group of the Śvetāmbara Jain canonical literature. According to the Jain tradition, like the other Aṅgas, the *Sūtrakṛtāṅga* is also supposed to have been preached by Lord Mahāvīra, the twenty fourth Tīrthaṅkarā who lived sometime during 567-487 B.C. and was put down in writing by Gaṇadharas, who are the direct disciples of Mahāvīra. A number of Jaina literary works such as the *Nandisūtra*, the *Samavāyāṅga*, the *Śramaṇasūtra*, the *Rājavartika*, the *JayaDhavalā*, the *Aṅgapannati* refere to the contents of the *Sūtrakṛtāṅga*[1] which is unequivocally regarded as the most ancient Āgamic text.

Despite the varied terminology of its Prākrait names in the Śvetāmbara and Digambara Jain traditions, the word 'Sūtrakṛta' denotes the demonstration of the meaning of the various contents of the text in a simplified form.[2] The etymological meaning of different Sanskrit forms of the name of this sutra as well as the interpretations of Jaina Ācāryas like Sri Bhadrabāhu testify its authorship and compilation. According to the general opinion of the scholars the whole Jain Āgama literature may be dated roughly between 6th to 3c B.C. However, ten or twelve centuries after Mahāvīra's Parinirvāṇa their composition took place i.e. probably during the second half of the 4c. A.D. As regards the date of the composition of the *Sūtrakṛtāṅga*, its antiquity goes as far back as Bhagavān Ṛṣabha the first and foremost Jaina Tīrthaṅkara whose date is still not free from controversy. According to the available historical evidence, during the life time of the first nine Tīrthaṅkaras and the last nine Tīrthaṅkaras, the *Sūtrakṛtāṅga* was extant. The text consists of two Śrutaskandhas which comprise of *Sixteen* and *Seven* adhyayās respectively. Whereas most of the first Śrutaskandha is written in the form of verse, the contents of most of the latter Śrutaskhandha are in prose. But according to the scholarly opinion the two parts of the *Śūtrakṛtāṅga* were not composed at a time. Some foreign scholars opined that the first Śrutaskandha of this sūtra and also that of the first parts of the *Ācāraṅga*, the *Uttarādhyāyana* and the *Dasavaikālika* were composed earlier than the rest of the Āgamas.[3] The Cheda sūtras succeeded the above four Āgamas and the former are followed by the second Śrutaskandhas of the *Ācāraṅga* and the *Sūtrakṛtāṅga*.[4] Basing on the epithets of Mahāvīra[5] we may presume that the second Śrutaskandha of the

Sūtrakṛtāṅga is later and that it is not earlier than even the second part of the *Ācāraṅga sūtra*. From the internal evidence of the text as well as its *Niryukti*, the *Sūtrakṛtāṅga* is supposed to have been written after the composition of the two Aṅgas viz., the *Sthānāṅga* and the *Samavāyāṅga* and its *Niryukti* must have been composed after the *Niryuktīs* on the two *Mūla sūtras* viz., the *Dasavaikālika* and the *Uttarādhyāyana*.[6]

The utmost popularity of the *Sūtrakṛtāṅga* is quite evident from its Prakrit Niryukti by Acarya Bhadrabāhu-II,[7] two Cūrṇis or the commentaries written in Prakrit or mixed Prakrit by Ācārya Jinadasagaṇi and Harshakula[8] three Ṭikās written by Ācārya Śīlāṅka,[9] Bahirgani and Pandit Ghasilalji Maharaj,[10] three Dīpikās by Harshukula, Sādhuraṅga and Jinahaṁsasūri and a Bṛhad Vṛtti in Sanskrit by Śīlāṅka Ācārya[11] besides its seven Hindi translations by Ambicadutta Ojha, Amolka Ṛṣiji, Ācārya Jawarharlalji, Pandit Hemacandraji, Muni Lalitaprabhāsāgar, Muni Nāthmalji Mahāprajñā besides others and one English translation by Hermann Jacobi.[12]

The *Sūtrakṛtāṅga* is extolled as the foremost of the eleven extant Aṅgas owing to its special emphasis on the Jain refutation of philosophical doctrines of their opponents and its significance of its contents. This text is devoted more to philosophy and hence it is called the foremost Aṅga which deals with Jain philosophy. This sūtra deals with three hundred eighty three heretical views. It intends to impart knowledge of Jain doctrines to the noices and also furnishes information about one hundred eighty Kriyāvādins, eighty four Akriyavādins, sixty seven Ajñānavādins, and thirty two Vinayavādins. This aṅga also elucidates the adherent on the path of liberation well illustrating the theme. The importance of this Aṅga lies in the fact that it contains arguments against those who belive in moral and spiritual actions (kriyāvādins), those who do not belive in moral and spiritual actions (Akriyāvādins), credulous persons (Vainayikas) and Agnostics (Ajñānavādins).[13] Besides, it contains the detailed exposition of Jain doctrines by refuting others.[14] The *Sūtrakṛtāṅga* describes all those religions and philosophical doctrines which are prevalent during the time of Mahāvīra.[15]

According to the *Samavāyāṅga* the term Gaṇipitak was used to be applied not only collectively to all Aṅgas but also individually to each of the Aṅgas. Bhagavān Mahāvīra is considered as the author of the impartation of the meaning of these sūtras. According to the *Cūrṇi* on the *Nandisūtra* the Śrutanpuruṣas are said to have shaped the twelve Aṅgas. The Gaṇadhāras who are these śrutapuruṣas who are known as the authors in the sense since they have framed their teachings in the shape of the words or śabda. Even though the intellectual Gaṇadhāras preached Bhagavān Mahāvīra's teachings in the form of twelve Aṅgas, but to the question why this aṅga only is called as *Sūtrakṛtāṅga* and not the rest of the Aṅgas which are also recorded by the Gaṇadhāras, the title of the *Sūtrakṛtāṅga* is justified as this sūtra discusses about the bondage of the soul and also its liberation from such bondage and since this sūtra alone consists the above theme it is named as the *Sūtrakṛtāṅga*.[16]

II

Themes of Metaphysics, Logic and Epistemology dealt in the Sūtrakṛtāṅga

The *Sūtrakṛtāṅga* discusses the themes of the inhabited universe (lokā) empty space (alokā), likālokā, soul (jīva), non soul (Ajīva), one's own doctrines (svasamaya) and the tenets of others (parasamaya). We come across the references of the contents of this sūtra from other Jaina literary sources. According to the *Rājavārttika*, in the *Sūtrakṛtāṅga*, the themes of Jñāna, Vinaya, Kalpīya and akalpīya, Chedopathāna, Vyavahāradharma etc., are dealt with. According to the *Jayadhavalā*, in this text the themes of Jain doctrines, doctrines of opponents, *Strīpariṇāma*, klibatva, the defilements of mind, lack of clarity, lust, delusion, the happiness derived from women etc., are discussed. According to the *Aṅgapannatti*[17] the following subjects viz., knowledge (*jñāna*), conduct (*Vinaya*), unperturbed study, Sarvasatikriya, prajñāpna, sukhatā, kalpīya, vyavahāra, dharma kriya, chedopasthāna, atisamaya, parasamaya and kriyābedha are demonstrated in the *Sūtrakṛtāṅga*.

According to Bhadrabāhu's *Niryukti*[18] among the sixteen chapters in the Pathama śrutaskandha, the following chapters lay emphasis on the Jain philosophy and Jain crituque of different doctrines of heretical views. Of these, the *first* chapter represents the "svasamya-parasamaya", the *second* one represents the virtues of Jaina Siddhānta and the defects of the non-Jaina doctrines. The *seventh* chapter tells that those householders devoid of character, the other Tīrthaṅkarās who are endowed with vices and others as a result of their service to a Nirgrantha become people of good character. The twelfth chapter provides information of the religious and philosophical views of three hundred and sixty three heretics who are divided into four kinds viz., Kriyāvād, Akriyāvād, Ajñānavād and Vinayavād and the Jaina criticism and refutation of their views and doctrines. The *thirteenth* chapter refers to the adherents' doctrines of Kapilagandha, Akshapāda, Buddha, Jaimini and points out their wrong views. The *Second tarūśkandha* consists of seven chapters. Of these, the first chapter deals with different heretical doctrines and Jaina refutation of the above. The second chapter deals with the twelve kinds of sinful deeds and sinless actions, conduct of virtuous monks and Jain refutation of the heretical schools. The sixth chapter deals with a conversation between Ārdraka and his disciple Gośāla and other heretical philosphers. This second śrutaskandha consists of the refutation of the doctrines of other schools especially Tajjīvataccharīravāda, the Creator aspect of Īśvara, Niyativād etc., Different components of Jain metaphysics viz., doctrines of self, karma liberation, hells and universe have been discussed as these are expounded in the text. Different viewpoints of the heretical schools viz., Sāṅkhya, Yoga Vedānta, Vaiśeṣika, Cārvākas, Buddhists etc., on the above metaphysical doctrines and the Jain refutation of those doctrines have been elucidated in the *Sūtrakṛtāṅga*.

In the *Sūtrakṛtāṅga*, we find Jaina refutation of the doctrines of Karma as expounded by the followers of different heretical schools viz., Brāhmanical philosophers, the adjerents of Sāṅkhya and Vedānta, the Buddhists and especially the Śūnyavādins, the Agnostics and Fatalists, the Lokāyatas and the Ājīvikas.[19] From Jain dialectical point of view Karman is conceived from different points of view as belonging to the agent and not belonging to the agent. In accordance with one's aggregates of karmas the transmigration of the souls from one body to another in different realms such as human, animal, celestial and infernal takes place. According to Jain doctrine of Karma not only voluntary but involuntary simple actions performed by five sensed to the one-sensed earth born beings result in the bondage of saṁsāra. Here, all the six classes of living beings[20] irrespective of their degree of intellect whether high, middle, or low are liable to sin. The Jains further assert themselves as Kriyāvādins and point out that suffering is caused by one's own acts but not due to the actions of others, viz., fate or Creator.[21]

In conformity with the doctrines of self and karma, the Jainas conceive the universe neither as non-eternal nor as annihilated.[22] From the Jain dialectical standpoint of view the universe is permanent, eternal and indestructible from the viewpoint (naya) of substance and from the view point of modes (paryāya) it is production, existence and destruction. The Jain doctrine of cyclical conception of the universe which is divided into two phases of evolution and involution (utsarpaṇī and avasarpaṇī) does not give any scope to postulate the existence of Omniscient, Omnipresent and Omnipotent God Creator who is belived by the heretics as responsible for the creation, sustenance and destruction.

The *Sūtrakṛtāṅga* provides information about the refutation of the different doctrines of liberation propounded by a number of heretical schools[23] viz., the Ajñānavādins, the Śaivās, the Ekadaṅdins, the Sāṅkhyas, the Vaiśeṣikas, the Buddhists, the Rasasiddhivādins, the Aṣṭasiddhivādins, the Vāribhadrakas and the Vinayavādins. In contrast to these doctrines, the Jains contend that liberation of Jīva can be attained by the two-fold practice of stoppage of the fresh inflows of the material particles (karmāvaraṇa) and the dissipation of karms (jñeyāvaraṇa) which lead to the goal of complete deliverence of the soul (sarvāvaraṇa vimuktir muktiḥ) from all evil and coverings of karma which will lead to the goal of complete deliverence of the soul from all evil and karmic coverings. From the Jain standpoint nirvāṇa which is the chief object of the law[24] has two stages subjective (bhāva) and objective (dravya). Of these, the subjective liberation is attained when the soul is released from the four obstructive (ghātin) karmas and the latter, the objective liberations is attained when the soul is released from the four unobstructive (aghātin) karmas. All this process ultimately leads a spiritual aspirant to attain the goal of pure and perfect knowledge (Kevala jñāna).[25] Different views on the doctrines of ignorance (Avidyā) and wrong world-views (mithya-jñāna) put forward by a number of heretical schools viz., Sānkhya, the Yoga, the Advaitavādins, the Buddhists have been refuted by Jains.

We come across some stray references to Jain Logic and Epistemology in the *Sūtrakṛtāṅga* more specifically in the *Dvitīya Śrutaskandha*. The Jaina theory of knowledge is primarily the Epistemology of experience which is of great antiquity. The Jain Tīrthaṅkaras Pārśva as well as Mahābīra who is believed to have preached the *Sūtrakṛtāṅga* have agreed upon the theory of knowledge to a great extent. The Jaina Āgamas such as the Upāṅgas like the *Rājaprasnīya*[26] as well as both the Jain sects have unanimously accepted the five-fold division of knowledge. According to jain philosophy the right knowledge (samyak jñāna) is considered as the only valid knowledge (pramāṇa). As regards the Jain conception of knowledge which is pre-canonical, it is five-fold. In the *Rājapraśnīya*, Pārśvanātha, the Twenty third Tīrthaṅkara is said to have referred to the five kinds of knowledge and Lord Mahāvīra to who the *Sūtrakṛtāṅga* is attributed is believed to have accepted the above tradition.

III

Jaina conception of different Heretical doctrine of 'self'

According to the *Sūtrakṛtāṅga commentary*[27] the Pañcabhūtavādins, the Vedāntins, the Tatjīva-taccharīravādins, the Ātmasastivādins, the Kṣanika-pañcaskandhavādins, the Caturdhātukavādins are the heretics according to whom the householders and the ascetics who dwell in forests, the mountain dwellers, the Sanyāsins who take pravadya and who adhere to different heretical doctrines are said to have liberated from all suffering so. Those who wear saffron robes, those who wear matted-hair, those who are shaven-headed, those who live nakedly will be free from all kinds of sufferings according to the above heretical thinkers.

The *commentary*[28] on the *Sūtrakṛtāṅga* while elaborating the Sāṅkhya conception of soul or the Puruṣa explains the Sāṅkhya doctrine of Akartrutva vāda. According to Sāṅkhya system Ātman or Puruṣa is intangible, permanent, all-pervading and it is devoid of any action. As distinct from Prakṛti which consists of twenty-four *tattvas* etc., since it is devoid of the three qualities viz., Sattva, rajas and tamas it does not perform any action and has no responsibility. It is ever conscious without indulging in any action whether meretorious or demeritorious. Nevertheless, due to '*mutraprat-ibimbanaya*' and *japarapatika naya*' Puruṣa enjoys the fruits of actions. Just as an object or one's face reflects in the mirror, similarly Puruṣa reflects in the mirror of Prakṛti. Likewise numerous actions of Prakṛti are reflected on Puruṣa. This is analogically compared to a red flower which due to its proximity to a white gem reflects redness on the stone which is absolutely devoid of any colour by itself. Thus according to Sāṅkhya doctrine although the Puruṣa is devoid of action due to its interaction with

Prakṛti reflects the action into it.[29]

The monistic doctrine of Vedānta is referred in the *Sūtrakṛtāṅga* as well as in its *commentary* wherein it is elaborately elucidated. Just as the same pile of earth appears in various shapes, so too, from the Advaitic standpoint Ātman which is identical with non-dual Brahman which pervades the entire universe with its diverse phenomena appear under various forms just as the universe.[30] Eventhough Brahman is the only real and Ultimate Truth, the world with its diverse objects are perceived by us as different due to one's ignorance (avidyā)[31] like a house, a tree, a body, an animal etc., Just as 'earthliness' pervades in different objects such as the hill, town etc., yet all these appear different from one another. Similarly, Ātman underlies the diverse phenomena of entire universe.[32] Despite the diversity of the upādānas the same Ātman appears differently, just as the same moon reflects in different water jars and appears as if there are a number of moons.[33] According to vedantic conception the invisible, everlasting, great and indestructible sould exceeds all other beings in each respect as a moon excels the stars. But Ācārya Sīlāṅka ascribes this Vedantic notion to the Ekadandins.[34] According to the *Sūtrakṛtāṅga commentary* on this verse, the Ekadaṇḍins who belong to Sāṅkyavādins point out the similarity in the Śāṅkya and Jaina notions of the self by concending that the self is jīvātmā and it is all-pervading permanent and imperishable consciousness and owing its incomprehensibility in both philosophical systems, it is known as indescribable (*avyakta*). Just as the moon is well connected with stars, so also Ātman is related with the body and its five elements. The Sāṅkhya conception of Puruṣa is Universal self. In view of these common attributes shared by both Sāṅkhya and Jains, the followers of Jains should adhere to the Sāṅkhya doctrine by abandoning the Jain doctrine. The Ekadaṇḍins who belong to Sāṅkhyavādins addressing ascetic Ārdraka endeavour to entice the Jains advising that they should adhere to their doctrines but not that of the Tīrthaṅkaras.[35] Besides, the *Sūtrakṛtāṅga* also refers to the Upanisadic conception of self[36] according to which each thing possess a self for its cause and objects and from self everything originates.

Different branches of Ātmasasthavāda have been referred in the text. According to one branch the five elements and soul are the six imperishable and everlasting. Sīlāṅkācārya[37] includes the Sāṅkhya and Śaivādhikariṇ philosophies in this school. The adherents of three schools viz., the Vedic doctrine, Sānkhya and Vaiśeṣika philosophers contend that the five gross elements viz., earth, water, fire air and space and Ātman which are in toto six padārthas are eternal and unproduced. According to them devoid of this presupposition liberation cannot be explained. According to these Satkāryavādins prior to its production the effect is not a 'new creation', but only a 'manifestation' since prior to its production the effect is implicitely contained in the cause. Thus the effect pre-exists in the material cause. The Sāṅkhya conception is known as Prakṛtipariṇāmavāda. In the *Sāṅkhyakārikā*[38] five arguments are produced in support of the doctrine of Satkāryavāda. The Nyāya-vaiśeṣikas are known as 'Ṇityapariṇāvamādins'. The Vaiśeṣikas as well as Buddhists are known as asatkāryavādins who hold that production is a new beginning and that the effect does not pre-exist in the material cause. According to them the effect is a new creation or a beginning since nothing is produced or caused from some other thing. According to the adherents of Ātmasadtvavādin school the validity of the six elements is proved by the authority of perception, inference and scripture (Pratyakṣa, Anumāna, Śabdapramāṇa). Both the Ātmasatavādins as well as Satkāryavādins commonly argue that Ātman is eternal since it is not regarded as doer or performer of any action and consequently, it does not bear any effect nor it suffers from any bondage of action. Consequently, it never accrues any rewards or retributions of actions of happiness as well as suffering. Atman is neither made nor produced by any outside agent whether a person or a thing. Like the Jains,[39] the Ātmasastavādins do not belive in the Sad-asatkāryavāda.

According to the Jain conception of Nāstikas (Cārvakas) presented in the *Sūtrakṛtāṅga*, the latter are those who have unique credence in the five gross elements viz., earth, water, fire, air etc., The Cārvākas are the ultra-materialists who believed in the non-existence of the soul, or God or rebirth.[40] The *Sūtrakṛtāṅga Commentary* elaborating Cārvāka position states that according to the Lokāyata doctrine the Ātman is produced out of the five elements as well as destroyed at the disintegration of these elements. According to these materialists there is no valid means to prove the existence of Ātman since the latter is neither perceived nor can be congised by Pratyakṣa which is the only means of valid knowledge. The other means of knowledge like anumāna (Inference) are not accepted as they are not directly connected with the sense-organs. To take inference as valid means is compared to a running of a blind person on an uneven path merely with the help of a touch of some other's hand. Due to the peculiar combination of the five great elements, the body is produced, just as due to the combination of jaggary, wine etc., the alcoholic power is produced. According to them just as the consciousness of the five great elements are not different from those elements, similarly the clay pot and other clay vessels are not different. So too, is the case of the Ātman and five elements.41 According to them life ends here with the termination of five elements or aggregates and there is no world beyond and there cannot be any effect whatsoever to good, bad, meritorious or demeritorious act performed by us. There is neither hell nor heaven nor any state of liberation.

According to Jain conception of Bauddhas as presented in the text, the Buddhists believe that the five skandhas are transitory; the self is neither produced from these elements nor is identical with them. It is neither everlasting. According to them 'self' is unsubstantial, for it changes at every moment. Between any two moments there is no actor although there occurs action. According to the *Sūtrakṛtāṅga commentary* the Buddhists are asatkāryavādins according to whom 'Rūpa' (mental form), 'Vedanā' (feeling), Vijñāna (consciousness), Sanjña (Perception) and Saṁskāra (coefficients of consciousness) are the five aggregates and all those whichever is existent is momentary. Right knowledge (Samyak dṛṣṭi) is the efficacious knowledge. That which is casually efficient is real (arthakriyā kāritva) and that which is causally inefficient is unreal. Reality is becoming or perpetual change. According to the doctrine of Pratītyasamutpāda (dependent origination) on avidyā (ignorance) whose beginning cannot be traced by many means of sensory knowledge, saṁskāra, vijñāna, nāmarūpa etc. depend. The *Sūtrakṛtāṅga* refers also to one school of Buddhists who maintain that the body is composed of four elements besides which there is no Ātman. Since there is no identical self in any two successive moments Ātman does not bear any fruit.

Those who adhere to the above doctrine are called as Aphalavādins.[42] Ācārya Śīlāṅka called Buddhists as Akriyavādins[43] since the latter do not admit that the action of the soul is transmitted to the future moments and as they did not admit the existence of soul.[44]

According to the doctrine of Niyativādins or Fatalists referred in the *Sūtrakṛtāṅga* misery, happiness and final liberation are not caused by soul or by others, but they are assigned by fate and each individual sould experience them.[45] According to the *Sūtrakṛtāṅga commentary* this school maintains that all these phenomena i.e. pleasures, pain, birth, death etc., are due to one's fate but not due to one's self or caused by one's own action or by others' actions. Neither due to passage of time nor by Īśvara nor by one's action (karma) or due to one's nature (sva-svabhāva) the fruits of pleasure and pain are obtained. The Niyativādins criticsied Kālavāda referred in the *Mahābhārata* (according to which the whole universe survives and is controlled by time) by refuting them that if everything is due to time there would not be difference in actions. Similarly, Īśvara whose existence and status can be clearly ascertained since whether he is tangible or intangible remains as a perennial question and his existence is logically untenable. According to Niyativādins 'Niyatī' is independent unalterable and inexorable principle from which substances are produced in a determined way.[46]

IV

Jain critique of the Heretical doctrines of 'Self'

The Jains levelled their criticism mainly against the doctrines of self of Ātmasastivādins, the Cārvākins, the Buddhists and Svabhāvavādins.

The Jains refuted the doctrine of Ātmasastavādins as

illusory (mithyā)[47] since they do not believe in the sadasatkāryavāda, like the former. The Jains vehemently refuted all the arguments of Cārvākin's conception of 'Self' at great length as follows: If there is no distinct Ātman other than the five elemetns, how can it be said with certainty that "A is dead?" The Cārvākin response to this question is that due to the leaving of the elements, i.e. air, fire etc., from the body a "person known as Devadatta is dead." When a person is dead there is nothing like a soul or a self leaves the body and such a thing is not perceived. The Jains refute the Cārvāka contention by stating that due to the special combination of the five great elements consciousness cannot be produced because from the association of the elements of different attributes an altogether new attribute will not be produced. The Jains contend that just as oil cannot be produced from the sand so too, Ātman does not emerge from the five elements.[48] Furthermore, it is also a fact that the knowledge of one's sense-organs cannot be obtained through another sense-organ since the qualities of the five great elements differ from one another. For instance, 'hardness' is the quality of earth; light is the quality of fire; movement is the quality of air etc.[49] The Jains hold the view that consciousness is not the quality of any of the five elements which are quite different in nature. They interrogate the Cārvākins by saying that when each of these five elements do not possess consciousness, how can then, the five elements as combined or when combined produce consciousness? Had there been any of these elements endowed with consciousness, then each of them would have appeared with the quality of consciousness. Hence the Jains conclude that the consciousness which appears in the body is the attribute of Ātman and not of the five elements. The elements are not based on consciousness.[50] Since the upādānas of the five sense-organs are not endowed with knowledge, consciousness cannot be the attribute of the combination of five elements. Since the Cārvākas do not regard a seperate Ātman apart from the five sense-organs, there is no subject which perceives the object. Further, according to Jains, since the knowledge of each sense-organ cannot be derived from another sense-organ, the collective knowledge and co-ordination cannot take place unless a conscious subject is admitted. The collective knowledge of the sense-organs cannot be obtained by any source except by means of a conscious subject. On the other hand, if we accept the Cārvākin proposition viz., that knowledge of each sense-organ can be obtained by another sense-organ, the knowledge obtained by 'A', i.e. (Devadatta) should be known to 'B', i.e. (Yagñadatta) which is not the fact from the point of view of our common experience. If the Cārvākins consider that sense-organs themselves are knowers, then the Jains raise the question whether knowledge is produced by the combination of all sense-organs or each of the sense-organs? If the former is the case, at the destruction of one's sense-organs the knower also should be considered as destroyed. In the case of the latter, for instance, when the external sense-organ, viz., eye is destroyed, the earlier experienced cognition should be memorised. But it cannot take place owing to the absence of the eye which is the knower. If it can be considered according to Cārvākins that the experience of 'A' can be derived from 'B' then the knowledge of omniscient person should be available to all of us. This again, is not a fact, from the experiential point of view.[51] The Jains interrogate the Lokāyatas by saying that on what strength the combination of the great elements produce consciousness? If the consciousness is considered as something different from the five elements, the combination should be regarded as a seperate element which is not accepted by Cārvākins. It is not possible through perception to grasp the combination of five elements. Since the Cārvākins do not accept the inference (anumāna) as well as verbal testimony (Scriptural evidence) as the valid means of knowledge, there is no other means to have such knowledge.[52] Similarly, from the Jain point of view, the heaven, hell, liberation, the *adṛṣṭa* cannot be denied by the Cārvāka, since for such denial there is no means of knowledge. Likewise according to Jains it is also to be argued that a Cārvāka who has no knowledge of heaven, hell etc., cannot also equally have a claim to have the knowledge of their non-existence.[53] For instance, one who has no knowledge of a 'Pot' cannot have any conception of a 'Pot', i.e. its presence or absence and so on. According to the *Sūtrakṛtānga and its commentary*[54] the Jains called the Cārvākins as Akriyāvādins who possess perverted mind and do not realise the action of the soul though it does exist, just like the blind persons though they have light cannot perceive colours due to their lack of eyesight. Having not comprehended the truth, they will undergo the cycle of births. The Jains equate the Cārvākins with Śūnyavādins (perhaps Mādhyamika Buddhists) who deny all phenomena which exist in the universe such as the Sunrise and Sunset, flowing water and moving air etc., has no existence, just as a blind person fails to see the objects despite the presence or aid of light. Similar is the case with Lokāyatas who due to their deluded knowledge deny the action which is in front of them.[55]

According to Jain standpoint, if as Buddhists hold that the physical body emerges due to the combination of skandhas (aggregates) then whoever follow such a doctrine irrespective of their dwelling in a house, wood or a hill should be free from misery.[56] The Jains who do not admit the Kṣaṇikavāda of Buddhists due to their doctrinal framework consider the latter as ignorant and foolish. For Jains devoid of the existence of Ātman, human experiences of pleasure and pain cannot be explained. The Jains viewed that the Buddhist doctrine of Pratītya Samutpāda which regards the production as the cause of destruction is a misnomer.

The Jains refuted the doctrine of Svabhāvavāda. According to Jain critique, if one's self-nature (svabhāva) is to be regarded as the cause of pleasure and pain, fortune or misfortune etc., one's effort (i.e. self-effort) would be futile. It seems that this is also not true. The jains raise the question whether the self-nature is different from Puruṣa or not differeent? If the former is true, it cannot be the cause of pleasure and pain. On the otherhand, if the latter is true, even then, it cannot be the cause of pleasure and pain because it is not different from Puruṣa. Thus the Jains endeavored to establish neither Puruṣa, nor time, nor Īśvara nor one's innate nature nor svabhāva (self-nature) canbe regarded as causes of one's pleasure and pain.

V

Jain doctrines of 'Self' as presented in the Sūtrakṛtānga

According to Jain conception the existence of Ātman may be proved through the knowledge of presupposition, implication (arthāpatti). Arthāpatti is the assumption of unperceived fact in order to reconcile two apparently perceived facts. When Jains establish the existence of Self/Ātman on the basis of logic, the question arises as regards Ātman whether it is permanent or impermanent. From the standpoint of Jaina Anekāntavāda, it is contended that just as the 'Pot' is eternal from the viewpoint of substance (dravya) and from the viewpoint of monodic form (paryāya) such as its newness, oldness etc., it is non-eternal. Similarly, the Ātman from the viewpoint of its (āvaraṇa) such as childhood, youth, oldage, it is non-eternal. In a nutshell it is neither solely eternal nor non-eternal.[57] According to Jains a thing is pariṇāma-nitya. Ātman is the basis of all knowledge. Since the self undergoes transmigration, it is impermanent; but its original nature is undestroyed as it is pure consciousness.

According to Jaina philosophical conception jīvas are souls, which are substantial, perpetual, infinite, uncreated imperceptible and indestructible. Jīvas are imperceptible due to their formlessness. Eventhough they are devoid of form, owing to the fruits of their varied karma, they are reborn among the six kinds of living beings that are formed out of earth, water, fire, air, seed and egg. Lokākāśa (occupied space) possess an absolute number of immaterial soul (jīva). Each possess an uncountable (asaṁkhyāta) number of space-points (pradeśa) and exists within the physical limits of its current corporal shape. Jīvas are of two types viz., Liberated, which are pure and perfect and possess four infinities, viz., infinite faith (ananta darśana), infinite knowledge (ananta jñāna), infinite bliss (ananta sukha) and infinite power (ananta vīrya).[58] The other type, i.e. the worldly souls are characterised having subdivided themselves into two types (a) mobile (trasa) which are again classified into four groups - Five-sensed to two-sensed depending upon the number of their senses, (b) the immobile soul (sthāvara) inherit only one or single sense, i.e. the sense of touch. These are further subdivided into five groups, viz., earth, water, fire, air and plant-bodied. The jīva gets confined and involved in the cycle of karma which is a mark of impurity (aśuddha) and when jīva attains liberation by the two āvaraṇās (kleśāvaraṇa and jñeyāvaraṇa), it becomes pure (śuddha). Pure consciousness (upayoga) is the innate attribute of a jīva and since it cannot be perceived by one's sense-organs, its existence may be proved only by means of presupposition (arthāpatti).[59] According to Jain metaphysical conception, a jīva is not only the enjoyer of fruits of karma (bhoktā), but also is the actor (Kartā) deeply involved in the mundane affairs and is responsible for one's deeds. In its innate nature it is self-existent Ultimate Reality without neither beginning nor end. Eventhough, it is metaphysically formless, it has to take shape or undergo rebirth by virtue of its own karma in different realms of saṁsāra viz., Heaven, Hell, Purgatory etc., until it finally realises itself absolutely from the fetters of bondage. That is why the *Sūtrakrtāṅga* reiterates that a pious monk who meditates on the teachings of Tīrthankaras,[60] whoever subdue their senses,[61] who are endowed with all virtues and abstain from all sins attain liberation which is characterised as the final beautitude.[62]

Footnotes

1. Bechards Doshi, *Jain Sāhitya ka Bṛhad Itihāsa, Part-I*, P.V. Reserch Institute, Varanasi, 1989, p. 172 (Here after abbreviated as JSBI-Part I).
2. *Ibid.* p.174.
3. Dr. Muni Nagaraj, *Jain Āgam Digdarshan*, Rajasthan Prakrit Sansthan, Jaipur, 1980, See. Dalsukhbhai Malvania's Preface p.v. (Hereafter abbreiated as JAD).
4. *Ibid.* p. vi.
5. Pandit Sri Hemachandra Ji (Tr. Comm.) *Sri Sūtrakṛtāṅga Sūtra* (Prathama Sruta-skandha), p. 9. fn. 1 (Hereafter abbreviated as Sukr, Prs.).
6. Dr. Mohanlal Mehta, *Jain Sāhitya kā Bṛhad Itihāsa, P.V. Research Institute,* 1989, p. 58. (Hereafter abbreviated as JSBI, Part-III).
7. *Ibid.* p. 6.
8. *Ibid.* pp. 267-268; JAD, p. 56.
9. *JSBI* Part-III, p. 357.
10. *Sukr.*, (Prs), p. 23.
11. *Ibid.* p. 27.
12. *JAD.* p. 56.
13. S. Gopalan, *Outlines of Jainism;* Wiley Eastern Pvt. Ltd., 1973. p. 31.
14. *Sukr.*, (Prs) p. 11.
15. *Ibid.* p. 20
16. *Ibid.* p. 6.
17. JSBI - Part I, p. 173
18. JSBI - Part III, p. 6.
19. J. Jacobi (Tr.) *Jaina Sutras, Part II*, Motilal Banarsidass, Delhi, 1973 Reprint pp. 237, 241-42, 245, 316-17, 343, 346, 415, 417 (Hereafter abbreviated as JS, Part II).
20. *Ibid.* p. 317.
21. *Ibid.* 311.
22. *Ibid.* p. 245

23. *Ibid.* pp. 268, 245-46, 294, 316, 331, 417.

24. *Ibid.* p. 299.

25. *Ibid.* p. 380.

26. See. *Rāya-Pāseniya-sutta.* 165

27. Sukr (Prs) pp. 125-27.

28. *Ibid.* p. 96; Munishri Punya Vijayaji (Ed.), *Sūyagadāṅga Sutta*, Part 1 (with Bhadrabahu's Niryukti and Curni) Prakrit Text Society, Ahmedabad, 1975, pp. 10-11 (Herafter abbreviated as SSBn & C, Part I).

29. Sukr (Prs) pp. 98-99.

30. Js, Part II, p. 237.

31. Sukr (Prs), p. 84; SSBn&C Part I, p. 9.

32. Sukr (Prs) p. 85.

33. *Ibid.* p. 86.

34. JS, Part II, pp. 417-18.

35. Paditratnasri Hemacandraji (Tr. & Commy), *Sri Sūtrakṛtāṅga Sūtra* (Dvitiya srutaskandha) ed. by Amar Muniji & Munisri Nemicandraji, Atma Jnana Peeth, Manasa, 1976, p. 380 (Hereafter abbreviated as Sukr, Dvs).

36. JS, Part II, p. 344.

37. *Ibid.* p. 238.

38. "asadkāraṇāt, upādānagrahaṇāt, sarvasaṁbhavābhāvāt, śaktasya śakyakaraṇāt kāraṇābhāvāccda satkāryaṁ - *Śāṅkhya-Kārikā, 9.*

39. Sukr (Prs), pp. 113-14; SSBn&C, Part I, pp. 11-12.

40. JS, Part II, p. 236.

41. Sukr (Prs), pp. 62-67; SSBn&C, Part I, p.7.

42. Sukr, (Prs), p. 119.

43. JS, Part II, p. 316.

44. *Ibid.* p. 315.

45. *Ibid.* pp. 239-240

46. Sukr (Prs) pp. 142-48; SsBn&C, Part I, pp. 21-22.

47. Sukr (Prs) p. 114.

48. *Ibid.* pp. 62-67
49. *Ibid.* p. 68
50. *Ibid.*
51. *Ibid.* pp. 68-69.
52. *Ibid.* p. 70.
53. *Ibid.* p. 76.
54. JS, Part II, pp. 316-17; Sukr (Prs), pp. 867-68; SsBn&C, Part I, pp. 210-11.
55. *Ibid.*
56. JS Part II, p. 238.
57. Sukr (Prs), p. 78.
58. *Ibid.* pp. 119-124.
59. *Ibid.* pp. 77-78.
60. JS, Part II, pp. 300-301.
61. *Ibid.* pp. 306, 314.
62. *Ibid.* p. 355.

MALLAVĀDĪ KṢAMĀŚRAMAṆA ON THE SELF-EFFULGENCE OF OBJECTS

Aruna Ranjan Mishra

In the Seventh Chapter (named as *Vidhi-niyama-ubhayāra*) of his celebrated book on Jaina logic and epistemology entitled *Dvādaśa-ara-naya-cakram (D.A.N.C)* the Jaina philosopher Mallavādī Kṣamā-śramaṇa (M.K.) (450 A.D.)[1] takes a very unusual stand that an object (*vastu*) which is inherent in its cause (*vṛttam*) gets connected (*sambadhyate*) with the state of cognition of the substance etc. (*dravyādi-pratyayatvādinā*) of its own accord (*svata eva*).[2] Thus the self-illumination of an object is not dependant on any qualifier (*viśeṣaṇa*) or on any known (*siddha*) object.[3] And it doesn't need a second illuminator like (*dravyatva* or *gotva*) class (*jāti*) etc. for getting cognised.[4] That means the cognition of '*gau*' (cow) is just the cognition of '*gau*' and is not like '*gotva-viśiṣṭaḥ gauḥ*'.

And the object is the illuminator not only of its own, but also of its class.[5] Through the illumination existent in the object, the class (of that object) also gets illuminated.[6]

So the class (*jāti*) is illuminated by its particular (*vyakti*). When the object is self-effulgent, the class and particularity existent in it become cognised after the cognition of the object.[7]

It is not that the relations like *sattā* and *dravyatva* etc. shall not have the scope for existence because of the self-effulgence of the object. As they are also cognised through the cognition of the self-illuminatory object, there shall be no hindrance to these relations which are accepted mainly to facilitate the understanding of varied groups under the umbrella of *sattā dravyatva* or any other class.[8] Ācārya Vijaya Labdhi Suri (A.V.L.S.) explains it saying that for the enjoyment of the living beings the world has been full with varied creations. Each cause has its effect. It being impossible to have the idea of groups encircling some of these objects without the concept of class etc., the *sattā* and *dravyatva* etc. are conceived. And the self-effulgence of objects doesn't attack upon the indispensability of *sattā* and *dravyatva* etc. The only difference is that the self-illumination of objects subsequently illuminates the class. So the cognition of an object gives rise to the cognition of class and not vice-versa.[9]

How does an object illuminate itself and its class? Answering the querry, M.K. places forth the following reasons- (1) An object is self-illuminatory like a candle. (2) It doesn't depend upon any other agency for illuminating itself. (3) It, being an effect, rises from various (*pravibhakta*) causes (*viṣayaḥ*) which are different from each other.[10]

The third reason explains all the intensions of M.K. The *dravya* etc. have their varied causes which are different from each other. And because of these causes, as object is self-illuminatory Siṁhasuragaṇi Vādī

Kṣamāśramaṇa (S.V.K.) shows the variety of such causes as- (1) the collection of causal factors (*Kāraṇa-sāmagrī*), (2) the conjunction of the parts of equal types (*tulya-jātīyạ-avayava-saṁyogādiḥ*), (3) the precedence of the *guṇas* of the cause (*kāraṇa-guṇa-pūrva-kramaḥ*), and (4) the *guṇas* (like *saṁyoga*) that generate the action in the loci of the effect (*sva-āśraya-āśrayāntara-kriyā-ārambhi-guṇādi-kṛtaḥ*).[11] Because of the varied and different causes, the effects vary from one another.[12] Actually this makes them *svaprakāśaka*. So they don't need the help of class to be cognised.

Moreover, since each object has different set of causal factors, they are cognised to be different and although they are different from one another, their grouping under a class makes them behave non-differently. So there is no necessity of *viśeṣya-viśeṣaṇa-sambandha* (like that in the knowledge of *ghaṭatva-viśiṣṭaḥ ghaṭaḥ*) for the knowledge of an object.[13]

A.V.L.S. explains it, saying - since there is the usage of the cognition of the objects differently and the usage of behaving them non-differently too, there are two types of activities (*puruṣārthas*).[14] These two types of activities being there, there is no necessity of imagining the *viśeṣaṇas* like *sattā* and *dravyatva* etc. for and before the cognition of objects—such an imagination for the knowledge of an object being purposeless.[15]

Thus, because of the collection of causal factors and hence, because of the self-effulgence of objects, the classes like *ghaṭatva, gotva, manuṣyatva* etc. are subsequently cognised automatically.[16] In other words, as the object is the illuminator, its qualifiers like *sattā* etc. are automatically illuminated by it.[17]

At this juncture, the *Vaiśeṣikas* seem to have a complaint against the self-effulgence of object. To them, when an object, by the virtue of its self-effulgence, gets its class cognised (or illuminated), that class is related to that object only and not to any other object. Thus there arises the one to one relationship between the particular and the class (*tat tat jāti-sambandha*).[18] So there shall be innumerable classes (*gotva*) for innumerable objects of the same kind (*gau*).

As a matter of fact, such a situation cannot arise since class is not produced but just illuminated for cognition by the self-effulgence of object and since class is accepted to be permanent (ie. non-productible), one and inherent is many.[19] However, in order to bring home that the self-effulgence of object is nothing but as *atiśaya* produced in it by its causal factors of a particular set, M.K. reminds how the *Vaiśeṣika* has already accepted *atiśaya* (speciality) in objects. He says[20], you Vaiśeṣika have said two things–

(1) Do you ascertain the *svarūpa* of effect (*Kāryadravya*) as that which is produced from the collection of causal factors and is inherent in the (inherent) cause? But that cannot be. Because if that is accepted then there shall be one to one relationship between the object (effect) and its qualifier (*pratiniyata-viśeṣaṇa-sambandhaḥ*). Because there is no speciality or *atiśaya* conceived in the effect. So in order to avoid such a situation, it should be accepted that the effect like *dravya* etc., inherent in cause and without depending on anything is the illuminatior of and connected with the qualifier like *dravyatva*.[21]

(2) Even without the *viśeṣaṇa-sambandha* the mutual-

excellence (*parasparātiśaya*) exists among the objects. And by that mutual excellence, the purpose of avoiding the *viśeṣaṇa-sambandha* is fulfilled.

It might be improper to give self-effulgence to objects (you *Vaiśeṣika* have thought). So it is better to conceive a speciality (in effect/object) which is produced from the collection of causal factors. The difference of causal factors for different objects creates mutual excellence in them (the objects).[22] But such a mutual excellence may also be impossible (you *Vaiśeṣika* think) and hence it is safer to conceive an *atiśaya* as noticed in *Pradhāna* of the *Sāṁkhya* system. In the *Sāṁkhya* system, the *pradhāna-tattva* formed through an equilibrium among *sattva, rajas* and *tamas* the seed of all modifications like mahat etc., non-different in any form, is still different, in speciality, from all *guṇas* and other things only because of the speciality caused by the imbalances of three *guṇas*.

M.K. shows that the same is the case with as effect or object which has the *atiśaya* produced from the variety of causal factors. And such a production of *atiśaya* is without a *viśeṣaṇa-sambandha.*[23]

Now, after arguing in favour of the *sva-prakāśakatva* of object caused by an *atiśaya* which is prepared by a unique set of causal factors and after reasoning in favour of objects non-dependence on any *viśeṣaṇa-sambandha*, M.K. proposes some inferences for the same purpose.

Inference-I

na dravyādi anyādheya-svaprakāśam[24] *sattvāt*

yat sat, na tat anyādheya-svaprakāśam sāmānyādivat.[25]

Inference-II

na dravyādi anyādheya-svaprakāśaṁ sātmakatvāt[26]

yat sātmakaṁ, na tat anyādheya-svaprakāśam

Thus M.K. takes a very unusual and controversial stand which is widely different from that of other systems on the necessity of the knowledge of the qualifier and that of class for the knowledge of an object. A wider space is necessary for a study of the class and self-effulgence of objects according to M.K. vis-a-vis other systems. M.K. is very clear that he doesn't mean as indeterminate cognition (*nirvikalpaka pratyakṣa*) of an object when he says that the object is cognised without a qualifier as it is *svaprakāśaka* by nature. Because in an indeterminate cognition, the perceived object is not different from any object and the perception is that of *sattā* (something). But to M.K., although the self-effulgence of an object doesn't make it dependent on the knowledge of proper name (*nāma*), class (*jāti*), quality (*guṇa*) and action (*kriyā*) - the ingredients for the determinate knowledge[27], it makes it an object of cognition as different from the cognition of other objects. Probably he thinks that when a boy sees a cow for the first time, his perception of cow is not non-different from that of pot or cloth etc. Nor can we say that even after seeing the cow he doesn't have the knowledge of cow on the ground that he doesn't know cow-ness. Even without knowing the cowness he may have positive (*pravṛtti*) or negative (*ninvṛtti*) behaviour with it. M.K. perhaps means to say that the self-effulgence of the objects (produced by *atiśaya*) explains such human behaviour.

Such a stand, again M.K. would mean, doesn't violate the maxim that justifies determinate cognition. 'One cannot cognise the qualified without first knowing the qualifier' (*na agṛhīta-viśeṣaṇā buddhir viśeṣyam upasaṁkrāmati*). Because when the maxim means that only the qualified objects depend upon the qualifiers in order to be cognised, M.K. holds that the objects need not be qualified at all to be cognised. So to him the *viśeṣaṇas* are just ornamental to the objects and are not indispensable or fundamental. Therefore, in the cognition of *daṇḍī puruṣa*, he doesn't decline to the knowledge of *daṇḍa* before knowing *daṇḍī puruṣa*. What he asserts is that even *puruṣa* can be known without the knowledge of *daṇda* and *puruṣatva*.

Moreover, although all the systems accept that the shape indicates class, they assert the knowledge of both of them at the same time when as object is perceived. M.K. on the other hand, would accept a sequence between the two and would hold that the knowledge of the object comes first and then that of class from the shape of many objects of the same kind. This *svaprakāśakatva* theory deduces *jāti* not only as *ākṛtivyangyā* but as '*aneka-samākāra-vyakti-vyaṅgyā*' and thus gives *jāti* a position subordinate to that of *vyakti*.

The article is dedicated to my beloved teacher Prof. V.N. Jha, Director C.A.S.S., University of Poona. I thank Sri Rameshwar Bhattacharya, lecturer in Sanskrit Agartala, Tripura and Sri Niranjas Purohit, lecturer in Sanskrit, Purulia, West Bengal for their kind and fruitful discussions with me on the topic.

Notes and References

1. In his extensive foreword to the Part-4 of *D.A.N.C.* (Pub.1960), Shri Vikrama Vijayaji fixes the date of M.K. as 450 A.D. (vide pp. 34-39).
2. *tata etad āpannaṁ, svata eva vṛttam vastu dravyādi-pratyayatvādinā sambadhyate - D.A.N.C.* of M.K., Part-3, critically Edited by Acharya Vijaya Labdhi Suri, Pub. by Chandulāl Jamnādas Shāh, Shri Labdhi Suriswar Jain Granthamālā, Chhāṇi (Baroda), 1957, p. 652.
3. *viśeṣaṇa-vyatiriktam anapekṣa-siddhaṁ prakāśate svata eva, prakāśāntareṇa nārtha iti uktaṁ bhavati - Nyāyāgamānusāriṇī (N.A.A.)* Commentary (on *D.A.N.C.*) by siṁha-suragaṇi Vādī Kṣamāśramaṇa, ibid.
4. *dravyatvādi-viśeṣaṇa-rahitam itara-anākāṅkṣaṁ svata eva pratibhāṣate, bhāsakāntareṇa dravyatvādinā na tasya kiñcit prayojanam iti bhāvaḥ - Viṣama- pada-vivecanam (V.P.V.)* by Ācārya Vijaya Labdhi Suri, ibid.
5. *tasmād eva tu nyāyāt svasāmānyasya api prakāśakaṁ tad eva - D.A.N.C., op.cit.*
6. *vastumātre vṛttena prakāśena jātiḥ svata eva prakāśata iti uditena nyāyena ityarthaḥ -V.P.V., op.cit.*
7. *vastumātram āvirbhūtan, tad āśrayatvād sāmānya-viśeṣādeḥ - N.A.A., op.cit.*
8. *yad api uktam vicitra-upabhoga-kriyā-prasiddhyarthaṁ sattā-dravyatvādi-sambandhaḥ kalpyata iti so'pi anenaiva pratipāditaḥ - N.A.A., op.cit.*
9. *prāṇinām upabhogāya vicitra-viśva-racanā-prapañca iti abhisandhāya prati niyata-kāraṇa-janya-pratiniyata-kārya-vyakter anuvṛttākāra-pratyaya-abhidhāna-nimittatva-asaṁbhavena sattā-dravyatvādayas tad hetutvena kalpyanta iti trayā yad uktam, tad api anenaiva - V.P.V., op.cit.*, pp. 652-53.
10. *pradīpavad bhūtād, vastunaḥ prakāśāntara-nirapekṣāt, tasmād eva pravibhakta-viṣaya-anvayāt-D.A.N.C. op.cit.*, p.652.
11. *pravibhakto viṣayaḥ dravyādeḥ, kāraṇa-sāmagrī-viśeṣaḥ, tulya-jātīya-avayava- saṁyogādiḥ, kāraṇa-guṇa-pūrvakramaḥ, svāśraya-āśrayāntara-kriyārambhi-guṇādikṛtaḥ - N.A.A., op.cit.*, p. 653.

12. *pravibhakta-kāraṇa-kāryatvāt kārya-vastunaḥ parasparaṁ vyatireka-rūpatā* - *V.P.V. op.cit.*, p. 653.

13. *vicitra-upabhoga-kriyā-prasiddher, bhinneṣu abhinna-vyavahāra-prasiddheś ca na viśeṣaṇa-sambandhaḥ kalpyaḥ* - *D.A.N.C., op.cit.*, p. 652.

14. *vyāvṛtta-rūpatvād vicitra-upabhoga-kriyāḥ, sāmānya-rūpatvāt abhinna-vyavahāra-prasiddhir iti puruṣārtha-dvayaṁ vyañjayati* - *V.P.V., op.cit.*, p. 653.

15. *tādṛk pravibhakta-viṣaya-anvayāt, tasmād eva vastuno vicitra-upabhoga-kriyā-prasiddheḥ bhinneṣu abhinna-vyavahāra-prasiddheś ca iti dvi-prakāram puruṣārthaṁ darśayati anayoś ca puruṣārthayor uktavad eva siddher na viśeṣaṇa-sambandhaḥ kalpyaḥ-sattā-dravyatvādi-viśeṣaṇa-sambandho na yuktaḥ kalpayitum, ānarthakyād iti* - *N.A.A. op.cit.*, p. 653.

16. *sarvatra tu ghaṭatvādau api tattvaṁ svata eva iti tvadvacanād eva pratiprāptam* - *D.A.N.C., op.cit.*, p. 652.

17. (a) *tad eva ca viśeṣaṇasyāpi prakāśakam iti sthitam* - *D.A.N.C., op.cit.*, p. 652.

(b) *svato'nuvṛtta-vyāvṛttātmakaṁ kārya-vastu eva prakāśakatvāt sva-viśeṣaṇānām api sattādīnāṁ prakāśakam* - *V.P.V., op.cit*, p. 653.

(c) *idaṁ tu prasphuṭataraṁ viśeṣaṇa-sambandha-prakāśaṁ vastu, tena ca vastunā na apekṣitaḥ sāmānyena saha sambandhaḥ, sāmānyam eva vastunā saha sambandham apekṣata iti* - *D.A.N.C., op.cit.*, p. 653.

It is to be noted that the phrase '*viśeṣaṇa-sambandha-prakāśaṅ vastu*' here is explained in *V.P.V.* as '*vastu eva prakāśakaṁ viśeṣaṇasya dravyatvādeḥ*'

(d) *idaṁ ca atyantaṁ spaṣṭam eva yat sattā-dravyatva-ādi-sambandhaḥ vyaktyā prakāśate, vyaktis tu svataḥ prakāśa-rūpa pradīpakalpā na prakāśāntaraṇ apekṣate, jātir eva tu svaprakāśe vyakti-sambandham apekṣata iti* - *V.P.V., op.cit.*, p. 653.

18. *vastu eva prakāśaṁ viśeṣaṇasya dravyatvādeḥ, vastu ca svaprakāśe sāmānya-sambandhaṁ na apekṣate, sāmānyam eva svaprakāśe vastu-apekṣate evam ca vastu yat sāmānyaṁ prakāśayati, tad eva sāmānyaṁ tatra eva sambadhyate, na anyatra, na anyad vā. tat tat jāti-sambandhaṁ niyama-yituṁ*

vaiśeṣika-ukta-vacanaṁ pradarśayati – *V.P.V., op.cit.*, p. 653-54.

19. *nityam anekānugatam sāmānyam, dravya-guṇa-karma-vṛtti. Tarka Saṅgraha (T.S.)* of Annaṁbhaṭṭa Ed. Athalye & Bodas, 1930. p. 60.

20. *tat (viśeṣaṇa-) sambandha-niyamāya (1) tad vyaktataraṁ vastu eva arthāntara-nirapekṣaṁ viśeṣaṇānām api prakāśakam iti, (2) athavā viśeṣaṇa-sambandham antareṇa api vastu mātrāṇāṁ paraspara-atiśayo'sti, tena viśeṣaṇa-sambandha-niyama-siddhir iti vadatā tvayā (Vaiśeṣikena) api abhypagatam* - *D.A.N.C., op,cit.*, p. 653.

21. *kāraṇa-sāmagrī-prabhavaṁ kāraṇa-samaveta-mātraṁ kāryadravyam iti svarūpam avadhāryate cet na, tarhi tatra pratiniyata viśeṣaṇa-sambandhaḥ kartuṁ śakyaḥ, tat-sambandha-niyāmakasya kasyacid api atiśayasya kārya-dravya-mātre abhāvā diti āśaṅkārthaḥ. tat parihāraṁ vaiśeṣiko brūte-tad vyaktataram iti-kāraṇa-samavetaṁ dravyādi-kāryam apara-anapekṣam svata eva pratiniyataṁ sat dravyatvādinā viśeṣeṇa sambadhyate iti bhāvaḥ* - *V.P.V. op.cit.*, p. 654.

22. *nanu dravyādeḥ svataḥ prakāśakatvam ayuktam iti vicintya kāraṇa-sāmagrī-viśeṣa-janyaṁ kārye vailakṣaṇyam abhyupagamya yad uktam tad darśayati (-tathā yad uktam iti). idam ca vacanam, kāryadravyādau kāraṇa-sāmagrī-viśeṣa-prasūtava-lakṣaṇātiśaya-prakāśakasya pūrvoktasya tat tulya-jātīya-avayava-saṁyoga-ārabdha-avayavi-dravya-kāryam ityādi-vacana-pratipādita-nyāyasya smārakam (iti āha yathokteti)* - *V.P.V., op.cit.*, p. 654.

23. (a) *codya-parihāro'pi kathaṁ paraspara-atiśaya iti cet katham prāk..... atiśayaḥ syāt. na, dṛṣṭāntāt, yathā para-(sāṁkhya)-pakṣe sattva-rajas-tamasām paraspara-atiśayas tathā iha-api rajas-tamasām paraspara-atiśayas tathā iha-api syāt;*

na, dṛṣṭāntāt yathā parapakṣe sattva-rajas-tamasām paraspara-atiśayas tathā ihāpi syāt, sāmānyādivad vā- *D.A.N.C.*, p. 653.

(b) *evaṁ paraspara-atiśaya-asambhavam āśaṅkya vaiśeṣikeṇa pradhānavat sāmānyādivat vā yo atiśayo vyavasthāpitas tām vyavasthām upadarśayati (-etasmin ca artha iti-) sāṁkhya-abhimatam avikṛtaṁ sattva-rajas-tamaḥ-sāmya-avasthā-svarūpa-pradhānatvam nikhila mahad ādi vikāra-bīja-bhūtam abhinnam api guṇa-vaiṣamya-lakṣaṇa-atiśaya-vimarda-vaśena kramavat mahadādi-vilakṣaṇa-nānā-vikāra-kāritvād vilakṣaṇaṁ tathā kāraṇa-sāmagrī-viśeṣa-prasūtatvam eva-atiśayaḥ kāryasya viśeṣaṇa-sambandha-vyatirekeṇa api sambhavati iti bhāvaḥ - V.P.V., op.cit,* p. 654

24. *yasya dravyādeḥ prakāśo anyena yena kenacid ādhātuṁ yogyo na bhavati iti sādhyārthaḥ etena kāraṇa-sāmagrī-viśeṣa -ārabdhaṁ kārya-dravyādi svayameva prakāśata iti uktam bhavati - V.P.V., op.cit.,* p. 655

25. Explaning the *dṛṣṭānta-'sāmānyādivat'*- S.V.K. says- "*yathā sāmānya-viśeṣa-samavāyāḥ santo na anyādheya-svaprakāśa-nādheya-sattvādayas tathā dravyādini - N.A.A., op.cit.,* p. 655

26. *sātmakatvāt-śaśa-viṣāṇādivat nirātmaka-tva abhāvād ityarthaḥ sattādi-sambandhāt tasya sad-rūpatve anyena tasya sadrūpatā-āpattyā svato nirātmakatvaṁ syāt. tat ca na iṣṭam, ataḥ sātmakatvāt na tad-anādheya-svaprakāśādi iti bhāvaḥ.*

27. (a) *nirvikalpakasya lakṣaṇam āha-niṣprakārakam iti. viśeṣaṇa-viśeṣya-sambandha-anavagāhi jñānam ityarthaḥ*

    (b) *savikalpakaṁ lakṣayati-saprakāraṁ nāma jātyādi-viśeṣaṇa-viśeṣya-sambandha-avagāhi jñānam ityarthaḥ-Tarka Dīpikā, T.S., op.cit.,* p. 30.

Prabhacandra's Critique of Jayanta's General Definition of Pramana

V.N. Jha

We acquire the knowledge of the world of our experience and when the knowledge reflects its content with clear form and name we behave with it being guided by our desires and inclinations. We acquire such knowledge through a particular process of knowing. In Indian Philosophical traditions various philosophical tradtions have suggested various processes of knowing. In the tradition of Nyāya school, four such processes of knowing have been suggested *pratyakṣa* (perception), anumāna (Interence), *Upamāna* (Analogy) and *Śabda* (verbal testimony). It is through these processes we acquire the knowledge of the world and behave with it. A proper process presents the world in its real form and a wrong process presents in its unreal form. *Pramāṇa* corresponds to the proper process and *pramāṇābhāsa* corresponds to the wrong process.

Various traditions have proposed various definitions of the general notion of *pramāṇa*. Jayantabhatta proposed the following definition : *avyabhicāriṇīm asandigdhām arthopalabdhim vidadhatī bodhabodhasyabhava samagra pramanam* (Nyayamanjari, Mysore Edn. p.31) That is, a collection of fators consisting of both knowledge and non-knowledge and which produces a cognition which is neither erroneous nor doubtful is called *pramāna.*

This general definition of pramāna is criticised by Prabhācandra Suri in his *Prameyakamalamārtaṇḍa* (pp. 7-13, 1990 Edn. Indian Books center Delhi).

Jayanta's dininition includes all factors which may be either of the form of knowledge or of the form of non-knowledge. Thus, in the process of perception *(pratyakṣa), ātman* (soul), *manas* (mind), *indriya* (sense-organ), *artha* (object) and their contacts are the factors of the nature of non-knowledge *(a-bodha)* and the *niryikalpaka-pratyakṣa* (indeterminate cognition) arising after those contacts is of the nature of cognition. All these are required for producing the perceptual cognition and hence all these are to be treated as the factors which produce perception.

This stand of Jayanta is challenged by Prabhācandra Sūri in his *prameyakamala-mārtaṇḍa.* According to Prabhācandra, knowledge alone can be *Pramāna* because it is the knowledge that reveals an object. Thus, a revealer is the *pramāṇa.* According to him there should be on intervention by any factor between a *pramāṇa.* and *phala.*

If Jayanta's view is accepted then there is some intervension and so his view is not acceptable to him.

Prabhācandra concludes.

Kārakasākalyasya svarupena asiddheh siddhau vā jñānena vyavadhānāt na prāmaṇyan(Prameyakama-lamārtanda Indian Books centre, 1990, p.13

If we examine both the views closely we will find that the notion of *pramāna* i.e. an instrument of Jayanta is different from that of Prabhācandra. While Jayanta's notion of *karaṇa* or instrument is the notion of a producer of a result, whereas the notion of Prabhācandra is that of a revealer. It is the knowledge that immediately reveals an object and hence knowledge is to be treated as the instant revealer and hence the *pramāna.* In the notion of Jayanta the idea of 'a process' is involved and hence all the factors involved in that process is the instrement. Naturally, before the final result appears there are many intervening factors including cognition. Even in the process of producing a determinate perception an indeterminate perception precedes the determinate perception. In the case of other processes off knowing like inferene, Analogy and Verbal testimony, it is obvious that various knowledges precede the final resultant knowledges. Thus, for the illumination of an object other knowledges come on the way. Therefore, only the final knowledge after which the object is illumined is fit to be called a *pramāna* recording tto Prabhācandra.

Thus, I think that it is the difference in the notion of Karaṇa that accounts for the difference in the opinions of Jayanta and Prabhācandra on the issue of the general definition of *Pramāṇa.*

Refutation of God in Jainism

Shripad Bhat

Before we going to discuss the problem it is to be clarified that whether Jainism is atheistic. The answer to this question naturally depends upon the meaning we attach to the word atheistic. If we take it in the sense of heterodox (*nāstika*) which is its commonly accepted Sanskrit equivalent, the answer is clear. For the word, '*nāstika*' means one that does not believe in a life beyond (paraloka)[1], i.e. one does not believe in a surviving self. The word 'nāstika' is used as the result of later modification in its meaning to describe that refute the authority of the Veda. In that sense Jainism is nāstika for its antagonistic to the Hindu scriptures and there it sides with Cārvāka and Buddhism. On the otherhand if we take 'atheistic' as not believing in God Jainism is considered to be atheistic, because it believes in no God. If there is a God he should be understood as a supreme personality and responsible for the creation of the world. It deliberately rejects such conception as well as argues that there is no God and world was not created. Regarding this the Jainism is curiously enough in agreement with the views of Mīmāṁsakas, the upholder of strict orthodoxy.

The Jaina philosophy was developed out of the canonical works of Jainas. Many glosses and commentaries were written in the sacred texts. Jainism more than any other system gives absolute religious importance as well as independence and freedom to man. Hence philosophical literature was first written in Prakrit and then in Sanskrit. Here, as far as the topic is concerned, Prameyakamalamārtaṇḍa of Prabhācandra (825 A.D.) Vītarāgastotra of Hemacandra (1088-1173) Syādvādamañjarī of Malliṣeṇa (1292 A.D.) Tarkarahasyadīpikā of Guṇaratna and his commentary on Ṣaḍdarśaṇasamuccaya of Haribhadra Sūri (1129 A.D.) Sarvadarśanasaṅgraha of Mādhavācarya (14th cent.) are important works.

According to all traditional exponents Udyotakara, Vācaspati and Udayana, Nyāya system is theistic. It accepts a personal God as the creator of the universe and as the bestower of fruits in accordance with one's *karma*.

अक्षपादमते देवः सृष्टिसंहारकृच्छिवः।
विभुर्नित्यैकसर्वज्ञो नित्यबुद्धिसमाश्रयः॥

In the faith of the followers of Akṣapāda, the deity is Śiva, creator and destroyer omnispresent eternal omniscient, and the abode of eternal cognition.[2]

An argument regarding God very famous in Nyāya works[3] is that the world is an effect, like a pot, it must have an intelligence cause (author). The world is an effect, because it is composite (*sāvayava*) and all composite things have an author, because, otherwise composition (*racanā*) is impossible.

God is the efficient cause (*nimittakāraṇa*) of the world. He has created the world out of pre-existing eternal atoms which are its material cause (*upādānakāraṇa*). The world is not infinite, it is of intermediate magnitude it consists of parts so it is of the nature of an effect. It is produced by an intelligent agent viz., God who has direct knowledge of the material cause or atoms, desire to create the world and the volition to do so.[4]

However, the Jaina refutes the nature of the world as an effect. He raises some questions regarding the nature of the world as an effect. Does Naiyāyika mean by effect that which consists of parts[5] (*sāvayavatva*)?

(1) If a substance made up of parts means that which has conjunction with parts (*avayavasanyogitva*) then ether (*ākāśa*) consists of parts and is an effect since it has conjunction with parts.[6] But Naiyayika holds that *ākāśa* is one, partless and eternal.[7] So the first alternative is wrong.

(2) If a substance made up of parts means that which inheres in parts (*avayavasamavāyitva*) then generality (*sāmānya*) consists of parts and is an effect, since the genus of jar (*ghaṭatva*) inheres in individual jar and in all its parts.[8] But Naiyāyika holds that a generality is one, partless and eternal.[9]

(3) If a substance consisting of parts means that, which is produced by parts (*avayavajanyat*) then there is no difference between middle term (*sādhana*) viz., effect. A substance produced by parts (*sādhana*) is identical with an effect (*sādhya*). Therefore they are identical with each other.[10]

(4) If a substance consisting of parts means a substance which possesses the mere relation of inherence (*samavetadravyatva*)[11], then, ether (*ākāśa*) consists of parts and is an effect, since its quality and the genus of substance inhere in it. But the Naiyāyika holds that ether is eternal.[12]

(5) If a substance consisting of parts means a substance inhering in other parts[13] (*anyatra-samavetadravyatva*) then there is no difference between the middle term (*sādhana*) and the major term (*sādhya*). Inherence of a composite substance in its parts which are its material cause has to be proved. The Jainas reject this.[14]

(6) If a substance consisting of parts means that which is apprehended as consisting of parts (*Sāvayavabuddhiviṣayatva*) then the self consisting of parts and is an effect, since it is apprehended as consisting of parts and pervading the body. But the self is eternal. It is not an effect. If the self is said to be partless (*niravayava*) and yet extensive (*vyāpaka*) then a partless atom also will be extensive. But an indivisible atom has no extensive magnitude. So all six alternatives are wrong. Therefore a substance consisting of parts cannot be an effect and the world is not an effect, because it consists of parts.[15]

Further, Jaina argues that if God is creator of the world, he creates it with a body or without a body. He cannot create it without a body, just as a jar is not created by a potter without a body. It is not perceptible, since grass, plants, rainbow, clouds, and like are found to be spontaneously generated without its aid. If God's body is imperceptible, a special greatness (*māhātmyaviśeṣa*) is its cause, there is no reason to prove it and it involves mutual dependence. God's imperceptible body depends upon his special greatness and that depends upon his imperceptible body. Our body is caused by our merits and demerits. But God's body cannot be caused by his merit and demerit. Therefore God cannot have a perceptible or imperceptible body. He cannot create the world.[16]

Again, if it is produced by one God, all effects in the world, such as human productions may be produced by him and particular causes of particular effects are not necessary.[17]

Further, the world may be produced by the co-operation of many gods, as a palace made by the co-operation of men, as a bee-hive is made by the co-operation of many bees. The Naiyayika argument that many Gods will conflict with other and frustrate one another. If a society of bees can construct a bee-hive, a society of Gods can create the world.[18]

Does god create variety in the world with the aid of the merits and demerits of the creature or without their aid? If he depends on them, he ceases to be the independent Lord. If he does not depend upon them why does he make some creatures happy and others unhappy? Then he is kind to some and kindless to others and thus guilty of partiality. If merits and demerits of creatures make them happy and unhappy, they become the Lord (Īśvara) and ceases to be the Lord (Anīśvara).[19]

Even if God exists he cannot be eternal. If he is of the nature of creative act which is external he can never desist from creating the world. If he desists from the creative act, he cannot be of the nature of creative act. Until the creative act is completed not a single effect can be produced. If he is not of the nature of creative act, he can never create the world, since he cannot acquire creativity. Moreover, if he is absolutely eternal, he can neither create the world nor destroy it, since creation and destruction imply change and God is admitted to be unchangeable and immutable. Creation and destruction are two different acts. They cannot be made by an eternal God who is not liable to change and God does not destroy the world by the same nature by which he creates the world. If he does so by a different nature then he is liable to change and is not eternal.[20]

If God is the creator of the world, what is the motive of his creation? An intelligent being exerts himself owing to self interest or compassion for others. So God being intelligent must create the world to serve his self interest or out of compassion for his creatures. But he is an eternally fulfilled being. He has no unfulfilled desires. He has no self interest. So he cannot create the world to fulfill his selfish end. Nor can he be moved by compassion for creatures. Compassion is desire to remove the sufferings of others. But before creation there is no suffering which is felt by the self through the mind, body and sense organs in intercourse with objects which are not yet created. If God feels compassion for sufferings of creatures before their creation, then creation will depend upon compassion and compassion will depend upon creation and sufferings consequent on it. Hence God has no motive for creation.[21]

If God creates the world in sport (*krīḍā*) then his creative act is purposeless, like the play of the child. If creation follows from his nature (*svabhāva*) then all effects may spring from the nature of other causes and the hypotheisis of God is unwarranted.

God cannot be ubiquitous. Is he ubiquitous through his body or through his knowledge? If he pervades the universe through his body there is no scope for the production of effects by human agents. All human productions must be ascribed to God. But this contradicted by perception. If God pervades the universe through his knowledge, the Jainas also admit that an omniscient person (*sarvajña*) and he pervades the universe with an overflow of his omniscience. But they do not believe in God. If God creates the world directly through his bodily activity, like a carpenter, he will take infinite time to create mountains and other effects. If he creates it by mere will (saṅkalpamātra) then other Gods also may create them by mere will. Moreover, if God is all-pervading, he creates impure creatures in hell also.[22]

God cannot be omniscient. His omniscience cannot be proved by perception, inference and testimony. Perception is produced by the intercourse of the sense-organs with sensible objects. So it cannot be apprehend the omniscience of God which is supersensible.[23]

Devine omniscience cannot be proved by inference which depends upon the recollection of invariable concomitance (*vyāpti*) between the mark of inference (*liṅga*) and the inferred property (*liṅgin*) after perception of the mark of inference. But there is no mark of inference (*hetu*) which is invariably accompanied by omniscience of God which is the object of inference.[24]

Testimony also cannot prove omniscience of God. If it depends upon God he loses his greatness, because great souls do not boast of their own glories. Further, scriptures consist of letters and sounds produced by different parts of the body. God has no body. So he cannot be the creator of the scriptures. If the scriptures depend upon some other agent, he is omniscient, then there are two omniscient beings. However the theist does not admit two omniscient beings. He believes in one God only who is omniscient.[25]

The Jainas do not recognize the existence of God. They do not believe in his eternity, ubiquity, independence, mercifulness and omniscience. If any one tries to justify the existence of God, he finds that it is a hopeless task according to Jainas.

The world is eternal and self existent. Particular things

in the world are created out of their material causes and destroyed into them. There is no creation out of nothing. There is no destruction of something into nothing. The phenomena in the world are governed by the law of causality subservient to the moral law of *karma*.

However a similarity can be found in the Mīmāṁsā, a strict orthodox system of the Indian philosophy. The question of the creator God is raised in connection with the eternality of word and its meaning and the relation between two, an authorship of the Veda and creation of the world. There are a number of verses in the *Sambandhākṣepaparihāra* chapter of the Ślokavārttika of Kumārila.[26] He delebarately rejects creatorship of the world of God and his omniscience.

The Buddhists point out that the individual should strive to attain perfection and should not unnecessarily speculate on some such identity who may be looked upon as the author of creation. It is an undeniable fact that the world is full of miseries and the individual should set himself to the task of overcoming these miseries by personal efforts and without seeking aid from any external agent, such as God, for the purpose. According to Buddhists, the hypothesis of a personal God is inconsistent with the law of karma.[27]

Bhāvaviveka refutes God in the ninth chapter *Mīmāṁsātattvanirṇayāvatāra* of Madhyamakahṛdayakārikā as refutation made by Jainas.[28]

Although the Jainas do not believe in God, they believe in the innate devinity of each soul. Every soul can realize its intrinsic devinity by self effort. Jainism also believes in the souls transmigration. As heat can unite with iron and water with milk, so *karma* unites with the soul and soul so united with the *karma* is called a soul in bondage. If through proper discipline all *karma* is worked out and there arises the full blaze of omniscience in the *Jīva*, it becomes free. When atlast it escapes at the time of death from the bondage of body it rises until it reaches the top of the universe described as Lokākāśa and there it rests in peaceful bliss for ever.

The Jainas find God in the shape of object of worship. According to them, Jina is the only object of worship who is free from all attachment and has conquered all passions and removes all ignorance.[29] It is clearly said in Āptaniścayalaṅkāra, that the devine Arhat is the supreme lord (Parameśvara), the omniscient, who has overcome all faults and desire.[30] He is omniscient but not creator of the universe. In this sense, Jainism is not atheism. Hence, it can be easily said that the Jaina's refutation of God is against the Naiyāyika's argument, that the world is an event, it must have a cause and the cause is no other than God. Therefore Jainism should be considered as the system which refutes only the creatorship of God of the universe.

Footnotes

1) Pāṇini 4.4.60
2) *Ṣaḍdarśanasamuccaya* of Haribhadra, verse 13.
3) *Nyāyamañjarī* of Jayanta Bhaṭṭa; *Nyāyakusumāñjali* of udayana etc.
4) Sinha J.N. History of Indian Philosophy, Vol. II, pp. 266-67.
5) *Sarvadarśanasaṅgraha* of Sāyaṇa-Mādhava p. 59
6) Ibid.
7) *Tarkasaṁgraha* of Annam Bhaṭṭa. p. 8
8) *Sarvadarśanasaṅgraha* of Sāyaṇa-Mādhava p. 59.
9) *Tarkasaṅgraha* of Annam Bhaṭṭa, p. 36
10) *Sarvadarśanasangraha* of Sāyaṇa-Mādhava pp. 59-60.
11) Ibid.
12) *Tarkasaṅgraha* of Annam Bhaṭṭa p. 8.
13) *Sarvadarśanasaṅgraha* of Sāyaṇa-Mādhava, p. 60.
14) Sinha J.N., History of Indian Philosophy, Vol. II p. 268.
15) Ibid.
16) *Syādvādamañjarī* of Malliṣeṇa, p. 44.
17) Ibid. p. 46.
18) Ibid.
19) Ibid p. 53
20) Ibid p. 55.
21) Ibid.
22) Ibid.
23) Sinha J.N., History of Indian Philosophy, Vol. II, p. 272
24) Ibid.
25) Ibid.
26) *Ślokavārttika* of Kumārila pp. 453-82; Wide. Bhat Shripad, Mīmāṁsādarśanātīla Īśvaraviṣayaka dṛṣṭikona, Parāmarśa, November 1992, pp. 43-51.
27) Bhattacharyya Gopikamohan, Studies in Nyāya-Vaiśeṣika Theism, p. 42.
28) Bhat shripad, Refutation of the Mīmāṁsakas by the Buddhists, pp. 118-122.
29) Jinendro devatā tatra rāgadveṣavivarjitaḥ/

Hatamohamahāmallaḥ Kevalajñānadarśanaḥ//45//
Ṣaḍdarśanasamuccaya of Haribhadrasūri.

30) Sarvajño jitarāgādidoṣastrailokyapūjitaḥ/
Yathāsthitārthavādī ca devo'rhan Parameśvaraḥ//

Sarvadarśanasaṅgraha of Sāyaṇa-Mādhava, p. 56.

References

1) Bhat shripad, *Mīmāṁsādarśanātīla Īśvaraviṣayaka dṛṣṭikona*, Parāmarśa research journal (Marathi) Quraterly, Deptt. of Philosophy, University of Poona, Pune November, 1992.

2) *Refutation of the Mīmāṁasakas by the Buddhists*, M.Phil. thesis. (unpublished) T.M.V. Pune, 1991.

3) Bhattacharyya Gopikamohan, *Studies in Nyāya Vaiśeṣika Theism*, Sanskrit College Calcutta, 1991.

4) *Nyāyakusumāñjali* of Udayana, Bharatīya-Vidya-Prakashana, Varanasi, 1968.

5) *Nyāyamañjarī* of Jayanta Bhaṭṭa, Ed., Suryanaryana Shukla, Çhowkhamba Sanskrit Series, Varanasi, 1971.

6) *Pāṇinīyam vyākaraṇam*, Ed., Harikrishna Pandeya published by Chandrakanta Pandeya Patna, 1938.

7) *Prameyakamalamārtanḍaḥ* of Prabhācandra, Ed. Mahindrakumar Shastri, Published by Satya-bhāmabai Pandurang, Bombay, 1941.

8) *Ślokavārttikam* of Kumarila Bhaṭṭa, with the commentary of Nyāyaratnākara, Ed. Swami Dwarakadas Shastri, Ratna Publications, Varanasi, 1957.

9) *Sarvadarśanasaṅgraha* of Sāyaṇa-Mādhava, Ed. T.G. Mainkar, with the commentary of Vasudev Shastri Abhyankar, B.O.R.J. Poona, 1978.

10) Sinha J.N., *History of Indian Philosophy*, Central Book Agency Calcutta, 1952.

11) *Syādvādamañjarī* of Malliṣeṇa, Ed. Jagadeesh Chandra Shastri, Paramashrutamandala, Bombay 1935.

12) *Ṣaḍdarśanasamuccaya* of Haribhadra, with the commentary of Manibhadra, Chowkhamba Sanskrit Series Varanasi, 1957.

13) *Tarkasaṅgraha* of Annam Bhaṭṭa, Ed. K.C. Mehendale, Bharat Bharati Bhandar, Delhi 1992.

Refutation of the Jaina Darśana by Śaṅkarācārya with special reference to Syādvāda in the Brahmasūtraśāṅkarabhāṣya

Vijay Pandya

Śaṅkarācārya has refuted some of the tenets of the Jaina system of thought in his *bhāṣya* on the Brahmasūtra 2-2-33 to 36. The second quarter of the second *adhyāya* of the Brahmasūtra has been traditionally designated as the Tarkapāda, indicating its content being based on logic.

The main thrust of the Śaṅkarācārya's arguments is against the Syādvāda or Anèkāntavāda and Saptabhaṅgīnaya, although not synonyms but interconnected with each other, as one philosopher of this system of thought puts it अनेकान्तात्मकार्यकथनं स्याद्वादः।[1] Syādvāda and Anekāntavāda can be said to have the relation of Vācyavācakabhāva - Anekāṅtavāda is intended to be expressed with the help of Syādvāda, as another work Syādvādamañjarī explains स्यादित्ययमनेकान्तद्योतकं ततः स्यादवादोऽनेकान्तवादः।[2]

The most singular contribution of the Jaina system of thought to Indian thought is Syādvāda or Anekāntavāda, and

Jaina system of thought has been almost identified with the Syādvāda, at times to the exclusion of other important ideas of the system, also. So it is not surprising that Śaṅkarācārya has specially targeted the Syādvāda arising out of the Saptabhaṅginaya, for his attack on the Jaina system of thought.

First of all, Śaṅkarācārya directs his attack on the Saptabhaṅginaya, and says that one object cannot contain in itself, contradictory attributes simultaneously. न हि एकस्मिन् धर्मिणि युगपत् सत्-असत्-त्वादिविरुद्धधर्म समावेशः संभवति। An object cannot be existent and non-existent at the same time. Moreover, according to Śaṅkarācārya, the corollary of this doctrine would be that, even the seven *padārthas* viz. *Jīva, ājīva, āśrava, saṁvara, nirjara, bandha* and *mokṣa* would not have any definiteness about them. A doubt will arise regarding, first of all, about the number of the entities, and then their nature and so on. Hence everything would be of indefinite nature and so, the knowledge would be of doubtful nature, which cannot serve as a means of knowledge. Resultantly, the tirthaṇkara would not be able to lend any certainty to his preachings regarding the valid means of knowledge (*pramāṇa*), the objects of knowledge (prameya), agent of knowledge (*pramātā*) and the resulting knowledge itself all of which have a non-determinate form. If there is any certainty, then only people can follow a certain path without any hesitation. So the teacher's preachings would not be acceptable to the people and hence, they are liable to be rejected like the prattling of a maniac.[3]

Now Śaṅkarācārya's dialectics in his refutation of the Anekāntavāda is remarkable. But, it may be pointed out that, it does not take the real position of Anekāntavāda into account. Śaṅkarācārya's representation of the Anekāntavāda is rather a simplification of things. Śaṅkarācārya seems to be identifying the Syādavāda with the agnosticism which was, once, articulated by one Sanjaya Belatthiputta (अत्थि पि मेनो, नत्थी ति पि मेनो अत्थि च नत्थि च ति पि मेनो नेवेत्थि न नत्थि ति पि मेनो) Sanjaya had said 'I cannot say if it is, and I cannot say, if it is not.' Syādvāda would say 'I can say that the thing in a sense is, and I can say, that the thing in a sense is not.' So, this is certainly not saṅśayavāda or agnosticism as Śaṅkarācārya would make it out to be. Anekāntavāda purports to grasp the polarity of the truth. This leads us to Saptabhaṅginaya viz. (i) स्यादस्ति घटः, (ii) स्यान्नास्ति घटः, (iii) स्यादस्ति स्यान्नास्ति घटः, (iv) स्यादवक्तोव्यो घटः, (v) स्यादस्ति वक्तवयो घटः, (vi) स्यान्नास्ति अवक्तव्यो घटः, (vii) स्यादस्ति नास्ति अवक्तव्यो घटः

Now when a statement is made that a jug exists, jug exists from its own nature स्वरूपेण अस्ति and पररूपेण नास्ति i.e. it does not exist in the form of पट, घटः स्वरूपेण अस्ति and पररूपेण नास्ति both statements are possible at the same time about घट and similarly, other remaining भङ्गीऽ also can be worked out. So, as it has been explained प्रश्नवशात् एकस्मिन् वस्तुनि अविरोधेन विधिप्रतिषेधकल्पना सप्तभङ्गी। तद् यथा स्याद् घटः स्वात्मना, स्याद् अघटः परात्मना। Everything exists from its own nature and does not exist from the nature different from its own; as has been elucidated in one verse

सर्वमस्ति स्वरूपेण पररूपेण नास्ति च।
अन्यथा सर्वसत्त्वं स्यात् स्वरूपस्याप्यसंगवः॥

So everything exists from its own nature and does not exist from the nature different from its own. If Syādvāda is root taken from this point of view, then, as pointed out in the above verse, every thing would be everything and there would not be any difference between the two things. If the Syādvāda arising out of the *saptabhangīnaya* is taken literally, at its surface value, then, there would be anarchy in the world. As Dharmakīrti would poke fun at the Syādvāda in the following couplet

सर्वस्योभयरूपत्वे तद्विशेषनिराकृतेः।

चोदितो दधि खादेति किमुष्ट्रं नाभिधावति॥[4]

With the differentiation removed, all things would be having dual nature, then, if somebody is implored to eat curds, why does he not eat the camel?

This is an extreme view taking the Syādvāda in a very surfacial manner. If it is said that, an entity is of dual nature, i.e. existing and non-existing, it means applying to an illustration given by Dharmakīrti, curds exist from the nature of curds and does not exist from the nature of a camel. So, if a person is asked to eat curds, then why should he run to eat a camel?

Or as Akalaṅka would issue a rejoinder

पूर्वपक्षमविज्ञाय दूषकोऽपि विदूषकः।

सुगतोऽपि मृगो जातः मृगोऽपि सुगतः स्मृतः॥

तथापि सुगतो वन्द्यो मृगः खाद्यो यथोच्यते।

तथा वस्तुबलादेव भेदाभेदव्यवस्थितेः।

चोदितो दधि खादति किमुष्ट्रमभिधावति॥[5]

Without properly understanding the primafacie view, if a person criticises that view, then he is only a Vidūṣaka and not a critic. Buddha was born as a deer and deer was born as Buddha, and not, Buddha is adorable, and the deer is only food. Similarly, due to the strength of an entity with its difference and non-difference specified, nobody would eat a camel if he is implored to eat curds.

As Amṛtacandra elcidates यदेव तत् तदेव अतत् यदेवैकं तदेवानेकं, यदेव सत् तदेवासत्, यदेव नित्यं तदेवानित्यं, इत्येक वस्तुनिस्वादक- परस्परविरूद्ध शक्तिद्वयप्रकाशमनेकान्तः।[6]

Or as one Acārya clarified with an illustration of a cowherd woman churning the curds

एकेनाकर्षयन्ती श्लथयन्ती वस्तुत्वमितरेण।
अक्षेन जयति जैनीनीतिर्मन्थानुनेत्रमिव गोपी॥[7]

The Jaina system of thought while deemphasizing one strand of thought, emphasizes another thought, just like a cowherd women, while churning the curds, straightens one end of a rope, loosening the other end.

So Saptabhaṅgīnaya is employed either from the point of view of *sakaladeśa* or *vikalādeśa* i.e. from a holistic point of view or from a partial point of view. Syādvāda itself is a holistic point of view. Syādvāda is dependent upon the Saptabhaṅgīnaya as acārya Samantabhadra says सप्तन्याङगनभयशः स्याद्वादः।[8] So Syādvāda attempts to accommodate all the differing points of view and hence this characteristic is in fact an ornament or a plus point, स्यात्कारः सत्यलांछनः and not a flow as Śaṅkarācārya tries to make it out to be.

Further, Śaṅkarācārya argues that pursuing the Syādavāda to its logical conclusion would lead one to doubt the doubting self, as there would be indeterminacy regarding the number of āstikāyas and their nature and so on,[9] and thereby Syādavāda would topsyturvy everything in the Jaina system of thought, by its own indeterminate nature. Śaṅkarā cārya's incisive logical faculty seems to be flowless. But, he does not seem to notice that such a situation is inherent in the doctrine itself. In fact, this possibility of Syādvāda applying its own doctrine to itself has been perceived in the Jaina system of thought. Samantabhadra, perceiving this possibility or rather contingency writes

अनेकान्तेऽप्यनेकान्तः प्रमाणनयसाधनः।
अनेकान्तः प्रमाणत्ते तदेकान्तेऽर्पितान्नयात्॥[10]

From the point of view of *pramāṇa* it is *anekānta*, and from the point of view of Naya it is *ekānta*. So, *anekānta* is *anekānta* as well as *ekānta*. As noted earlier, Naya is a partial point of view. Naya has been explained as प्रमाणगृही तार्थैकदेशग्राही प्रमातुरभिप्रायविशेषः नयः। Naya grasps only a part of an object cognised by pramāṇa. Or Naya leads an various entity to its partial nature, excluding other characteristics नानास्वभावेभ्यः व्यवृत्य एकस्मिन् स्वभावे वस्तुं नयतीति नयः।" So Naya is neither pramāṇa nor apramāṇa. Naya is a part of a pramāṇa. Naya cognises a thing only partially and not wholly.[12] Thus Naya is a pramāṇa as well as apramāṇa. Similarly, Anekāntavāda is also anekānta as well as ekānta. Anekānta reconciles all differing partial positions.[13]

So anekāntavāda or Syādvāda boldly faces and does not shy away from facing its own logical consequences.

En passent it may be remarked that, Jaina system of thought is not 'anxious to prove their padārthas, any more than the Vedāntins are to prove their Brahman'.[14] The existence of the padārthas depends upon the authority of the Āgama as a Vedāntin would depend upon the Śruti. Of course, there is a difference too, between the two systems. As the God, the creator of the universe, is unavailable to the Jaina system of thought as they do not believe in creator of the universe, and hence God does not lend any authority to the Āgamas. But, Śaṅkarācārya also, does not lay much stress upon this argument. As noted in the beginning of this essay, Śaṅkarācārya's main thrust is against the syādvāda.

Moreover, Śaṅkarācārya finds fault with one of the Saptabhanginaya i.e. स्यादवक्तव्यः About this Śaṅkarācārya remarks that if it is inexpressible, it cannot be expressed, and if it is expressible, or expressed, it is not inexpressible. न चैषां पदार्थानामवक्तव्यत्वं संभवति। अवक्तव्याश्चेन्नोच्येरन्। उच्यन्ते चावक्तव्याश्चेति विप्रतिषिद्धम्।[15]

Śaṅkarācārya forgets for the time that, his conception of the Māyā is also, open to the same change.

Thus, it will be seen that, Śaṅkarācārya has not been able to do full justice to the multihued splendour of Syādvāda. It is quite probable that, the great ācārya, as he was, might have been led by a contemporary consideration of his days, which were the days of great upheaval, affecting the destiny of an entire nation. But, the Jaina system of thought and especially its main plank Syādvāda is a distinct contribution to the Indian thought. In its Syādvāda tenet, the Jaina system of philosophy appears to be most vital and resilient. It can be said to be relevant even to day, and Śaṅkarācārya's refutation of it has a little impact on the subsequent course of Indian thought.

Notes and References

1. Akalaṅka in his Laghiyastrayatīka 62.
2. Syādvāda mañjari-5.
3. See the Śṅkarabhāṣya on 2-2-33: निरङ्कुशं ह्यनेकान्तत्वं सर्ववस्तुषु प्रतिजान्पनस्य, निर्धारणस्यापि वस्तुत्त्वाविशेषात्, स्यादस्ति स्यान्नास्तीत्यादि विकलपोपनियातादनिर्धारणात्मकतैव स्यात्।... एवं सति कथं प्रमाणभूतः संस्तीर्थकरः प्रमाणप्रमेय प्रभातृमितिष्वनिर्धारितारूपदेष्टुं शक्नुयात्, कथं वा तदभिप्रायानुसारिणस्तदुपदिष्टेऽर्थे निर्धारितरूपे प्रवर्तेरन्। ऐकान्तिकफलत्व निर्धारणे हि सति तासाधनानुष्ठानाय सर्वो लोकोऽनाकुलः प्रवर्तते, नान्यथा। अतश्चानिर्धारितार्थं शास्त्रं प्रणयन् मत्तोन्मत्तवदनुपादेयवचनः स्यात्।
4. Pramāṇavārtika 3-181.
5. Akalaṅka in his Nyāyaviniścaya 203,204
6 Amṛtacandra in his Ātmakhyāti commentary.
7. Amṛtacandra in the Puruṣārthasiddhi 225.
8. Samantabhadra in his Āptamīmāṁsā 14.
9. तथा पञ्चानामस्तिकायानां पञ्चत्वसंख्यास्ति वा नास्ति वेति विकल्यमाना, स्यात् तावदेकस्मिन् पक्षे, पक्षान्तरे, तु न स्यात्, इत्यतो न्यूनसंख्या त्वमधिकसंख्यात्वं वा प्राप्नुयात्। Śāṅ.
10. Samantabhadra in Svayambhūstotra 103.
11. Devasena in Nayacakra
12. नायं वस्तु न चावस्तु वस्त्वंशः कथ्यत्ते यतः। नासमुद्रः समुद्रो वा समुद्रांशो यथोच्यते।। Tattvārthaśloka vārtika 1-6.
13. परमागमस्य बीजं निषिद्धजाव्यन्तसिन्धुरविधानम्।
    सकलन्यविलसितानां विरोधमथनं नमाम्यनेकान्तक।।

    Amṛtacandra in Puruṣārthasiddhi 2
14. Belvelkar S.K., The Brahmasūtras of Bādarāyaṇa 2-1,,2, Notes, p. 181 15 Śāṅkarabhāṣya 2-2-33.

Is there Salvation for Women?

Nirmala Kulkarni

I.O.O Introduction

Ancient Indian systems of philosophy and religion as well unanimously accept *Mokṣa,* as the highest goal of human life. They describe the concept of *Mokṣa* in the light of the philosophical tenets of their own.

A question comes to our mind immediately, "Who are the persons eligible to attain *Mokṣa*?" and a woman in the 20th century who is more alert about her equal status and rights would anxiously ask– "Is a woman considered eligible for the highest goal of human life?" To answer her question a scholar of theistic philosophies would get puzzled for a moment, since there is no explicit statement. But a scholar of Jainalogy would immediately answer her question. For the affirmative answer he would point out to the Śvetāmbara Jaina view and for the negative one to that of a Digambara Jaina's.

I felt necessary to write on this particular issue for the following reasons.

(1) Only the Jaina texts reserve separate chapters for this issue.

(2) It is the main point of difference between the Śvetāmbaras and the Digambaras.

(3) The rationale put forth by both these subsystems would enable us to lay hold on their views about women though it is not the prime concern of this particular seminar.

Many texts discuss this issue theoretically.

Among these the following are the Śvetāmbara texts :

(1) स्त्रीमुक्तिवाद
(2) सन्मतितर्कटीका
(3) ललितविस्तर
(4) शास्त्रवार्तासमुच्चय etc.

The Digambara texts could be cited as

(1) प्रमेयकमलमार्त्तण्ड of प्रभाचन्द्र
(2) गच्छाचारप्रकीर्णकवृत्तिः
(3) भावसङ्ग्रह and
(4) न्यायकुमुदचन्द्र of प्रभाचन्द्रसूरि

Among these the *Nyāyakumudacandra* gives us crystal clear picture of both the views. The Śvetāmbaras declaring salvation for women come here as पूर्वपक्ष and the Digambaras dening the same are the *Siddhāntins*.

Let us see how these two sects argue with each other.

I.1.0 The Digambaras open the discussion with the following argument–

मुक्तिः पुंसः एव, न स्त्रियाः।

तस्याः नपुंसकवत्तदयोग्यत्वात्।
तन्मुक्तिप्रसाधकप्रमाण-असंभवाच्च।

Tr. Salvation is meant only for men and not for women, for two reasons.

(1) They are not capable of attaining it.

(2) Secondly, there is no sound reason to establish salvation for them.

(Obj) Immediately, the Śvetāmbaras come forward with the evidence to establish women's right on salvation. They argue - What is the cause of salvation? The threefold causal complex रत्नत्रय i.e. सम्यग्दर्शन, सम्यग्ज्ञान and सम्यक्चारित्र्य. It exists along with all these three features in women. Therefore, there is salvation for them.

अस्ति स्त्रीणां निर्वाणम्।

अविकलकारणत्वात्।

पुंवत्।

(Sid) Here, Digambara catches him-When does the *Ratnatraya* act as cause? In its ultimate state or without reaching to its ultimate height? We cannot say that it before reaching to its ultimate height becomes cause, because then even a householder also will attain salvation. Thus, the *Ratnatraya* only in its ultimate state becomes the cause. Since the *Ratnatraya* in its ultimate state is not in women. Therefore, we cannot establish salvation for them. To say–

स्त्रीषु मोक्षाभावः।

मोक्षप्रसाधकस्य प्रकर्षपर्यन्तप्राप्तस्य रत्नत्रयस्य तत्र अभावात्।

गृहस्थादिवत्।

(Obj) The Śvetāmbara asks - Do you see रत्नत्रय reached to its heights? If not, then how do you cognise its absence? अदृष्टे विरोधप्रतिपत्तेः अनुपपत्तेः।

Because, it is illogical to cognise absence of an unseen thing.

न खलु प्रकर्षपर्यन्तप्राप्तं रत्नत्रयम् अस्माकं दृश्यम्, न च अदृश्यस्य विरोधः प्रतिपत्तुं शक्यः, अतिप्रसङ्गात्।

(Sid) Digambara says – It is true, that we cannot cognise absence of an unseen thing, however, only by perception. By other means of cognition *anumāna* etc. we do cognise it. Here is our argument–

निर्वाणकारणज्ञानादिपरमप्रकर्षः स्त्रीषु नास्ति।

परमप्रकर्षत्वात्।

सप्तमपृथिवीगमनकारण-अपुण्यपरमप्रकर्षवत्।

Since any kind of ultimatum is absent in women, even रत्नत्रय in its ultimatum is absent in them. As they do not posses the ultimate sin leading to the seventh hell. We say, that प्रकर्षनिर्वर्त्तनसमर्थककर्मार्जनसामर्थ्याभाव is in women i.e. a woman does not have capacity to attain *karma* either the ultimate good or the ultimate bad, leading to मोक्ष or to the last hell respectively. Because womanly body is obtained by a *jīva* because of his extreme demerit.

न स्त्रीशरीरं सकलकर्मक्षपण-अप्रारम्भहेतुः।

महता पापेन मिथ्यात्वसहायेन उपर्जितत्वात्।

नारकादिशरीरवत्।

To quote some supporting verses from भावसंग्रह (244-47)

सदैवाशुद्धता योनौ गलन्मलाश्रयत्वतः।
रजःस्खलनमेतासां मासं प्रति प्रजायते॥
उत्पद्यन्ते सदा स्त्रीणां योनौ कक्षादिसंधिषु।
सूक्ष्मापर्याप्तका मर्त्यास्तद्देहस्य स्वभावतः॥
स्वभावः कुत्सितस्तासां लिङ्गं चात्यन्तकुत्सितम्।
तस्मान्न प्राप्यते साक्षात् द्वेधा संयमभावना॥
उत्कृष्टसंयमं मुक्त्वा शुक्लध्याने न योग्यता।
नो मुक्तिस्तद्विना तस्मात्तासां मोक्षोऽतिदूरगः॥

I.2.O Now we give you our second argument to establish absence of salvation in women. We say–

नास्ति स्त्रीणां मोक्षः।

वादादिलब्धि-अभावात्।

गृहस्थादिवत्।

Women do not possess special capacities such as (1) वादादिलब्धि i.e. to establish one's own stand by getting hold of dialectics. वादादिलब्धिः खलु इन्द्राद्यास्थानेषु बृहस्पत्यादिषु प्रतिबन्धकेषु सत्सु छलजात्यादिपरिहारेण स्वतत्त्वप्रतिपादनसामर्थ्यम्।

(2) They do not have विक्रियालब्धि i.e. the capacity to take form of Indra etc. इन्द्रादिरूप-उपादानशक्तिः।

(3) Also they do not have *cāraṇa labdhi* i.e. गगनगमनसामर्थ्यम्। Capacity to fly in the air.

These three special capacities are not seen in women. Because these are the results of a particular kind of *saṁyama*, i.e. अचेलसंयम. Such संयम is denied for women in the *āgamas*.

Therefore, we say यतः यत्र ऐहिकवाद-विक्रिया-चारणादिलब्धीना मपि हेतुः संयमविशेषो नास्ति तत्र मोक्षहेतुरसौ भविष्यति इति कः सुधीः श्रद्दधीत?

(Obj) Here, the Śvetāmbaras contradict – If अचेलसंयम is denied for them in the *āgamas* then let them deny निर्वाण also. But it is not denied. आगमे वादादिलब्धि-अतिशय-अभाववत् मोक्षाभावोऽप्युच्येत?

(Sid) We say, by rejecting अचेलसंयम, they have rejected निर्वाण for women.

आचेलक्यादिसंयमविशेषनिषेधादिव आगमे तासां मोक्षा-भावप्रतिपादनप्रसिद्धेः।

I.3.0 Here is our third argument to deny salvation for them.

नास्ति स्त्रीणां मोक्षः।

परिग्रहवत्त्वात्।

गृहस्थवत्।

Women cannot have salvation. Since they possess clothing as belongings, as householders.

(Obj) The Śvetāmbaras regard clothing not as परिग्रह but मुक्त्यङ्ग, like प्रतिलेखन i.e. the broom. They say that it (garment) is prescribed for women in the *āgamas*.

The Digambaras reject their stand on the following grounds:

(1) मुक्त्यङ्ग i.e. means of salvation are prescribed for संयम. Cloting cannot be मृक्त्यङ्ग because it disturbs संयम. We define संयम as बाह्य-आभ्यन्तर-परिग्रहपरित्यागः। स च याचन-सीवन-प्रक्षालन-शोषण-निक्षेप-आदान-चौरहरणादि मनःसंक्षोभकारिणि वस्त्रे गृहीते कथं स्यात्?

Therefore, instead of being संयमपालनाङ्ग it becomes संयमउपघातक.

(2) Secondly, since it has relation with *himsā*, it cannot be मुक्त्यङ्ग.

(3) Thirdly, it is said that one who is desirous of salvation must give up clothing. मुक्त्यार्थिना तत्त्यागस्य कर्तव्यतया उपदिश्यमानत्वात्।

(4) Moreover, even प्रतिलेखन etc. which are prescribed as मुक्त्यङ्ग are given up in the last stage of salvation. But a woman should never give up clothing

Thus, clothing cannot be मुक्त्यङ्ग.

(Obj) The Śvetāmbaras still insist that वस्त्र is not परिग्रह. According to them ममत्वमेव परिग्रहः। आर्यिकायाश्च ममत्वाभावात् अम्बरमपरिग्रहः।

(Sid) Here the Digambaras ask - If the garment falls down does she not pick it up intentionally? बुद्धिपूर्वं हि पतितं वस्त्रं हस्तेन आदाय परिदधानाया मूर्च्छारहितत्व-अनुपपत्तेः।

Thus, since she has ममत्त्व it becomes परिग्रह.

(Obj) Then let सचेलसंयम be the cause of salvation for them, and अचेलसंयम for men.

(Sid) Then there would be two types of salvation. *Sacela saṁyama* would lead to one type of salvation and *acela-saṁyama* to the other. But infact salvation is one. न च मुक्तेः भेदः अस्ति। कारणभेदात् मुक्तेः अवश्यमुपसज्येत भेदः।

(Obj) Then let there be वस्त्रपरिग्रह as a meagre fault. All other rules and regulations she follows sincerely. वस्त्रे तु सति तत्परिग्रहमात्रं दोषः, सकलशीलपरिपालनं तु गुणः।

(Sid) We do not disagree on this point. Our point of disagreement is salvation. We say, because of wearing garments a woman possesses belongings and therefore, her conduct is contaminated with *himsā*. Thus, in spite of the strict observances her behaviour does not lead to *Mokṣa*, same as that of a householder. तच्छीलं हिंसाशबलितत्वात् न मोक्षप्रसाधनाय प्रभवति।

I.4.0 Now, here is our fourth argument.

नास्ति स्त्रीणां मोक्षः।

पुरुषेभ्यो हीनत्वात्।

नपुंसकवत्।

Women do not have salvation.

Because, they are inferior to men.

Like impotents.

The following are the evidences of their inferior status.

नास्ति स्त्रीणां मोक्षः।

पुरुषैः अवन्द्यमानत्वात्।

(Obj) Here, the Śvetāmbaras say, अवन्द्यमानत्व cannot be the reason to reject salvation. Because, the *gaṇadharas* who have actually attained salvation are not paid respect by अर्हत्s. Thus, they are अवन्द्यमान still have attained salvation.

(Sid) Here the Digambara's explain what we mean by अवन्द्यमानत्व is different from what you intend. We say in the hierarchy of respectable persons women do not have any place. अवन्द्यमानत्व means यतिगृहदेवपदअनर्हत्व। i.e. They are not paid respect by यति, गृहस्थ or देव.

Besides there are more proofs to establish her inferiority. These are as follows:

1.4.1 In each house a man is sovereign and not a woman.

प्रतिगृहं च प्रभुत्वं पुंसामेव, न स्त्रीणाम्। तथा पितरि सत्यसति च पुरुषस्यैव लघोः विरूपकस्यापि सर्वत्र कार्ये अधिकारः, न पुत्रीणां महतीनां सुरूपाणामपि। अतः यासां सांसारिकलक्ष्म्यामपि अधिकारो नास्ति तासां मोक्षलक्ष्म्यामधिकारो भविष्यति इति किमपि महाद्भुतम्।

Everywhere the behaviour towards men and women shows striking contrast.

पुत्रवर्गात् पुत्रीवर्गस्य सकलव्यवहारेषु लोके अत्यन्तविलक्षणतया प्रसिद्धेः।

1.4.2 Secondly, the whole behaviour of women depends upon men. सारणवारणचोदनानि पुरुषाः स्त्रीणां कुर्वन्ति। (सारणा - हिते प्रवर्तना, वारणा - अहितान्निवारणा, चोदना-संयमयोगेषु स्खलितास्सन् न युक्तमेतद् भवादृशां विधातुम् इत्यादिवचनेन प्रेरणा।)

In this way the life of women is governed by men.

1.4.3 Moreover, there are no women तीर्थंकरऽ - तीर्थंकर आकारधराश्च पुरुषाः, न स्त्रियः।

(Obj) The Svetāmbaras do accept inferiority of women, but they do not accept it as the cause for *Mokṣa*. They argue :

न हीनत्वमधिकत्वं वा मुक्तेरङ्गम्। किन्तु शिष्य-आचार्यवत्। शिष्या आचार्येभ्यों हीनाः, ते तु तेभ्योऽधिकाः, अथ च उभयेषां मुक्तिः, तद्वत् आर्यणाम् आर्यिकाणां च सा भविष्यति।

(Sid) The Digambaras defend : We have already proved that the three fold causal complex existing in men and women varies in degree. Women cannot have it when it is in its ultimatum and therefore they do not have capacity to achieve salvation.

नहि प्रचण्डमार्त्तण्डप्रसाध्ये कार्ये प्रदीपस्य स्वप्नेऽपि सामर्थ्यं प्रतीयते।

Thus , to summarise,

Women cannot obtain salvation, because

(1) They do not possess *Ratnatraya* in its ultimatum.

(2) They do not possers special capacities such as *vādādilabdhī,* since they do not observe अचेलसंयम.

(3) They have clothing as belonging .

(4) and finally in many respect they are inferior to men.

Conclusion

In the introductory part of this article we have seen that this issue is raised only in the Jaina literature specifically in the post-*āgama* philosophical texts. The following are the possible reasons behind it.

(1) Because of the strict observances of Jaina religion, even the philosophy had to group together सम्यक्ज्ञान, सम्यक्चारित्र्य and सम्यक्दर्शन as the causal complex for salvation. Therefore, even a slight fall in behaviour holds back the *mumukṣu* and throws on the subsequently inferior step of the 14 *guṇasthānas*. Thus, *aparigraha* in its extreme state was given importance since it bridles *himsā*. However, it resulted into considering even the minimum and low priced garments as परिग्रह. Thus, अचेलसंयम gained it roots in Jainism. The social circumstances however, did not allow a woman to follow अचेलसंयम. Therefore, she can not

possers the *ratnatraya* in its ultimatum and thus was deprived of *Mokṣa*.

(2) Because, in the Jaina philosophy *Ātmā* has limited size and therefore has *gati.* The Ātman of a woman though moves but can not more to the both extreme steps. Therefore, salvation was denied.

(3) Though in contrast to the Brahmanical philosophical tradition, Jainism has allowed Saṁnyāsa to women in Jaina system *saṁnyāsa* became invitable for salvation. However, since the social image of a woman was inferior they could not uplift her up to salvation. Even the Śvetāmbaras who argue for salvation, say that a woman gets salvation by changing herself mentally to man. Therefore, they call the *Tirthaṅkara* Malli as Mallinātha.

(4) Other systems of philosophy do not explicitly take up this issue for discussian. Because, for them knowledge alone is the cause for salvation. 'ज्ञानादेव तु कैवल्यम्' The code of conducts are not tricky like अचेलसंयम. Saṁnyāsa was not inevitable. Moreover, when *saṁnyāsa* was prescribed for women it was अश्रौत and in the form of कामनात्याग. Thus, any soul if possesses knowledge gets liberated. Therefore, we find characters such as चूडाला etc. in the *Yogavāsiṣtha* are depicted as *jīvanmukta*. She is not at all *hīnasattva* since she trains her husband Śikhidhvaja in the Yogic capacities leading to salvation.

Thus, since *jñāna* alone was postulated as the cause of *Mokṣa* some issues like salvation of women or *saṁnyāsa* for women did not find place in the philosophical discussions.

Concept of Avadhi in Jaina Epistemology

Ujjwala Panse

सम्यगर्थनिर्णयः प्रमाणम्। (प्रमाणमीमांसा 1.1.2)

Pramāṇa in general is defined by Hemachandra in these words. सम्यगर्थनिर्णयात्मकता is the property (धर्म) of the *dharmin* namely *pramāṇa*. What is *nirṇaya* in the definition? *nirṇaya* is the knowledge/cognition without *saṁśaya, anadhyavasāya* and *avikalpakatva.* Thus, doubt which is a (false) type of cognition and also *indriyasannikarṣa* which is not a knowledge - both are excluded from the domain of the definition of *pramāṇa*. (तत्र निर्णयः संशयाऽनध्यवसायाविकल्पकत्वरहितं ज्ञानम्। ततो निर्णयपदेनाज्ञान-रूपस्येन्द्रियसन्निकर्षादेः, ज्ञानरूपस्यापि संशयादेः प्रमाणत्वनिषेधः। Pramānamimāṁsā p. 3)

Now let us see what *artha* is: *Artha* is that which is to be accepted or rejected or ignored. We cannot drop the third category of *artha* as it can be neither rejected nor accepted. (अर्यतेऽर्थ्यते वा अर्थो हेयोपादेयोपेक्षणीयलक्षणः, हेयस्य हातुम् उपादेयस्योपादातुम् उपेक्षणीयस्योपेक्षितुमर्थ्यमानत्वात्। न चानुपादेयत्वादुपेक्षणीयो हेय एवान्तर्भवति अहेयत्वादुपादेय एवान्तर्भावप्रसक्तेः। उपेक्षणीय एव मूर्च्धाभिषिक्तोऽर्थः योगिभिस्तस्यैवार्यमाणत्वात्। अस्मदादीनामपि हेयोपादेयाभ्यां भूयानेवोपेक्षणीयोऽर्थः; तन्नायमुपेक्षितुं क्षमः। अर्थस्य निर्णय इति कर्मणि षष्ठी, निर्णीयमानत्वेन

व्याप्यत्वादर्थस्य। अर्थग्रहणं च स्वनिर्णयव्यवच्छेदार्थं तस्य सतोऽप्यलक्षणत्वादिति वक्ष्यामः। (ibid p. 3)

By saying *arthagrahaṇa* i.e. cognition of *artha,* cognition of self (itself i.e. of cognition) is excluded. Hemachandra explains '*samyak*' as follows:

सम्यग् इत्यविपरीतार्थमव्ययं समञ्चतेर्वा रूपम्। तच्च निर्णयस्य विशेषणम्। तस्यैव सम्यक्त्वासम्यक्त्वयोगेन विशेष्टुमुचितत्वात्; अर्थस्तु स्वतो न सम्यग्। नाप्यसम्यगिति सम्भवव्यभिचारयोरभावान्न विशेषणीयः। तेन सम्यग्योऽर्थनिर्णय इति विशेषणाद्विपर्ययनिरासः। (ibid p. 3)

Samyak stands for correct, other than incorrect and qualifies the cognition. Because it is adequate to qualify knowledge/cognition only by this word *samyak*. As far as the object *artha* is concerned it cannot be correct or incorrect. It remains as it is. And hence by qualifying the cognition (*nirṇaya*) by *samyak* incorrect or erroneous cognition is excluded from being *pramāṇa*. While explaining the title of the book Hemachandra observes: प्रकर्षेण संशयादिव्यच्छेदेन मीयते परिच्छिद्यते वस्तुतत्त्वं येन तत्प्रमाणं प्रमायां साधकतमं तस्य मीमांसा - उद्देशादिरूपेण पर्यालोचनम्। (ibid p. 2)

That (knowledge) is *pramāṇa* which reveals forth the true object setting aside doubt etc. and that is thus the instrument of valid knowledge. Discussion and explanaton of that instrument of valid knowledge is *pramāṇamīmāṁsā*.

Thus defining *pramāṇa* in two places, the author of the *Pramāṇamīmāṁsā* divides *pramāṇa* into two *pratyakṣa* and *parokṣa* i.e. direct and indirect. He has defined *pratyakṣa* in his *sūtra* 1.1.13: विशदः प्रत्यक्षम्। So *viśadatva* or *vaiśadya* is the definition of *pratyakṣa*. He comments upon it as follows: सामान्यलक्षणानुवादेन विशेषलक्षणविधानात् सम्यगर्थनिर्णय इति प्रमाणसामान्य-लक्षणमनूद्य विशद इति विशेषलक्षणं प्रसिद्धस्य प्रत्यक्षस्य विधीयते। तथा च प्रत्यक्षं धर्मि। विशदसम्यगर्थनिर्णायात्मकमिति साध्यो धर्मः। प्रत्यक्षत्वादिति हेतुः। यद्विशदसम्यगर्थनिर्णयात्मकं न भवति न तत्प्रत्यक्षम्। यथा परोक्षम् इति व्यतिरेकी।

(Commentary of Hemacandra on the *sūtra* 1.1.13. ibid).

And then defines *vaiśadya* in the next *sūtra* i.e. 1.1.14. प्रमाणन्तरानपेक्षेदन्तया प्रतिभासो वा वैशद्यम्। (ibid 1.1.14).

This is explained by the author in the commentary as: प्रस्तुतात् प्रमाणाद्यदन्यत् प्रमाणं शब्दलिङ्गादिज्ञानं तत्प्रमाणान्तरं तन्निरपेक्षता वैशद्यम्। न हि शाब्दानुमानादिवत् प्रत्यक्षं स्वोत्पत्तौ शब्दलिङ्गादिज्ञानं प्रमाणान्तरमपेक्षत इति एकं वैशद्यलक्षणम्। लक्षणान्तरमपि 'इदन्तय। प्रतिभासो वा' इति इदन्तया विशेषनिष्ठतया यः प्रतिभासः सम्यगर्थनिर्णयस्य सोऽपि वैशद्यम्। वा शब्दः लक्षणान्तरत्वसूचनार्थः। (Commentary of Hemacandra on 1.1.14. ibid).

After defining *vaiśadya* in this way, the author proceeds to the definitions of two types of *pratyakṣa*. As we have seen before *pratyakṣa* is divided into *mukhya-pratyakṣa* and *sāṁvyāvahārikapratyakṣa*. तत्सर्वथावरणविलये चेतनस्य स्वरूपाविर्भावो मुख्यं केवलम्। (ibid, *sūtra* 1.1.15). केवलप्रत्यक्ष is defined in this aphorism as the manifestation of the real nature of the ātman which is nothing but *prakāśasvarūpa*.

This *pratyakṣa* being the main is called *mukhya* and because the *ātman* does not require the help of sense organs etc. for this knowledge this is called *kevala*.

Then the author enters into the interesting discussion on the *prakāśasvabhāvatva* of the *ātman*. He establishes it on the basis of *asandigdhasvabhāvatva, boddhṛtva* and *kriyākartṛtva*.

Then comes the question: if such is the nature of the *ātman* then how is he covered by any type of cover? In answering this question, Hemachandra gives the example of the moon and the sun who are *prakāśasvabhāva* but are covered by *rajas, nīhāra abhrapaṭala* etc. As these covers are removed by *prabalapavana* i.e. very strong wind so also by *dhyāna, bhāvanā* etc. the *āvaraṇa* of the *ātman* is also *taken* off.

Then continuing the discussion on this line he speaks about the *kevalapratyakṣa* which is possible in the case of a *sarvajña*. There is very interesting discussion on the possibility of a human being becoming *sarvajña* in the light of the objections taken by Kumārila against such a possibility in his *Ślokavārtika*. Then the author describes two more types of supernatural perception or direct knowledge namely: *avadhi* and *manaḥparyāya* in the *sūtra* 1.1.18. *tattāratamye'vadhimanaḥparyāyau ca.* So, *Kevalapratyakṣa* is the direct knowledge where the cover of *karman* etc. on the soul is totally removed and this removal (*vilaya*) is in the form of two knowledges namely *avadhi* and *manaḥparyāya* or *manaḥparyaya* or *manaḥparyava*.

The *avadhi-jñāna* as the name suggests has certain limits as it has as its object only *rūpavat dravyas* substances with colour. Hemachandra writes: तत्र अवधीयत इति अवधिः मर्यादा सा च "रूपिष्ववधेः" (तत्त्वा 1.28) इति वचनात् रूपवदद्रव्यविषया अवध्युपलक्षितं ज्ञानमप्यवधिः।

And मनःपर्याय literally means modes of mind. मनसः द्रव्यरूपस्य पर्यायाश्चिन्तनानुगुणाः परिणामभेदास्ताद्विषयं ज्ञानं मनःपर्याय। (ibid, p. 15) Let us now confine ourselves with the *avadhijñāna* which is the variety of super-normal perception in Jaina Epistemology, as we have just seen.

The अवधिज्ञान is defined by *Yaśovijaya* as: सकलरूपिद्रव्य-विषयकजातीयम् आत्ममात्रापेक्षं ज्ञानम् अवधिज्ञानम्। (जैनतर्कभाषा, Pub. Motilal Banarasidass p. 7)

So what is *avadhijñāna*? It is the knowledge i.e. supernormal, perceptual knowledge of material objects only. Thus its area of apprehension is limited: hence the name: *avadhi*.

Division of Avadhi

Hemachandra divides *avadhi* into two: *bhavapratyaya* -

and *guṇapratyaya*. To quote *Pramāṇamīmāṁsā*: स द्वेधा भवप्रत्ययो गुणप्रत्ययश्च। तत्राद्यो देवनारकाणां पक्षिणामिव वियद्गमनम्। गुणप्रत्ययो मनुष्याणां तिरश्चां च। (ibid, p. 15)

Bhavapratyaya is natural type of *avadhi* with which a being is born i.e. it is something innate '*sahaja*' we may say. The example given by Hemacandra makes it clear: it is like the capacity of flying in the birds. A bird only becauseit is a bird has the capacity to fly. So also any being born in the heaven or hell is endowed with *avadhijñāna*. Thus, *bhavapratyaya-avadhi* i.e. *avadhi* caused by birth can be present in either the gods or in the beings in he hell.

The second type is *guṇapratyaya-avadhi* i.e. *avadhi* caused by merit. Human beings and animals are said to have this type of *avadhi*.

This has another name namely: *kaṣāyopaśmapratyaya* i.e. caused by the removal of *avadhijñānāvaraṇa*.

Here, let us, in brief look into the concept of knowledge in general as per the Jaina system (which would throw light on) and the concept of *kaṣāyopaśama*.

According to them cognition is a permanent quality of the soul. It is not an accidental phenomenon produced by external factors. We know that Nyāya system holds the view that *buddhi* is produced by certain external and internal causal (complex) factors and it is momentary not in the sense of the buddhists of course. (They have defined क्षणिकत्व also in their system: तृतीयक्षणवृत्तिध्वंसप्रतियोगित्वं क्षणिकत्वम्। Vide *Nyāyasiddhāntamuktāvali* on *kārikā* 27) Further in this system it is accepted that in the state of *suṣupti* i.e. sound sleep and also in the state of liberation cognition is totally absent in the soul.

But according to the Jaina system the knowledge is natural. A soul is omniscient as far as its nature is concerned.

This is one point.

Secondly, the soul is the only real caụse of cognition all other things namely senses, light, object, etc. are merely the (*sahakārikāraṇas*) helping factors which are necessary only occassionaly. They are not essential. The soul plays both the roles: the role of the agent as well as the role of the instrument.

The real value of knowledge is its ethical utility. The three virtues, namely, Right attitude (*samyagadarśana*), Right knowledge (*samyagjñāna*) and Right conduct (*samyakcaritra*) lead one to the state of liberation. The result of Right conduct is freedom from wordly miseries and its cause is *samyagjñāna*: Right knowledge; but it itself is not possible without the Right attitude. In short, we may say:

Right Attitude leads to Right knowledge this leads to Right Conduct it again leads to State of Liberation. Thus, knowledge i.e. Right knowledge plays the vital role in the achievement of liberation. Right knowledge followed by Right conduct will ultimately result into the state of liberation.

But it is not that simple! There are hindrances on the way to liberation. And they are the vices like ignorance (*ajñāna*) and attachment or passions (*kaṣāyas*). Ignorance is removed by Right knowledge (and attachment by Right conduct.)

Now, to come to our point, the capacity of *bhavapratyaya avadhi* is fixed according to the region where a being is born. e.g. the being in the hell cannot perceive beyond six miles.

But it is not so with the *guṇapratyaya avadhi*. It varies according to *kaṣāyopaśama* and thus is divided into the six varieties i.e. *anānugamika* etc. to be found in the *Tarkabhāṣā* of Yaśovijayagaṇi.

Hemacandra, however, explains the exact difference between *manaḥparyāya* and *avadhi*. The point of similarity between the two is both have *rūpidravya* as their object and also both cause *kaṣāyopaśama*.

The points of difference, however are: *visuddhi kṣetra, svāmin* and *viṣaya*. To quote Hemacandra: विशुद्धिक्षेत्रस्वामिविषयभेदात् तद्भेदः। (ibid, *sūtra* 1.1.19)

He explains viśuddhi as: तत्र अवधिज्ञानात् मनःपर्यायज्ञानं विशुद्धतरम्। यानि हि मनोद्रव्याणि अवधिज्ञानी जानीते तानि मनःपर्यायज्ञानी विशुद्धतराणि जानीते। (ibid p. 15)

Then he explains *kṣetrakṛtabheda*: क्षेत्रकृतश्चानयोर्भेदः - अवधिज्ञानं अङ्गुलस्यासङ्ख्येयभागादिषु भवति आ सर्वलोकात्, मनःपर्यायज्ञानं तु मनुष्यक्षेत्र एव भवति। (ibid, p. 15)

Svāmikrtabheda is: अवधिज्ञानं संयतस्यासंयतस्य संयतासंयतस्य च सर्वगतिषु भवति, मनःपर्यायज्ञानं तु मनुष्यसंयतस्य प्रकृष्टचारित्रस्य प्रमत्तादिषु क्षीणकषायान्तेषु गुणस्थानकेषु भवति तत्रापि वर्धमानपरिणामस्य नेतरस्य। वर्धमानपरिणामस्यापि ऋद्धिप्राप्तस्य नेतरस्य। ऋद्धिप्राप्तस्यापि कस्यचित् न सर्वस्येति। (ibid, p. 15)

Viṣayakṛtabheda is: रूपवद्द्रव्येष्वसर्वपर्यायेष्ववधेः विषयनिबन्धः तदनन्तभागे मनःपर्यायस्य इति। (ibdi, p. 15) and then says: *avasitam mukhyam pratyakṣam*. (ibid, p. 15). This is all Hemacandra has to say about *Avadhi* in his available portion of the work *Pramāṇamīmāṁsā*.

There is also division of *avadhi* into *deśāvadhi paramāvadhi* and *sarvāvadhi* in the *Viśeṣāvaśyakabhāṣya* (Gathas 690-99), *paramāvadhi* has wider scope than *deśāvadhi* and *sarvāvadhi* has wider scope than *paramāvadhi*. According to *Śvetāmbara* school *paramāvadhi* results into *Kevalajñāna*.

Observations

As for the Jaina side of the coin one needs still more efforts to understand the concept of *Avadhi* in the light of modern psychology. To compare this concept with the Nyāya Vaiśeṣika concept of *alaukikapratyakṣa*, I have a few points to make:

The most conspicuous point of contrast is that according to Jaina Epistemology, there is no contact between the sense organ and the object the sense organ and the mind - the mind and the soul as the Nyāya-vaiśeṣika (NV) system contends. No. They say this knowledge occurs in the soul itself without the others having any role to play.

The *Nyāya Vaiśeṣika* system accepts *alaukikasannikarṣa* that produces *alaukikapratyakṣa*. There are three types of *alaukikapratyakṣa* namely:

(1) ज्ञानलक्षणाप्रत्यासत्तिजन्य,

(2) सामान्यलक्षणाप्रत्यासत्तिजन्य, and

(3) योगजप्रत्यासत्तिजन्य

The first two are possible in case of normal or average human beings - this is true about the *avadhi* also but the point of difference is that *avadhi* requires no सन्निकर्ष as such.

The third category i.e. *Yogipratyakṣa* is divided into two: *yuñjāna* and *yukta Nyāyasiddhāntamuktāvali* in its *Pratyakṣakhaṇḍa* says: युक्तस्य तावद्योगजधर्मसहायेन मनसा आकाशपरमाण्वादिनिखिलपदार्थगोचरं ज्ञानं सर्वदैव भवितुमर्हति। द्वितीयस्य चिन्ताविशेषोऽपि सहकारीति।

It is clear that mind is the instrument through which the *yogin* perceives all the things present past and future.

However the Jaina will say *Ātman* himself plays the role of instrument and also that of an agent.

There could be objections to this but they are also answered by the Jainas.

When I first read the description of *Avadhi* I was

wondering whether such a type of knowledge is accepted in the *Nyāya Vaiśeṣika* system and I was all through thinking about the *prātibhajñāna* like, 'श्वो मे भ्राता आगन्ता' accepted in this system. This knowledge we cannot group under *anumiti, upamiti* or *śābdabodha* for obvious reasons; this has to come under the perview of percption. What type of process shall we give here that is responsible in producing this knowledge. There is no object no sense-organ no contact. It is mere intuition of a sister and very much valid as the brother really comes home the next day and the sister is very happy. So it stands the test of validity even in the *Nyāya Vaiśeṣika* system and therefore is accepted as a valid type of knowledge.

My contention got a stronger foundation when I came across T.G. Kalghatgi's book *Some Problems in Jaina psychology* (Published by Karnataka University Dharwad). He says that on rare occassions we get a flash of intuition as for instance when a girl perceives in a heart of her heart that her brother will come tomorrow (p. 133).

And then after a few pages observes that this clairvoyance can be compared with *anavasthita avadhi* - which sometimes increases and some times decreases. We sometimes read in news-papers that such and such person remembers his past birth and so on. This, I think, could also be included in the sphere of *avadhi*.

* This paper is based mainly on the *Pramāṇamīmāṁsā* of Hemcandra. (Edited by Pt. S. Sanghavi, Published by Saraswati Pustak Bhandar, Ahmedabad, 1989.)

Prabhācandra's Concept of Smṛti

S.C. Dash

O. The Jaina system of Logic considers *smṛti* to be a *pramāṇa* and classes it under non-perceptual (*parokṣa*) *pramāṇa*. It is based on earlier experience and treated as a valid organ of knowledge. But in some logical schools the validity of *smṛti* is challenged.

Prabhācandra in his *Nyāyakumudacandra* devoted a full chapter on discussing the validity of accepting *smṛti* as a *pramāṇa*. He first of all records the opponents views and raises his objections to them. Further he gives his own arguments for accepting it under non-perceptual *pramāṇa*. The paper aims at discussing the validity of *smṛti*.

1.0. In the beginning of the second part of the text *Nyāyakumudacandra*,[1] the *Kārikā* starts discussing about the *parokṣa pramāṇa*.[2] Then the *vivṛti* starts explaining it. After that, Prabhācandra starts analysing the *kārikā* in a normal way beginning the argument of the opponents with *nanu* etc.

1.1. Now, the opponents (Buddhists) raise objections that what is the nature and need of *smṛti* and with reference to what it is non-erroneous?[3] If it is said that its nature and characteristics refer to the object which is expressed by *smṛti*, then what exactly it is? Is it of the type of a knower or knowledge. (Reply) If it is the first i.e. *jñātā* 'the knower' then it is not possible because nobody has the knowledge of something other than the knowledge of the previous or subsequent that of a knower. And, if it is the second i.e. *jñāna* 'knowledge', then there can be two alternatives namely- i) it is only the knowledge or ii) it is the object of that which is already experienced.

Now one may further ask that, if the first one is accepted, then the knowledges like perception etc. would be treated as *smṛti* and other than that of *smṛti* the difference among *smṛti* and perception, inference etc. would be ruled out. Then if the second alternative is accepted then in case of the experience of the object by Devadatta, there will arise the perceptual knowledge of Yajñadatta which would be treated as *smṛti*.[4]

Moreover, if someone holds the view that what is experienced or known earlier by the help of that previous knowledge, the knowledge of that is called the remembrance. It is not so, it is rather a mere statement because there will arise the contingency of continuous perception being included under *smṛti*. The opponents further ask - by the explanation that *smṛti* is *anubhūte jāyamānam*, the question is through what it is known either by experience on by remembrance or by both? the reply is - the first one is not possible, since by the time of *anubhava*, the very idea of *smṛti* is impossible[5]. It is further explained and elaborated that, if a thing is nonexistent, one cannot have it as one's object of knowledge as it will be a far - fetched or over-extensive statement. The example is given as that of a rabit's horn.

And naturally, it is true that, when something is not an object of knowledge, how can one say that in that or through that something is produced or generated? If it is so, there will be *atiprasakti* which is not desirable.

It is true that, whatever is not the object of knowledge, that does not produce the knowledge of that afterwards through the earlier experience. As for example, when in sleep, one gets a dream of the blue, red colours and pleasure of something etc., since it is not the object of that knowledge - it does not appear in the knowledge of a person in an awakening state. Then, whether *smṛti* is that which does not become the object of knowledge through one's experience but through the sense of past events related to experienced objects. That is also not tenable, because that kind of (*smṛti*) knowledge does not arise from experience[6].

The second alternative is also not proper, since the object and the experience are not treated to be the object of one's knowledge, by remembrance one cannot have the knowledge but is produced in that which is experienced as the expression, *anubhūte' ham utpannā* etc. Then the next point arises that, if it is argued that the state of being experienced '*anubhūtatā* is realised through perception, then one can know also remembrance through the experience of the expression mentioned above. This also follows the same pattern of experiencing as we have examined earlier - in case of the first alternative.

Again, if it is said that *smṛti* is based on perception, it is not proper because it is known only through the state of being that which is being experienced[7]. So, one cannot say that, *smṛti* is produced by *smṛti*, and also one cannot argue that *smṛti* is produced by both *anubhava* and *smṛti*, since both the cases are faulty. And hence, the nature of *smṛti* now remains to be discussed.

Further the opponents argue that if *smṛti* is accepted from the standpoint of the object and if so, then is it mere the object itself which is the content of *smṛti* or this object is qualified by the state of being that which is being experienced? The reply is — no. *Smṛti* is not only the object because in such case all the knowledges will be treated as *smṛti*.

Then the second option also is not proper - that the object is not qualified by *anubhūtatā* in the case of the object experienced by Devadatta, there will arise the contingency of the continuous knowledge of the knowledge arisen in yajñadatta being included in *smṛti*[8].

So one can not accept the validity of *smṛti* as a *pramāṇa* with reference to the object which becomes the content of that which is experienced earlier, since it does not remain to be a content of knowledge at the time of remembrance. Whatever does not appear as the content of knowledge, that can not be treated as *pramāṇa* like the knowledge of a bunch of hair remaining in the sky as it is not experienced. As a matter of fact, the content of knowledge which is not present but is intended as the content of the knowledge of the object experienced earlier and that is called the knowledge of remembrance. In this way, if the validity of *smṛti* is accepted, then it will be over-extensive and far-fetched.

2.0 (Reply) Now, the reply of the opponents is given by Prabhācandra. To the earlier argument that whether *smṛti* is knower or knowledge, it is not proper because sometimes the term *jñāna* refers to the word *smṛti* also. One cannot deny this that, *smṛti* does not follow in each and every knowledge, because *smṛti* is not used only in the sense of a specific knowledge. Now, he defines *smṛti* as-the content of the knowledge of an object experienced earlier and it is produced by a particular *saṁskāra* which is a particular type of knowledge.[9] To the question that whether *smṛti* is treated as knowledge and there is no difference between the two, we say that there is a difference no doubt. *Smṛti* is different from other types of knowledges like perception, inference etc. and this difference is on the basis of *kāraṇa* 'causal factors', *svarūpa* 'nature' and *viṣya* 'the content of knowledge'.

i) ***kāraṇa bheda*** : The first differenciating feature is causal factor and *smṛti* has strong impressions '*saṁskāra*' as its cause where as for perception etc. the eyes etc. are the causes which help in producing the knowledge.[10]

ii) ***svarūpabheda*** : This is the second one. In the case of *smṛti*, one mentions or refers to that object '*tat*' where as in perception etc., one refers to this object '*idam*'.

iii) ***viṣayabheda*** : The third one is *viṣayabheda*. In case of *smṛti*, one gets the knowledge of the object which is already experienced in the past, where as in perception etc., one gets the knowledge which has a content of this object being present now in the present moment.[11]

As to the argument, whether *smṛti* is produced by *anubhava* on *smṛti* itself or by both it is not proper, since that type of arguments are not logically expressed due to ignorance. To that, our reply is - the knower gets the knowledge with reference to the object known in the past and even now at present. As you have raised earlier that a knower does not have the knowledge of both since the earlier knowledge is not present now, and the present one will not remain in future. It is not true, as this will be discussed later on in another discussion where by chain of knowledges or repeated knowledges is refuted.

The argument that *smṛti* is not *pramāṇa*, because it involves the state of being known which is already known '*gṛhītagrāhitva*', this is also not proper, because through the restriction of the past time, when one experiencing, the state, of being experienced '*anubhūtatā*' is not possible. And because of that, the presence of a knower only cannot become a subordinate factor '*aṅga*' to the knowledge of the state of being experienced.

The role of the knower in a knowing process is that it helps to remember an object and brings the *anubhūtatā* in that object where as in the case of that of perception etc. the helping factor is *anubhūyamānatā*.[12] So, in this ground *smṛti* is different from perception etc. and hence included in *parokṣa pramāṇa*. Now he proves that *smṛti* is a *pramāṇa* by giving an inference. It says that - *smṛti* is *pramāṇa* because it is the delimitor of that portion of the unseen factor which is through some part of the past events etc., which is represented by some object different from a normal instrument of knowledge. And it is supported by that, whatever is represented like that type of unseen factor i.e. as an intermediate factor, and that is considered as *pramāṇa*. As for example, for the operation of inference, the perception etc. are the instruments as also the remembrance as necessary an operating instrument for the production of knowledge. Hence, *smṛti* is accepted as *pramāṇa* which cannot be ruled out.[13]

As the opponents mainly the Buddhists have different definitions those are also ruled out through the earlier arguments of whether *smṛti* is a knower on knowledge itself or the object itself which is already answered. And now, Prabhācandra further points out those definitions of

Buddhists and rules out one by one. The definition *gṛhītagrāhitvam* also is discussed earlier and ruled out.

Further, he points out that one cannot say that, the state of being that what possesses the qualities of contradiction on inconsistency is the cause of *smṛti* not being valid, but we say it is not true, whatever is consistent to that knowledge, that only is the cause of that knowledge. As for example a perceptual object is the cause of producing a perceptual cognition. Hence, *smṛti* is non-erroneous or non-contradictory because it tries to present to remembrance of that object which is present now. So, the remembrance of a sky-flower or rabit's horn does not arise, since they are non-perceptible objects. And suppose there are such objects remembered which are non-existent, it is to be treated as the superimposition of *smṛti*,[14] like that of perception as in the case of rope and snake. To those, who argue that, *smṛti* is not a *pramāṇa* because there is not basis of becoming a necessary factor for the production of a knowledge, we say that it is not proper to argue like this, because we see that the person gets involved in the process of inferings something on the basis of the relation of invariable concomitance which he has already known earlier or experienced earlier.[15]

Unless one has the knowledge of *vyāpti* earlier how can he remember now and unless he remembers, how can there will be inference possible? So, *smṛti* is a necessary factor for the production of inference also and one cannot deny its validity because it is a subordinate factor in an inference. And, whatever is a subordinate factor in the process of an inference, that is a *pramāṇa*, as in the case of perception. Likewise, here also the remembrance. Hence, *smṛti* is also a valid *pramāṇa*.[16] And, on the basis of causal factor, nature or characteristic feature and the content, *smṛti* is different from perception.

3.0 Conclusion

From the above discussion, we may conclude the following:

1. *Smṛti* is not a knower since a knower is he who wants to know something or about something. But *smṛti* is the earlier experience, which is a remembering process.

2. Prabhācandra proves that *smṛti* is different from the knowledges like perception, inference etc. on three grounds. They are causal factor, characterisitic feature and the content of knowledge.

3. *Smṛti* refers to the experience of the past events, where as perception etc. referes to present experience.

4. The knower remembers the earlier experience and to that *anubhūtatā* is the helping factor, where as in perception etc. the knower is required to have *anubhūyamānatā*. This is the basic reason, why *smṛti* is included in *parokṣa pramāṇa*.

5. Prabhācandra refutes all the earlier definitions and gives his own definition as - *jñānaviśeṣa eva hi saṁskāraviśeṣa prabhavaḥ tadityākāro 'nubhūtārtha-viṣayaḥ smṛtirityucyate.*

6. *Smṛti* is an operating instrument for the production of knowledge, as it is proved in the case of the remembrance of *vyāpti* in case of *anumāna* also and hence different from inference and called a *pramāṇa*.

7. *Smṛti* is non-erroneous with reference to the object of the earlier experience and helps in bringing out the revival of the past impressions which is required for *dhāraṇā* in Jaina tradition.

Notes and References

1. *Nyāyakumudacandra* of Prabhācandra, a Commentary on Bhaṭṭakalaṅkadevaś *Laghīyastraya* Ed. by Pt. Mahendra Kumar Nyāyācārya, Sri Satguru Publications, Indian Books Centre, New Delhi, Reprint 1991.
2. *jñānamādyaṁ matiḥ saṁjñā cintā cā" bhinibodhikam. prāṅ nāma-yojanācchesaṁ śrutaṁ Śabdānuyojanāt* p. 403.
3. *nanu smṛteḥ svarūpato viṣayataśca vicāryamāṇā yā anupapatteḥ kasyāvisaṁvādaḥ prārthyeta* p. 405.
4. *dviṭīyavikaelp'pi devadattānubhūte'rthe yajñadatta-pratyakṣādijñānasya smṛtitva prasaktiḥ.* Ibid.
5. *na, tāvadanubhavena, tatkāle smṛterevā'sambhavāt.* Ibid.
6. *tanna, anubhavāttathāpratītiḥ.*
7. *anubhūyamānatā. mātee eva asya paryavasānāt.* p. 406.
8. *nāpyunubhūtatāviśiṣṭaḥ, devadattānubhūte'rthe yajñadāttajñānasya dhārāvāhikasya ca smṛtitva prasaṅgāpādanāt,* Ibid.
9. *jñānaviśeṣa eva hi saṁskāra viśeṣa - prabhavaḥ tadit-yākāro'nubhūtārtha viṣayaḥ smṛtirityuvyate.* Ibid.
10. *tatra kāraṇabhedaḥ - paṭutacasaṁskāra kāraṇakatvāt, pratyakṣādīnāmca cakṣurādihetukatvāt.* Ibid.
11. *viṣayabhedo'pi - smṛteḥ anubhūtārthagocaratvāt, pratyakṣādīnāñca vartamānādyarthaviṣyatvāt,* p. 407.
12. *smṛtisahāyo hi pramātā arthe'nubhūtatāṁ pratipadyate pratyakṣasahāyastu anubhūyamānatāṁ iti.* Ibid.
13. p. 408.
14. *avisamvādo hi gṛhīte'rthe prātiḥ, ... yatra tu visamvādaḥ sā smṛtyābhāsā pratyakṣābhāsavat.* p. 410.
15. *anumāna-pravṛttilakṣaṇasya tatsādhyaprayojanasya sad-bhāvāt.* Ibid.
16. *yadanumānapravṛtter-aṅgaṁ tat-pramāṇam yathā pratyakṣam, tathā ca smaraṇam, tasmāt pramāṇa miti* p. 411.

नोचितं प्रभाचन्द्रस्य प्रत्यभिज्ञानिरूपणम्

डॉ. रमाकान्तपाण्डेयः

परिचयः

'प्रतिगता अभिज्ञाम्' इति विवक्षायां 'प्रति' 'अभि' उपसर्गपूवकात् 'ज्ञा अवबोधने' इत्यस्माद् धातोः अङ्टाप् इत्यादिप्रत्ययनिष्पन्नोऽयं 'प्रत्यभिज्ञा' शब्दो बोधकस्तद्देशकालविशिष्टैतद्देशकालावच्छिन्नस्य संस्कारेन्द्रियोभयजन्यज्ञानस्य। अर्थात् तद्देशकालविशिष्टस्य पूर्वदृष्टपदार्थस्य यदा कालान्तरे जायते पुनरन्यत्र साक्षात्कारस्तदा 'तदेवेदम्' इत्याकारकं यद्धि ज्ञानमुत्पद्यते तत्प्रत्यभिज्ञानमिति।

न्यायशास्त्रे प्रत्यभिज्ञायाः स्वरूपम्

न्यायशास्त्रे लभ्यतेऽस्य ज्ञानस्य यद्यपि प्रत्यक्षज्ञानत्वेन व्यपदेशस्तथापि प्रतीयते पूर्ववर्त्तिनां केषाञ्चिन्मते मिश्रितज्ञानताऽप्यस्य। यथा च सङ्गिरन्ते स्म भाष्यकारा वात्स्यायनपादाः-

'पूर्वपरयोर्विज्ञानयोरेकेस्मिन् विषये प्रतिसन्धिज्ञानं प्रत्यभिज्ञानम्'[1]

पूर्वानुभूतस्य पश्चादनुभूतस्य च पदार्थस्यैकस्मिन्नेव विषये या ह्येकत्वप्रतीतिः, सैव प्रत्यभिज्ञा। यथा- 'तमेवैतर्हि पश्यामि यमज्ञासिषम्, स एवायमर्थः'। पूर्वानुभवावगाहिज्ञानस्य चाधिकरणमिहापि यद्यपि प्रत्यक्षपदार्थ एव तथापि भाष्यकारो न तथा स्पष्टं वदति विषयेऽस्मिन् यथा पश्चाद्वर्तिभिर्व्याख्यातम्। 'स एवायम्' इत्यनेन प्रत्यभिज्ञानस्य वात्स्यायनाभिमतस्य तत्तावगाहित्वमिदन्तावगाहित्वं च व्यज्यते किन्तु 'विशुद्धप्रत्यक्षाकारकं भवतीदं ज्ञानं' विषयेऽस्मिन न किमप्युक्तं

तैरिति मिश्रितत्वमेव शक्यते वक्तुमस्य।

परवर्त्तिभिर्न्यायतत्त्वविद्भिः सर्वैः खलु व्याख्यातोऽयं विषयः किन्तु जरन्नैयायिको जयन्तः सविशेषं विविधसिद्धान्तखण्डनपुरस्सरं निश्चकार प्रत्यक्षतामस्य। पूर्वानुभवजन्यसहकृतेन्द्रियसन्निकर्षाज्जनेर्भेदोऽपि लक्ष्यते साधारणप्रत्यक्षापेक्षयेह। किन्तु न नैयायिकमते तत्तेदन्तयोरवगाहिज्ञानत्वाद् द्वित्वोपस्थापकज्ञानता प्रत्यभिज्ञाया अपितु सविकल्पकप्रत्यक्षतैव। यथा चाहुः-

'यत्तावदिदं विकल्पितं - 'स एवायम्' इति किमेकं विज्ञानम् उत द्वे? इति तत्रोच्यते सामानाधिकरण्येनैकविषयावद्योतनाप्रवणैक - प्रतीतिसंवेदनात् केयं द्वित्वाशङ्का? योऽयम् अयं सः सोऽयमित्येकत्त्वावमर्शिनी खल्वियमेका'[2]

तदेतदवगाहित्वान्न व्याहन्यतेऽस्याः ज्ञानता न च निश्चीयते पदार्थद्वयोपस्थापकता, प्रत्यक्षकाले कस्यचिदेकस्यैव पदार्थस्योपस्थितेस्तस्य च तदेतद्देशकालावच्छिन्नत्वात्। अर्थात् प्रत्यभिज्ञायां यो हि विषयः प्रतीयत इदन्तत्त्वेन स एव तत्तात्वेनापीत्यतो नेयं द्वित्वावमर्शिनी, पदार्थस्यैकस्यैव तदेतद्रूपेण प्रतीतेरित्यभिप्रायो मञ्जरीकारस्य। तथा च प्रत्यक्षज्ञानतामस्याः प्रतिपादयन्तो व्यावर्णयामासुः कुसुमाञ्जलिकारा उदयनपादाः-

''न च प्रत्यभिज्ञानमपि ग्रहणस्मरणाकारम्, विरोधात्'[3]

अथायमत्राशयः

प्रत्यभिज्ञाने या हि पूर्वानुभूतविषयस्य ज्ञातपूर्वावस्था तदित्यनेन भासते, तद्विषयस्य पूर्वानुभवत्वेनोत्पन्नाः संस्कारा न प्रत्यभिज्ञायाः प्रयोजका अपित्विन्द्रियसन्निकर्ष एव तज्जनकः। 'सोऽयं देवदत्तः' इत्यादिस्थले 'देवदत्तरूपपदार्थेन सह नेत्रेन्द्रियस्य संयोगो भवति सन्निकर्षः। अथ च तत्तापदार्थेन सह तस्यैव नेत्रेन्द्रियस्य 'स्वसंयुक्तविशेषणतया' अर्थात् यो हि पदार्थ इदानीं भजत इन्द्रियविषयत्वं स एव तस्मिन् देशे तस्मिन् क्षणेऽनुभूत इति रूपेण तद्विशिष्टतया भवति सन्निकर्षः। अतः प्रत्यक्षप्रयोजकेनेन्द्रियार्थसन्निकर्षेणैवोत्पत्तेः प्रत्यभिज्ञायाः प्रत्यक्षज्ञानतैव न च परोक्षज्ञानतेति। तस्याश्च कारणं संस्कार, उद्बुद्धेनैव तेन तज्जन्यत्वप्रसङ्गात्।

किन्तु प्रकाशकारो वर्द्धमानो न स्वीकरोति संस्कारकारणतामिह, तथात्वे तस्याः परोक्षज्ञानतापत्तेः। अतस्तेन निराकृत[4] उदयनसिद्धान्त इति विचार्यं सुधीभिः।

प्रत्यभिज्ञायाः प्रमाणता

भारतीयदर्शनसम्प्रदायेषु प्रत्यभिज्ञायाः प्रामाण्यविषयोऽवतरति विवादपथम्। तत्र त्रयः पक्षाः दृश्यन्ते। प्रथमो वैदिकदर्शनपक्ष इमां प्रत्यक्षस्मरणरूपां न वदति। तेषां प्रस्थानेषु ज्ञानमिदं प्रत्यक्षमेव। अस्माभिर्यच्चर्चितं पूर्वं तदनुसारिणी व्याख्यैव किञ्चिद् भेदेन सर्वत्र लभ्यते। अतो वैदिकसम्प्रदायेऽस्याः प्रमाणता।

सौगतास्तु स्मरणप्रत्यक्षरूपां प्रत्यभिज्ञां स्वीकुर्वन्ति। वस्तुतस्तु तेषां मते स्मरणप्रत्यक्षावगाहि यद्धि ज्ञानं प्रत्यभिज्ञारूपं न तस्यैकज्ञानताऽपि तु स्मरणाकारत्वात् प्रत्यक्षाकारत्वाच्च तस्योभयात्मकतेति ज्ञानसमुच्चयवादिनां बौद्धानां द्वितीयः पक्षः।

तृतीयस्तावज्जैनपक्षो विद्यते। येनेयं प्रमाणत्वेन स्वीकृता किन्तु न प्रत्यक्षज्ञानतयाऽपि तु परोक्षज्ञानतयेति भेदः। बौद्धानां ज्ञानसमुच्चयवादं वैदिकसूत्रकृतां प्रत्यक्षवादं चापाकृत्य जैनदार्शनिकैः स्थापिता परोक्षरूपाताऽस्याः। तत्र प्रत्यक्षपरोक्षभेदाद् द्वैविध्यं प्रमाणस्य।[5] परोक्षं पुनः स्मृति-प्रत्यभिज्ञान-ऊह-अनुमान-आगमभेदात् पञ्चविधम्।[6]

प्रभाचन्द्रमतानुसारि प्रत्यभिज्ञास्वरूपम्

माणिक्यनन्दिविरचितस्य परीक्षामुखसूत्रस्य व्याख्याग्रन्थे 'प्रमेयकमलमार्त्तण्डे' तत्कृता प्रभाचन्द्रेण मीमांसा-न्याय-बौद्धादिसिद्धान्तानां निरसनपूर्वकं पारम्परिकं तदेव प्रत्यभिज्ञायाः स्वरूपं निर्धारितं यत्खलु पूर्वाचार्यैराम्नातम्। न किमपि नूत्नत्वं तत्रेति तन्मात्रं प्रपच्यत इह। यथा च तत्र सूत्रम्—

दर्शनस्मरणकारणकं सङ्कलनं प्रत्यभिज्ञानम्।

तदेवेदं तत्सदृशं तद्विलक्षणं तत्प्रतियोगीत्यादि॥[7]

अयमर्थः

पूर्वदृष्टपदार्थस्य पुनः प्रत्यक्षकाले जायमाना या हि स्मृतिस्तज्जन्यं प्रत्यक्षभिन्नं स्मृतिभिन्नं चोभयोः सङ्कलनरूपं यज्ज्ञानं तत्प्रत्यभिज्ञानम्। अत्रोपस्थितपदार्थ एव स्वस्मृतेर्हेतुर्न च प्रणिधानादयो न्यायसूत्रोक्ता अन्ये हेतवः। एवं तद्दर्शनेनैव तद्विषयकसंस्कारोद्बोधजन्या स्मृतिस्तद्देशकालेन विशिष्य पदार्थं तमुपस्थापयति। तथा च साक्षादिन्द्रियार्थसन्निकर्षजन्यं प्रत्यक्षम् एतद्देशकालावच्छिन्नतयेति सहैव एतत्तदोर्व्यवहारः। तदित्याकारकत्वात् स्मृतित्वं न शक्यतेऽस्य वक्तुम्, इदमित्यनेनापि युक्तत्वात्। अत उभयोरेतत्तदोः सङ्कलनरूपमिदं ज्ञानमिति व्यपदिष्टं सूत्रकारेण।

अथ च व्याख्यायामपि प्रभाचन्द्रस्ततान तज्ज्ञानस्य प्रत्यवमर्शनरूपताम्—

'दर्शनस्मरणे कारणं यस्य तत्तथोक्तम् सङ्कलनं विवक्षितधर्मयुक्तत्वेन प्रत्यवमर्शनं प्रत्यभिज्ञानम्'।[8]

किं च आस्तिकसूत्रकृद्भिः प्रत्यभिज्ञा प्रत्यक्षज्ञानत्वेन स्वीकृतेति चर्चितचरमेव। प्रभाचन्द्रोऽत्र स्वसम्प्रदायसिद्धान्तानुरूपं तत्स्वरूपं विवृण्वन् मीमांसकमतमपाकरोति—

'ननु प्रत्यभिज्ञायाः प्रत्यक्षप्रमाणस्वरूपत्वात् परोक्षरूपतयाऽत्राभिधानमयुक्तम् तथा हि प्रत्यक्षं प्रत्यभिज्ञा अक्षान्वयव्यतिरेकानुविधानात् तदन्यप्रत्यक्षवत्। न च स्मरणपूर्वकत्वात् तस्याः प्रत्यक्षत्वाभावः, सत्सम्प्रयोगजत्वेन स्मरणपश्चाद्भावित्वेऽप्यस्याः प्रत्यक्षत्वा-विरोधात्।[9]

अयमभिप्रायः

मीमांसकेषु कौमारिलाः प्रत्यक्षेऽपि स्मृतेरनुविद्धतामङ्गीकुर्वन्ति। किन्तु प्राधान्यं प्रत्यक्षस्यैव व्यपदिश्यते तैरितीत्थं श्लोकवार्तिके प्रत्यक्षसूत्राध्याये सिद्धान्तितम्—

न हि स्मरणतो यत् प्राक् तत्प्रत्यक्षमितीदृशम्।
वचनं राजकीयं वा लौकिकं वापि विद्यते॥

न चापि स्मरणात् पश्चादिन्द्रियस्य प्रवर्तनम्।
वार्यते केनचिन्नापि तत्तदानीं प्रदुष्यति॥

तेनेन्द्रियार्थसम्बन्धात् प्रागूर्ध्वं चापि यत्स्मृतेः।
विज्ञानं जायते सर्वं प्रत्यक्षमिति गम्यताम्॥

इत्येषा श्लोकवार्तिककृदुक्तिः पिस्पर्द्धिषया यत् प्रभाचन्द्रेण निराक्रियते, तन्मन्ये नासमीचीनं, प्रत्यक्षस्य स्मृतिनिरपेक्षिज्ञानत्वात्। किन्तु तत्रैव "पुनर्दर्शने पूर्वदर्शनाहितसंस्कारप्रबोधोत्पन्नस्मृतिसहायमिन्द्रियं तज्जनयतीति" यदुक्तं तद् वस्तुतोऽधिरोहति विचारपदवीम्, तस्मिन्नेव प्रकरणे कुमारिलपादानामुक्तेरस्याः—

गृहीतिमपि गोत्वादि स्मृतिस्पृष्टं च यद्यपि।
तथापि व्यतिरेकेण पूर्वबोधात् प्रतीयते॥

देशकालादिभेदेन तत्रास्त्यवसरो मितेः।

य: पूर्वमवगतोऽथः स न नाम प्रतीयते॥

इदानीन्तनमस्तित्वं नहि पूर्वधिया गतम्॥

नेत्यप्यसारम्। निष्कर्षतया प्रभाचन्द्रस्याभिप्रायस्तावदेतदेव विद्यते यत्- "अव्यवधानेन प्रतिभासनलक्षणवैशद्याभावाच्च न प्रत्यभिज्ञानम्'। भवतु सम्प्रति ओम् इति ब्रूमः। तत्त्वं तु वक्ष्यते।

एवमत्र प्रत्यभिज्ञाया लक्षणमुपस्थाप्य सूत्रकार एव 'तदेवेदं', 'तत्सदृशं', 'तद्विलक्षणं', तत्प्रतियोगीत्यादिभेदांस्तस्याश्चकार।

निष्कर्ष

'तदेवेदम्' इति नूनं प्रत्यभिज्ञानमेव। प्रायशो न कस्यापि शास्त्रविदोऽत्रापत्तिः। किन्तु 'तत्सदृशम्' इति प्रत्यभिज्ञाभेदे नैयायिकानामुपमानप्रमाणस्य या हि अन्तर्भावकल्पना तत्र विचारोऽपेक्ष्यते। इह हि स्वसिद्धान्तमुपस्थापयता प्रभाचन्द्रेण निराकृतं न्यायसूत्रम्। तत्र तावदभिप्रायोऽयं तस्य - 'गौरिव गवयः' इत्युपमानवाक्याहितसंस्कारस्य पुनर्वने गवयदर्शनात् 'अयं गवयशब्दवाच्य' इति संज्ञासंज्ञिसम्बन्धप्रतिपत्तिरूपमानमिति नैयायिकमतमपि प्रयुक्तम्। यथैव ह्येकदा घटमुपलब्धवतः पुनस्तस्यैव दर्शने 'स एवायं घटः' इति प्रतिपत्तिः प्रत्यभिज्ञा। तथा 'गोसदृशो गवयः' इति सङ्केतकाले गोसदृशगवयाभिधानयोर्वाच्य- वाचकसम्बन्धं प्रतिपद्य पुनर्गवयदर्शनात् तत्प्रतिपत्तिः प्रत्यभिज्ञा किन्नेष्यते? न खलु पूर्वमप्रतिपन्नेऽपूर्वदर्शनात् स्मृतिर्युक्ता, यतस्तथा प्रतिपत्तिः स्यात्।

गोविलक्षणमहिष्यादिदर्शनाच्च 'अयं गवयो न भवति' इति तत्संज्ञासंज्ञि-सम्बन्ध- प्रतिषेधप्रतिपत्तिश्च यद्युपमानं प्रसिद्धसाधर्म्यात्साध्यसाधनमुपमानम्' इति व्याहन्येत। अथ प्रसिद्धार्थवैधर्म्यादपीष्यते। तर्हि 'प्रसिद्धार्थबैधर्म्याच्च साध्य-साधनमुपमानम्' इत्युपाख्यानं सूत्रे कर्त्तव्यम्।

उपर्युक्तं सर्वं प्रसमीक्ष्य ज्ञायतेयज्जैननये 'तत्सदृशम्' इत्याकारकज्ञानस्यापि प्रत्यभिज्ञानता। न वदन्ति ते नैयायिकवदुपमानं, प्रत्यभिज्ञायामेव तस्यान्तर्भावकल्पनात्। किन्तु यदा विचार्यते न तदा तेषां प्रत्यभिज्ञालक्षणस्य साधुत्वं घटते। यथा च तत्र स्मृतेः लक्षणं 'संस्कारोद्बोधनिबन्धना तदित्याकारा स्मृतिः' (प्रमेय. पृ. 335) संस्कारः पुनः सांव्यवहारिकप्रत्यक्षभेदो धारणा। तस्योद्बोधः प्रबोधः। स निबन्धनं यस्याः तदित्याकारो यस्याः सा तथोक्ता स्मृतिः।

संस्कारकारणं त्वनुभव एव। आद्यं देवदत्तदर्शनम्। अर्थात् पूर्वं कुत्रचिद् दृष्टस्य देवदत्तस्य पदार्थस्यान्यस्य वा पूर्वानुभूतस्य संस्कारा जायन्त इत्यतोऽनुभव एव संस्कारकारणम्।

यदि नाम समीक्ष्यते जैनशास्त्रे संस्कारोद्बोधकारणं तदा प्राप्यते यत् त एव लोकप्रसिद्धा हेतवस्तत्रापि कारणायन्ते ये हि शास्त्रेष्वन्येषु। तथात्वे सदृशपदार्थदर्शनेन तत्सदृशस्य स्मरणमेव भवितुमर्हति न च प्रत्यभिज्ञानं, सादृश्यस्यापि संस्कारोद्बोधे कारणत्वात् तत्स्मृतिजनकत्वात्। यथा च तत्पठितमेव स्मृतिनिमित्तहेतुषु मुनिना गौतमेन स्वीकृतं च भवद्भिःजैनदार्शनिकैस्तत्कारणत्वं तत्र। यतो हि देवदत्तसदृशदर्शनेन तस्य स्मृतिरेवोदेति न च प्रत्यभिज्ञानम्। देवदत्तसदृशोऽयमथवा देवदत्तस्येदमित्यादि तु स्मृतिजनकमेव। तर्हि कथं जैननैयायिकैः प्रत्यभिज्ञा स्मृतित्वेन व्यपदिश्यते। अथवा किमर्थं स्मृतेर्व्यामोहः प्रत्यभिज्ञास्मृत्योस्तथात्वे उभयोः एकरूपत्वात्। अपि च नह्येवं सदृशाकारमात्रेण न्यायशास्त्रस्योपमानं विनश्यति, तज्जन्यस्मृतेरूपमानशब्देनान्यपदेशात्।

स्यान्नाम। यदि त्वत्र तेषां प्रत्यभिज्ञालक्षणं निक्षिप्यते निर्णयनिकषे तदा तदेव पतति पङ्के। यथा च सूत्रितम्—

'दर्शन-स्मृतिकारणकं सङ्कलनम्'

अत्र संस्कारः कारणं प्रत्यभिज्ञायाः स्मृतिर्वा? स्मृतिरेवेति ज्ञायते लक्षणे तदुपदेशात्। तर्हि या हि स्वीकृता प्रत्यभिज्ञायाः परोक्षज्ञानता तैस्तत्रापि सन्देह एव।

स्मृतिकारणतया जन्या प्रत्यभिज्ञा। अतः स्मृतिस्तस्याः कारणम्। न च 'करणम्'। तेन ज्ञानरूपकारणजन्याया अपि प्रत्यभिज्ञाया ज्ञानाकरणकत्वम्। ज्ञानाकरणकज्ञानस्य अपरोक्षाकारत्वमेव न तु परोक्षाकारता। अतो जैनैः परोक्षस्वरूपनिर्धारणार्थं तस्यास्तस्यां संस्कारस्य हेतुत्वं प्रतिपादनीयम्। अर्थात् संस्कारकारणतया प्रत्यभिज्ञाजनिः स्वीकरिष्यते चेत् तस्याः परोक्षज्ञानतैव भविष्यति, संस्कारस्य पूर्वानुभवरूपकरणस्य व्यापाररूपत्वात्। संस्काररूपव्यापारजन्यत्वे तु संस्कारजनकपूर्वानुभवरूपकरणजन्यत्वं भविष्यत्येव। अतो न कापि भविष्यति विप्रतिपत्तिः परोक्षाज्ञानतायां भवदिष्टायां तस्याः। ज्ञानाकरणकात् अर्थात् ज्ञानरूपकरणाभिन्नकरणजन्यं ज्ञानमेव भवति अपरोक्षाकारकम्। यथा चोदयनमतमालोचयद्भिः प्रकाशकारेणोक्तम्—

वस्तुतस्तत्तास्मृतिजन्यमेव प्रत्यभिज्ञानं न तु संस्कारजन्यम्। अन्यथा संस्कारद्वारा पूर्वानुभवस्य तत्करणतया ज्ञानकरणतया तस्य परोक्षापत्तिः। तत्तास्मृतेश्च निर्व्यापारत्वेनाऽकरणत्वादिति तत्त्वम्।[10]

एतेनैतदायातम् - यज्जैनानां 'तदेवेदम्' इत्येव प्रत्यभिज्ञानिरूपणं साधु। किन्तु तत्रापि स्मृतिकारणत्वाज्जनेरसाधुत्वमेव। अतस्तेषां लक्षणे करणीयमेव 'संस्कार' इति पदस्योपाख्यानम्। 'तत्सदृशम्' 'तद्विलक्षणम्' इत्युभयोः स्वीकृतौ तस्याः स्मृतित्वापत्तिः, उभयोरनयोः स्मृतिनिमित्तत्वात। स्मृतिकारणतया तज्जन्यत्वोपदेशात् तस्याः परोक्षज्ञानता- बाध इत्यपि सुस्पष्टमेव। 'इदमस्माद्दूरं' 'वृक्षोऽयमित्यादयो भेदा एव न भवितुतुमर्हन्ति प्रत्यभिज्ञायाः। अतो नोचितं प्रत्यभिज्ञानिरूपणं प्रभाचन्द्रस्य अर्थात् जैननैयायिकानामिति मे धीरिति दिक्।

संदर्भ सूची

1. न्या. सू. 3.1.6 भाष्ये
2. न्यायमञ्जरी द्वितीयो भागः, आ. - 6, पृ. 329.
3. न्या. कु. का. - 4.4, पृ. 464.
4. तत्रैव प्रकाशटीका.
5. प्रमाणं द्विधा, प्रत्यक्षं परोक्षं च, प्रमाणमीमांसा-1.1.9-10
6. स्मृतिप्रत्यभिज्ञानोहानुमानागमास्तद्विधयः, तत्रैव 1.2.2
7. प्रमेय. पृ. 338.
8. तत्रैव।
9. तत्रैव।
10. न्या. कु. 4.4 प्रकाशटीका।